STAND STRONG

• DELUXE EDITION •

Stand Strong: 365 Devotions for Men by Men, Deluxe Edition
© 2020 by Our Daily Bread Publishing
All rights reserved.

Requests for permission to quote from this book should be directed to:
Permissions Department, Our Daily Bread Publishing, PO Box 3566, Grand Rapids, MI 49501,
or contact us by email at permissionsdept@odb.org.

ISBN: 978-1-64070-073-4

Printed in China

20 21 22 23 24 25 26 27 / 8 7 6 5 4 3 2 1

STAND STRONG

• DELUXE EDITION •

365 DEVOTIONS
FOR MEN BY MEN

OUR DAILY BREAD

Our Daily Bread
Publishing™

FOREWORD

It was one of the scariest moments of my life.

I was trying to be the cool dad, so I took my son into the waves to boogie-board. He was holding on to my back, and we took the first wave without a problem. He loved it, and I was the hero.

On the way back out, he and I broke a few waves before lying back down on the boogie-board. A large wave came, and I knew it was the one we should ride. I grabbed the board with my left hand and grabbed my son with my strong right hand. Unfortunately, the wave was larger than I realized, and it threw us off the board. My son fell off my back. I jumped up and looked around. For what felt like much longer than it probably was, I couldn't find him. I looked right and left, desperately searching for my boy. Finally, he came up for air.

Waves are strong. If you try to keep them from coming, well, you will look silly. You can try to keep yourself from being moved by a large wave, but it's nearly impossible. In the waves we struggle to stand firm because the sand moves with the tides and is stirred by the very waves that push us from here to there. We can't gain the footing we need.

Life often feels like standing in waves. Sometimes our lives are calm, and the waves undetectable as they roll in. Other times, life sends waves of change, anxiety, or problems that knock us down. The firm footing we thought we had in calm waters betrays us as our feet sink into the unsettled sand or get pulled out from under us with the current.

Unlike the ocean sand, however, there's a strong foundation available to us—a firm place to stand when life's waves are more than we can bear. The apostle Paul, a man who dealt with his share of storms, both literally and metaphorically, had a foundation to stand on. In Ephesians, a letter he wrote from prison (4:1), he gives us a hint as to what that foundation looks like.

> Then we will no longer be infants, tossed back and forth by the waves, and blown here and there by every wind of teaching and by the cunning and craftiness of people in their deceitful scheming. Instead, speaking the truth in love, we will grow to become in every respect the mature body of him who is the head, that is, Christ. . . . [You] were taught in him in accordance with the truth that is in Jesus. (4:14–15, 21)

How can we stand strong in a world full of powerful waves? By standing on the firm foundation of Jesus Christ. But what does that mean?

This book offers short, daily snidbits of how to stand strong because of the truth in Jesus. If you want to find that firm footing available to you through the Scriptures, this book is a great place to start. Our prayer for you is that God will use this devotional to strengthen your faith and help you *Stand Strong*.

May God give you eyes to see and ears to hear His voice in these pages.

Daniel Ryan Day
Author and cohost of the Discover the Word *radio program*

Stand Strong

2 TIMOTHY 4:1–8

I have fought the good fight,
I have finished the race, I have kept the faith.

—2 TIMOTHY 4:7

Andrew Carroll has been urging people not to throw away letters written by family members or friends during war times. Carroll, director of the Center for American War Letters, says, "Younger generations are reading these letters, asking questions, and saying, 'Now I understand what you endured, what you sacrificed.'"

When Paul was imprisoned in Rome and knew his life would soon end, he wrote a letter to a young man he considered a "son in the faith," Timothy. Paul opened his heart to him: "The time for my departure is near. I have fought the good fight, I have finished the race, I have kept the faith. Now there is in store for me the crown of righteousness, which the Lord, the righteous Judge, will award to me on that day" (2 TIMOTHY 4:6–8).

When we read the letters in the Bible from heroes of the Christian faith and grasp what they endured because of their love for Christ, we gain courage to follow their example and to **stand strong** for those who come after us.

❖ *David McCasland*

Strength of a Man

Be on your guard; stand firm in the faith;
be courageous; be strong.

—1 CORINTHIANS 16:13

Some years ago I found myself in an elevator with a couple of men. It was late at night, and we all looked weary. The elevator stopped, and a larger-than-life cowboy ambled in, wearing a battered hat, an old, stained sheepskin coat, and rundown logger boots. He looked us up and down and growled, "Good evening, men." All of us straightened up and squared our shoulders. We were trying to live up to the name.

Let's talk about living up to the name *man*. We try to be strong and macho, but often it's just a façade. Underneath the bravado we harbor a host of fears, insecurities, and shortcomings. Much of our manliness is pure bluff.

Paul was man enough to admit it: "We are weak," he said (2 CORINTHIANS 13:4). That's a humbling fact. Yet Paul also insisted that we are to "be courageous" (1 CORINTHIANS 16:13).

How can we be the strong person God meant for us to be? Only by putting ourselves in God's hands and asking Him to make us that way through His power and enablement.

❖ *David Roper*

The Best Is Yet to Come

DEUTERONOMY 34

The eternal God is your refuge, and underneath are the everlasting arms.
He will drive out your enemies before you, saying, "Destroy them!"

—DEUTERONOMY 33:27

Are the best days of your life in front of you? Our outlook on life—and our answer to that question—can change with time. When we're younger, we look ahead. Once we've grown older, we yearn for the past. But when we walk with God, whatever our age, the best is yet to come!

Over the course of his long life, Moses witnessed the amazing things God did, many of which happened when he was no longer young. Moses was eighty when he confronted Pharaoh and saw God miraculously set His people free from slavery (EXODUS 3–13). Moses saw the Red Sea part, saw manna fall from heaven, and even spoke with God "face to face" (14:21; 16:4; 33:11).

Moses lived expectantly, looking ahead to what God would do (HEBREWS 11:24–27). Even when he was one hundred twenty years old, he understood that his life with God was just getting started and that he would never see an end to God's greatness and love.

Regardless of our age, God's "everlasting arms" (DEUTERONOMY 33:27) faithfully carry us securely through each new day.

❖ *James Banks*

As Is

Therefore, if anyone is in Christ, the new creation has come:
The old has gone, the new is here!

—2 CORINTHIANS 5:17

The beat up old car sits on the used-car lot, rusty and forsaken. Years of abuse and hard driving have taken their toll.

A man walks onto the lot and is attracted to this rust bucket. He plunks down cash, and the salesperson hands over the keys while saying, "I'm selling you this car 'as is.'" The new owner just smiles. He knows his cars, and he's about to restore this castoff to its former beauty.

Across town, a troubled man sits in forlorn sadness, contemplating where he went wrong. Years of abuse and hard living have taken their toll. He's been rejected so many times he feels he has little value. After all that misery and pain, he's sure he will be left on life's junk heap forever.

Then someone tells him about Jesus. Someone mentions that Jesus specializes in castoffs and that He is waiting to transform anyone who trusts Him. Someone tells him that Jesus will take him "as is." He believes. He trusts. And Jesus begins to restore another lost person to the abundant life He has promised.

❖ *Dave Branon*

The Big Comeback

1 JOHN 1

*If we confess our sins, he is faithful and just and will forgive us our sins
and purify us from all unrighteousness.*

—1 JOHN 1:9

While playing in the NFL, Chad Pennington suffered multiple career-threatening type of injuries. Twice his injuries forced him to endure surgery, therapy, and extensive training to get back onto the field. He not only returned to playing but he also excelled so much he was twice named Comeback Player of the Year. Pennington's efforts were an expression of his determined spirit.

Spiritually, when sin and failure break our relationship with God and sideline our service, determination alone cannot restore us to rightness and usefulness. When we are sidelined by sin, the path to a comeback is confession. "If we confess our sins, he is faithful and just and will forgive us our sins and purify us from all unrighteousness" (1 JOHN 1:9).

For us to be able to recover from our spiritual failings, we depend on the One who gave himself for us. He gives us hope. Christ, who died for us, loves us and will respond with grace as we confess our faults to Him. Through confession, we can find His gracious restoration—the greatest of all comebacks.

❖ *Bill Crowder*

A Devoted Heart

He did what was right in the eyes of the Lord.

—2 CHRONICLES 20:32

A successful Christian businessman shared his story at church. Candid about his struggles with faith and abundant wealth, he declared, "Wealth scares me!"

"But," the businessman stated, "I've learned a lesson from Solomon's verdict on the abundance of wealth. It's all 'meaningless'" (ECCLESIASTES 2:11). The man determined not to let wealth get in the way of his devotion to God. Rather, he wanted to serve God with his assets and help the needy.

Throughout the centuries, God has blessed some people materially. We read of Jehoshaphat in 2 Chronicles 17:5, "The LORD established the kingdom . . . so that he had great wealth and honor." He did not become proud or bully others with his wealth. Instead, "his heart was devoted to the ways of the LORD" (V. 6). Also, "he followed the ways of his father Asa and did not stray from them; he did what was right in the eyes of the LORD" (20:32).

The Lord is not against wealth, but He is definitely against the unethical acquisition and wrong use of it. He is worthy of devotion from all His followers.

❖ *Lawrence Darmani*

Windtalkers

2 PETER 1:19–21

For prophecy never had its origin in the human will, but prophets,
though human, spoke from God as they were carried along by the Holy Spirit.

—2 PETER 1:21

Their contribution to victory in World War II was enormous, but few people even knew about them. In 1942, the US Army trained twenty-nine young Navajo Indians and sent them to a secret base. These people, called "windtalkers," had been asked to use their native language to devise a special code the enemy couldn't break. They succeeded! The code was never broken. It secured and speeded up war communications.

By contrast, the Bible was not sent down to us in some unbreakable code impossible to understand. Although it contains rich imagery, vivid metaphors, and the record of magnificent visions, it was written by human authors to give people the message of God's love and salvation.

That message is clear and unmistakable. The biblical writers were moved by God's Spirit to record exactly what He wanted us to know. For centuries people have been freed from their sin and guilt by believing His message.

We owe a great debt to the writers of Scripture, who received God's Word and wrote it down. So let's read it often. ❖ *David Egner*

The Power of Demonstration

2 TIMOTHY 3:10–17

*All Scripture is God-breathed and is useful for
teaching, rebuking, correcting and training in righteousness.*

—2 TIMOTHY 3:16

My attempts at fixing things around the house usually lead to paying someone else to undo the damage. But recently I successfully repaired a home appliance by watching a YouTube video with step-by-step details.

Paul was a powerful example to his young protégé Timothy, who watched him in action. From prison in Rome, Paul wrote, "You . . . know all about my teaching, my way of life, my purpose, faith, patience, love, endurance, persecutions, sufferings" (2 TIMOTHY 3:10–11). In addition, he urged Timothy to "continue in what you have learned and have become convinced of, because you know those from whom you learned it, and how from infancy you have known the Holy Scriptures" (VV. 14–15).

Paul's life demonstrated the necessity of building our lives on God's Word. He reminded Timothy that the Bible is our powerful, God-given source.

As we thank God for everyone who helped us grow in faith, we are challenged to follow their example as we seek to teach and encourage others.

That's the power of demonstration.

❖ *David McCasland*

By the Spirit's Power

ZECHARIAH 4:1–7

"What are you, mighty mountain? Before Zerubbabel you will become level ground. Then he will bring out the capstone to shouts of 'God bless it! God bless it!'"

—ZECHARIAH 4:7

What do you do when there is a mountain in your way? The story of Dashrath Manjhi from India can inspire us. When his wife died because he couldn't get her to the hospital, Manjhi did what seemed impossible. He spent *twenty-two years* chiseling—by hand—a gap in a mountain so others could get medical help!

Rebuilding the temple must have looked impossible to Zerubbabel, one of Israel's leaders who returned from exile. The people were discouraged, faced enemy opposition, and lacked resources. But God sent Zechariah to remind Zerubbabel that the task would take something more powerful than military strength or manmade resources. It would take the Holy Spirit's power (ZECHARIAH 4:6). With the assurance of divine aid, Zerubbabel trusted that God would level any mountain of difficulty that stood in the way (V. 7).

When there's a "mountain" before us, we can either rely on our own strength or trust the Spirit's power. When we trust Him, He'll either level the mountain or help us climb over it.

❖ *Marvin Williams*

Alone in Space

When Jacob awoke from his sleep, he thought,
"Surely the LORD is in this place, and I was not aware of it."

—GENESIS 28:16

Apollo 15 astronaut Al Worden knew what it felt like to be completely isolated. For three days in 1971, he flew alone in his command module, *Endeavor*, while David Scott and James Irwin were miles below on the moon's surface. Worden's only companions were the stars overhead.

As the sun went down on Old Testament character Jacob's first night away from home, he too was alone, but for a different reason. He was on the run from his older brother—who wanted to kill him for stealing the family blessing. On falling asleep, Jacob dreamed of a staircase joining heaven and earth. As he watched angels ascending and descending, he heard God's voice promising to be with him and to bless the whole earth through his children. When Jacob woke he said, "Surely the LORD is in this place" (GENESIS 28:16).

Jacob had isolated himself because of his deceit. Yet he was in the presence of the One whose plans are always better and more far-reaching than our own. Heaven is closer than we think, and the "God of Jacob" is with us.

❖ *Mart DeHaan*

Shaq and Me

PSALM 111

The fear of the LORD is the beginning of wisdom; all who follow his precepts
have good understanding. To him belongs eternal praise.

—PSALM 111:10

I'll never forget the time I had my picture taken with Shaquille O'Neal, one of the giants of professional basketball. I never thought of myself as short until I stood next to his 7'1" frame. With my head tucked under his arm, I suddenly realized that I wasn't as tall as I thought I was.

The psalmist wrote, "The fear of the LORD is the beginning of wisdom" (111:10). Fearing God requires that we get things in the proper proportion, like the fact that He is so much greater in every way than we are. "The works of the LORD" (V. 2) are the outworking of His love, strength, wisdom, foresight, will, and faithfulness. Fearing God means coming to grips with this truth.

It's easy to miss the point when we don't stay close to God. The closer we get to Him, the more we realize how much we are lacking and how desperately we need His far greater wisdom to direct our lives.

Wise people realize how little they know and how much they need the great wisdom of God.

❖ *Joe Stowell*

Drift

Do not be yoked together with unbelievers.
For what do righteousness and wickedness have in common?
Or what fellowship can light have with darkness?

—2 CORINTHIANS 6:14

Adrian Vasquez frantically waved from his tiny fishing boat. *A cruise ship was within sight!* After their boat's engine had failed, Adrian and two friends had been adrift for days on the ocean. Passengers aboard the cruise ship spotted the three and told crewmembers. Inexplicably, the ship didn't stop to help. When Adrian was finally rescued by a different ship *two weeks later,* both of his friends had perished.

The people in the church at Corinth seemed to be adrift, so Paul pled with them to turn back and take the "life ring" of true faith in Jesus. Some had been attending pagan religious services (1 CORINTHIANS 10:14–22). Embracing idolatry was a sign of drifting from true belief in God. So Paul asked, "What does a believer have in common with an unbeliever?" (2 CORINTHIANS 6:15). Paul told his readers not to be *of* the world but to stick to the moorings of holy living in Jesus.

Do you know a believer who's starting to drift? Don't just cruise by. Throw out that life ring.

❖ *Tom Felten*

Be Prepared to Tell

1 CHRONICLES 16:7–13

Give praise to the LORD, proclaim his name;
make known among the nations what he has done.

—1 CHRONICLES 16:8

When author Studs Terkel was looking for a topic for his next book, a friend suggested "death." While he resisted at first, the idea gradually began to take shape. Its voice became all too real when Terkel's wife of sixty years died. The book became a personal search: a yearning to know what lies beyond. Its pages are a poignant reminder of our own search for Jesus and our questions about eternity.

I'm thankful for the assurance that we will be with Jesus after we die if we have trusted in Him as Savior. There is no greater hope! It's our privilege to share that hope with others. First Peter 3:15 encourages us: "Always be prepared to give an answer to everyone who asks you to give the reason for the hope that you have." We have the opportunity from God to "proclaim his name; make known among the nations what he has done" (1 CHRONICLES 16:8).

The stories of so many people we love are not yet ended, and the privilege to tell them about the love of Jesus is a remarkable gift.

❖ *Randy Kilgore*

The Fingerprint of God

EPHESIANS 2:1–10

For we are God's handiwork, created in Christ Jesus to do good works,
which God prepared in advance for us to do.

—EPHESIANS 2:10

Lygon Stevens loved to climb mountains with her brother Nick. They were experienced climbers and both had summited Alaska's Denali, the highest point in North America. But in January 2008, they were swept off a Colorado mountain by an avalanche, injuring Nick and killing twenty-year-old Lygon. When Nick later discovered his sister's journal, he was deeply comforted by its contents. She wrote: "I am a work of art, signed by God. But He's not done; in fact, He has just begun. . . . I have on me the fingerprint of God. . . . I have a job to do in this life that no other can do."

Through the legacy of her life and her journal she inspires and challenges those she left behind.

Made in God's image (GENESIS 1:26), each person is a "work of art, signed by God." The apostle Paul says, "We are God's handiwork, created in Christ Jesus to do good works, which God prepared in advance for us to do" (EPHESIANS 2:10).

Praise God that He uses each of us to help others.

❖ *Dennis Fisher*

Minister of Reconciliation

2 CORINTHIANS 5:16–21

For if, while we were God's enemies, we were reconciled to him through the death of his Son, how much more, having been reconciled, shall we be saved through his life!

—ROMANS 5:10

As Dr. Martin Luther King Jr. preached on a Sunday morning in 1957, he fought the temptation to retaliate against a society steeped in racism.

"How do you go about loving your enemies?" he asked the Dexter Avenue Baptist congregation in Montgomery, Alabama. "Begin with yourself. . . . When the opportunity presents itself for you to defeat your enemy, that is the time which you must not do it."

Quoting from the words of Jesus, King said: "Love your enemies, bless them that curse you, do good to them that hate you, and pray for them which despitefully use you" (MATTHEW 5:44–45 KJV).

As we consider those who harm us, we are wise to remember our former status as enemies of God (SEE ROMANS 5:10). But "[God] reconciled us to himself through Christ and gave us the ministry of reconciliation," wrote Paul (2 CORINTHIANS 5:18). Now we have a holy obligation. "He has committed to us the message of reconciliation" (V. 19).

Ours is a "ministry of reconciliation" that imitates the selfless servant-heart of Jesus.

❖ *Tim Gustafson*

Intimate Details

You know when I sit and when I rise; you perceive my thoughts from afar.

—PSALM 139:2

The universe is astonishingly grand. The moon is spinning around us at nearly 2,300 miles an hour. Our Earth is spinning around the sun at 66,000 miles an hour. Our sun is one of 200 billion other stars and trillions more planets in our galaxy. Astounding!

In comparison to this vast cosmos, our little Earth is no bigger than a pebble, and our individual lives no greater than a grain of sand. Yet according to Scripture, the God of the galaxies pays attention to each microscopic one of us in intimate detail. He saw us before we existed (PSALM 139:13–16); He watches us as we go about our days and listens for our every thought (VV. 1–6).

When King David wrote Psalm 139, he was in the midst of crisis (VV. 19–20). And when Jesus said God counts each hair on our heads (MATTHEW 10:30), He was living in an age of crucifixion. Biblical talk of God's caring attention isn't a naïve wish. It is real-world truth.

The One who keeps the galaxies spinning knows us intimately. That can help us get through the worst of times.

❖ *Sheridan Voysey*

Human Chess

Dear friends, let us love one another, for love comes from God.
Everyone who loves has been born of God and knows God.

—1 JOHN 4:7

Chess is an ancient game of strategy. Each player begins with sixteen pieces on the chessboard with the goal of cornering his opponent's king. It has taken different forms over the years. One form is human chess, which was introduced around AD 735 by Charles Martel, duke of Austrasia. Martel would play the game on giant boards with real people as the pieces.

Could we be playing a human game of chess sometimes? We can easily become so driven by our goals that people become just one more pawn we use to achieve those goals. The Scriptures, however, call us to a different view of others. We are to see people as created in the image of God (GENESIS 1:26). They are objects of God's love (JOHN 3:16) and deserving of ours as well.

The apostle John wrote, "Dear friends, let us love one another, for love comes from God. Everyone who loves has been born of God and knows God" (1 JOHN 4:7). Because God first loved us, we are to respond by loving Him and the people He created in His image.

❖ *Bill Crowder*

Plod for God

MATTHEW 25:14–30

To one he gave five bags of gold, to another two bags, and to another one bag,
each according to his ability. Then he went on his journey.

—MATTHEW 25:15

This morning I was out jogging when I decided to walk a bit. Just then a trim runner sprinted past, glancing at his watch. "This is embarrassing," I thought. "What must he think of me?"

Sometimes I'm embarrassed by more gifted "runners" in God's kingdom as well. But I needn't be. God has given each of us responsibilities according to our abilities (MATTHEW 25:15). We who have "two bags of gold" need not be jealous of those who are given "five." God applauds faithfulness—not numbers. The diligent two-bag servant receives the same praise as the one who invests five (VV. 21–23).

William Carey was a poor, self-educated British shoemaker. He wasn't on anyone's fast track. But he said, "I can plod. I can persevere." His plodding and his enthusiasm for Jesus took him to India, where he became known as the father of modern missions.

Most of us can't run wind sprints in God's kingdom. But we all can plod. Day after ordinary day, we can work, serve, and pray. Then we will hear from God, "Well done, good and faithful servant" (MATTHEW 25:23).

❖ *Mike Wittmer*

Elephants Down

JONAH 4

Six days do your work, but on the seventh day do not work,
so that your ox and your donkey may rest, and so that the slave born
in your household and the foreigner living among you may be refreshed.

—EXODUS 23:12

When rainy-season storms caused flooding in Thailand, seven elephant calves became unlikely victims. As they tried to ford a river at their usual crossing point, strong currents swept them over a 250-foot waterfall. Wildlife advocates said the loss could have been prevented by better protective barriers.

Long before animal rights became a global issue, the story of Jonah shows the attention our Creator gives to all His creatures. As the story ends, the Lord expresses concern not only for the citizens of Nineveh but also for their livestock (JONAH 4:11). And earlier, God gave Moses laws that extended certain protections even to animals (EXODUS 23:4–5, 12).

Though humans alone are made in the image of God, the story of Jonah and other Bible texts show a link between caring for people and animals. The Creator gives us reason to provide appropriate, though different, attention to both.

If God cares even for livestock, how can we ignore the needs of any person for whom His Son died?

❖ *Mart DeHaan*

Those Old Sports Trophies

PHILIPPIANS 3:7–14

But whatever were gains to me I now consider loss for the sake of Christ.

—PHILIPPIANS 3:7

While in my son's garage, I found the trophies he had won in his years of athletic competition. They were in a box—about to be thrown out. I thought of the blood, sweat, and tears that had gone into gaining those awards, yet now he was dumping them. They no longer had value.

It reminded me of a whimsical children's poem by Shel Silverstein called "Hector the Collector," which describes the things Hector had. He "loved them more than shining diamonds, loved them more than glistenin' gold." Then Hector called to all his friends, "Come and share my treasure trunk!" They "came and looked and called it junk."

So it will be at the end of our lives. The things we spent a lifetime working for will be nothing but junk. We'll realize that the best things in life are not things.

But we can have Paul's perspective: "Whatever were gains to me I now consider loss for the sake of Christ" (PHILIPPIANS 3:7). Because we possess the surpassing greatness of knowing Jesus, we can keep a proper attitude about our possessions.

❖ *David Roper*

No Reverse

EXODUS 16:1–2

In the desert the whole community grumbled against Moses and Aaron.

—EXODUS 16:2

The first time I saw her, I fell in love. She was a beauty. Sleek. Clean. Radiant. As soon as I spied the 1962 Ford T-Bird at the used-car lot, her shiny exterior and killer interior beckoned me. So I plunked down $800 and purchased my very first car.

But there was a problem lurking inside my prized possession. A few months after I bought my T-Bird, it got a little cranky. It allowed me to go forward, but I couldn't go backward. It had no reverse.

Although not having reverse is a problem in a car, sometimes it's good to be a little like my old car. In our walk with Jesus, we need to refuse to go backward. Paul said we need to "press on toward the goal" (PHILIPPIANS 3:14).

Perhaps the children of Israel could have used my T-Bird's transmission. We read in Exodus 16 that they were in danger of putting life into reverse. Despite the miracles God had performed, they longed for old Egypt.

We need to keep moving ahead in our walk with God. Don't back up. Look forward. Press on.

❖ *Dave Branon*

Stewards Unaware

GENESIS 1:1, 20–28

And God said, "Let the water teem with living creatures,
and let birds fly above the earth across the vault of the sky."

—GENESIS 1:20

Recently I met the captain of a boat featured on *Wicked Tuna*, National Geographic Channel's reality TV show. The show follows the lives of bluefin tuna fishermen. Sadly, illegal practices and over-fishing have seriously threatened the population of that fish.

The captain told me of steps taken to protect the tuna population. When I remarked, "That's a fantastic act of stewardship," he asked, "Are you religious?" To him, *stewardship* was a religious word.

I told the captain I believe in a Creator-God who created human beings, and that we're to steward—to take care of—the earth (GENESIS 1:20, 27–28). I explained that even if people don't realize it, they practice stewardship because that's part of what God created us to do.

The captain admitted that seeing the intricate design of the bluefin tuna sometimes makes him want to be "religious." I responded, "I'm going to pray that you will find the Creator of the bluefin tuna."

You never know what conversations may open up when you affirm the efforts of others who unknowingly reflect what God created us to do.

❖ *Jeff Olson*

A New Friend

JOHN 15:9–17

I no longer call you servants, because a servant does not know his master's business.
Instead, I have called you friends, for everything that I learned from my Father
I have made known to you.

—JOHN 15:15

While flying from Europe back to the US, I sat next to a little girl who never stopped talking from the moment she sat down. She told me the history of her family and all about her puppy, which was in the hold of the plane. She pointed excitedly to everything around us. I couldn't help but think that eight hours of this could make for a very long flight!

We chatted for a while until she suddenly got quiet. She pulled her blanket up around her, so I thought maybe she was going to doze off. Soon, though, I felt a little elbow in my side. I looked down at her, and she threw out her little hand and said, "Hey, Joe, wanna be friends?"

My heart melted. "Sure," I said, "let's be friends."

In the midst of the turmoil of life, when we think all we want is to be left alone, Jesus extends His nail-scarred hand and invites us to be His friends (JOHN 15:14–15). We have a choice: keep to ourselves or open our heart to a friendship of unlimited love and guidance.

❖ *Joe Stowell*

Always in His Care

PSALM 32

I will instruct you and teach you in the way you should go;
I will counsel you with my loving eye on you.

—PSALM 32:8

Our youngest daughter was flying from Munich to Barcelona, so I visited a flight tracking website to follow her progress. After I entered her flight number, my computer screen showed that her flight had crossed Austria and was skirting the northern part of Italy. From there the plane would fly over the Mediterranean, south of the French Riviera toward Spain, and it was scheduled to arrive in Barcelona on time. It seemed that the only thing I didn't know was what she had for lunch!

Why did I care about my daughter's location and circumstances? Because I love her. I care about everything going on in her life.

In Psalm 32, David celebrated the marvel of God's guidance and concern for us. God knows every detail of our lives and the deepest needs of our hearts. And He promises, "I will instruct you and teach you in the way you should go; I will counsel you with my loving eye on you" (V. 8).

Whatever our circumstances, we can rely on God's care because "the LORD's unfailing love surrounds the one who trusts in him" (V. 10).

❖ *David McCasland*

Taking Risks

ACTS 15:7–26

So we all agreed to choose some men and send them to you with our dear friends Barnabas and Paul—men who have risked their lives for the name of our Lord Jesus Christ.

—ACTS 15:25–26

In his book *Stuntman! My Car-Crashing, Plane-Jumping, Bone-Breaking, Death-Defying Hollywood Life*, Hal Needham reflects on taking risks. Needham has slugged it out in fist fights, raced cars at high speed, walked on wings of airborne planes, and even been set on fire! He risks his life to entertain film audiences.

Paul and Barnabas were also "men who have risked their lives" (ACTS 15:26). But their motivation was far different. Their goal was to exalt Christ through the preaching of the gospel. As a missionary in the Roman Empire, Paul faced hazards that resulted in shipwrecks, beatings, persecution, and imprisonment—just to name a few (2 CORINTHIANS 11:22–30). But Paul was more than willing to take these risks to make Christ known.

God has provided His Spirit to empower you (ACTS 1:8) and His Word to make the message clear (ROMANS 1:16). Ask God for the courage to speak up and witness for the Savior. Taking the risk will be well worth it.

❖ *Dennis Fisher*

God's Compass

PSALM 119:105–112

Your word is a lamp for my feet, a light on my path.

—PSALM 119:105

During World War II, small compasses saved the lives of twenty-seven sailors three hundred miles off the coast of North Carolina. The SS *Alcoa Guide* was spotted by a German submarine, which opened fire. The ship was hit, caught fire, and began to sink. The crew lowered compass-equipped lifeboats into the water and used the compasses to guide them toward shipping lanes closer to shore. After three days, the men were rescued.

The psalmist reminded God's people that His Word was a trustworthy "compass." He likened it to a lamp. In that day, the flickering light cast by an olive oil lamp was only bright enough to show a traveler his next step. To the psalmist, God's Word was such a lamp, providing light to illuminate the path for those pursuing God (PSALM 119:105). When the psalmist was wandering in the dark, he believed that God, through the guidance of His Word, would provide direction.

When we lose our bearings in life, we can trust our God, who gives His trustworthy Word as our compass to lead us into deeper fellowship with Him.

❖ *Marvin Williams*

Leaving a Legacy

2 CHRONICLES 21:4–10

For even the Son of Man did not come to be served, but to serve,
and to give his life as a ransom for many.

—MARK 10:45

When a road-construction foreman was killed in an accident, the love of this man for his family, co-workers, and community resulted in an overwhelming sense of loss.At his funeral, the message was clear: Tim touched many lives in a way uniquely his. So many would miss his kindness, sense of humor, and enthusiasm for life.

As I returned from the service, I thought about the life of King Jehoram. What a contrast! His brief reign of terror is traced in 2 Chronicles 21. To solidify his power, Jehoram killed his own brothers and other leaders (v. 4). Then he led Judah into idol worship. The record tells us, "He passed away, to no one's regret" (v. 20). He is forever commemorated in Scripture as an evil man and a self-centered leader.

Jesus also was a king, but He came to Earth to be a servant. Today, Jesus's legacy includes those who understand that life isn't just about themselves. It's about Jesus—the One who longs to wrap His strong, forgiving arms around anyone who turns to Him.

❖ *Tim Gustafson*

"I'm Boss Around Here!"

Submit to one another out of reverence for Christ.

—EPHESIANS 5:21

A mild-mannered man was reading a book on being self assertive and decided to start at home. He stormed into his house, pointed a finger in his wife's face, and said, "From now on I'm boss around here! I want you to prepare me a gourmet meal and draw my bath. Then, when I've eaten and finished my bath, guess who's going to dress me and comb my hair!" "The mortician," replied his wife.

King Rehoboam tried that kind of self-assertiveness, and it turned Israel against him. When he came to the throne, the people pleaded for less oppressive taxation. His older advisors urged him to heed their request, but his young friends told him to be more demanding. Because he listened to his peers, ten of the twelve tribes of Israel seceded (2 CHRONICLES 10:16–17).

Good leaders don't rely on domineering self-assertion not at home, at church, or in business. Rather, they balance proper self-assertiveness with the principle of submitting to one another (EPHESIANS 5:21). They listen respectfully, admit mistakes, and mix gentleness with firmness. That's submissive leadership—and it works!

❖ *Herb Vander Lugt*

Fox Trouble

1 JOHN 1:5–10

If we claim to be without sin, we deceive ourselves and the truth is not in us.

—1 JOHN 1:8

The British are having trouble with foxes. According to *The Wall Street Journal*, the sly little fellows have moved into London and are making a general nuisance of themselves. They knock over rubbish cans, swipe shoes left outside, destroy gardens, and leave a foul odor. With the city borders being pushed farther into the countryside, the little troublemakers are adapting rather than moving—and Londoners are frustrated and upset.

When you stop to think about it, little "foxes" can become great aggravations for followers of Christ who want to honor Him. What we may consider "little" or "harmless" sins can be our downfall. "Stretching the truth," for example, is actually lying. And gossip is nothing less than character assassination. Those little sins will inevitably grow larger. Before we know it, we'll need to do some serious confessing.

If little foxes have crept into the backyard of your spiritual life, there's help. With the Holy Spirit's guidance, identify them. Admit your guilt, confess these pesky little practices to God, and get rid of them before they ruin the entire landscape of your life.

❖ *David Egner*

Where Are You?

GENESIS 3:1–10

The LORD God called to the man,
"Where are you?"

—GENESIS 3:9

The two teenage boys heard the sound of their parents' car and panicked. How would they explain the mess in the house? Their father's instructions had been clear that morning as their parents left for the day: no parties, no rowdy friends. But some unruly friends came and the boys let them stay. Now the house was trashed and the boys were disheveled. In fear, they hid.

That was how Adam and Eve must have felt after they disobeyed God and then heard the sound of Him approaching. In fear, they hid themselves. "Where are you?" God called (GENESIS 3:9). Adam responded, "I heard you in the garden, and I was afraid because I was naked; so I hid" (V. 10). Sin makes us feel afraid and naked, and we become vulnerable to even more temptation.

God is still calling to people: "Where are you?" Many run away, trying to hide from Him. Yet we cannot hide from God; He knows exactly where we are. Rather than hide in fear, we can respond in this way: "God, have mercy on me, a sinner!" (LUKE 18:13).

❖ *Lawrence Darmani*

The Day My Dad Met Jesus

1 TIMOTHY 1:15–17

But for that very reason I was shown mercy so that in me,
the worst of sinners, Christ Jesus might display his immense patience
as an example for those who would believe in him and receive eternal life.

—1 TIMOTHY 1:16

My father was a tough man who didn't appreciate people who "got up in his face about faith." When he was diagnosed with a rapid and deadly cancer, I took every opportunity to talk to him about Jesus's love. Inevitably he would end the discussion with a polite but firm: "I know what I need to know."

I promised not to raise the issue again but gave him a set of cards that shared God's forgiveness—cards he could read when he wanted. I entrusted Dad to God and prayed. A friend also asked God to keep my dad alive long enough to know Jesus.

One afternoon I got the call that Dad was gone. When my brother met me at the airport, he said, "Dad told me to tell you he asked Jesus to forgive his sin." "When?" "The morning he passed," Mark replied. God had shown him "mercy" as He had shown us (1 TIMOTHY 1:16).

God is a gracious God, and no matter what the outcome of our prayers and our attempts to share the gospel, He can be trusted.

❖ *Randy Kilgore*

Work Together
ROMANS 8:28–30

And we know that in all things God works for the good of those who love him,
who have been called according to his purpose.

—ROMANS 8:28

My wife makes an amazing pot roast dinner. She takes meat, along with sliced white and sweet potatoes, celery, mushrooms, carrots, and onions—and throws them into the slow cooker. Six or seven hours later the aroma fills the house, and the first taste is a delight. It's worth it to wait until the ingredients in the slow cooker work together to achieve something they could not achieve individually.

When Paul wrote the phrase "work together" in the context of suffering he used the word from which we get our word *synergy*. He wrote, "We know that in all things God works for the good of those who love him, who have been called according to his purpose" (ROMANS 8:28). He wanted the Romans to know that God would cause all their circumstances to cooperate with His divine plan—for their ultimate good, which is being "conformed to the image of [God's] Son" (V. 29).

Our heavenly Father takes all the suffering, distress, and evil in our world, and He causes them to work together for His glory and our spiritual good. It's worth the wait.

❖ *Marvin Williams*

Dog Tired?

MARK 2:23–28

The highest heavens belong to the LORD,
but the earth he has given to mankind

—PSALM 115:16

During the long, harsh Alaskan winter, Denali National Park rangers rely on teams of sled dogs to help them patrol the vast, snowy wilderness. Because Alaskan huskies live to run and pull, the dogs are always raring to go.

Those furry bundles of energy don't know when to stop, so park rangers have to make them rest. Otherwise, they'd run themselves until they collapse.

Sled dogs can remind us of our need to take a break. All of us have times when we need to stop, rest, and recharge. The biblical word for this is *sabbath*. Jesus explained that the Sabbath "was made for man" and not to be an oppressive religious rule to follow (MARK 2:27).

After God made the world, He "rested" on the seventh day (GENESIS 2:2). This doesn't mean God was tired and needed a day off. He rested by dwelling in, enjoying, and ruling over the kingdom He had completed.

So let's practice Sabbath by stopping to enjoy a much-needed rest. It's more than taking a break; it's a way to acknowledge the One who is ultimately in charge of this world.

❖ *Jeff Olson*

Super Bowl Light

For you were once darkness, but now you are light in the Lord.
Live as children of light

—EPHESIANS 5:8

For many years a friend of mine attended the Super Bowl as a journalist to gather interviews with Christian athletes and NFL personnel for a faith-based radio program.

He told me that when he first started covering the game, he grew disillusioned with the self-serving, pleasure-seeking atmosphere of Super Bowl week. "I found it to be a very dark place," he said.

One day he told a former NFL player, a Christian, how he was feeling. The athlete said to him, "Brother, you are being light in this dark place." That comment reminded my friend why he was there, and it helped renew his excitement for serving God in a place where the light of the gospel is needed. It spurred him to shine his light.

Perhaps you work in a setting where God is not acknowledged, faith is mocked, and godless living is applauded. Maybe it feels like "a very dark place."

Ask God to help you be a light (EPHESIANS 5:8)—through your smiles, kind words and deeds, and diligent work. You may be the only light a coworker sees today.

❖ *Dave Branon*

Walking on a Wet Log

1 CORINTHIANS 10:1–13

If you think you are standing firm, be careful that you don't fall!

—1 CORINTHIANS 10:12

My wife Carolyn and I were hiking on Mount Rainier in Washington when we came to a swollen, glacial stream. Someone had flattened one side of a log and dropped it across the river to form a crude bridge, but there was no handrail and the log was slippery.

The prospect of walking on the wet log was frightening, and Carolyn didn't want to cross. But she found the courage, and slowly, carefully she inched her way to the other side.

On the way back we had to walk on the same log, and she did so with the same care. "Are you afraid?" I asked. "Of course," she replied, "that's what keeps me safe."

Life poses many moral dangers for us. We shouldn't assume in any situation that we're incapable of falling (SEE 1 CORINTHIANS 10:12). All of us are capable of falling into any sin.

We must watch and pray and arm ourselves for every occasion by putting our total trust in God (EPHESIANS 6:13). "God is faithful" (1 CORINTHIANS 10:13), and He will give us the strength to keep from falling.

❖ *David Roper*

Time to Grow Up

1 CORINTHIANS 3:1–17

*Brothers and sisters, I could not address you as people who live by the Spirit
but as people who are still worldly—mere infants in Christ.*

—1 CORINTHIANS 3:1

While browsing through some birthday cards, I found one that made me laugh. It read: "You are only young once, but you can be immature forever." There's something kind of inviting about never having to grow up, as any fan of Peter Pan can attest.

But we all know that perpetual immaturity is not only inappropriate but it's also unacceptable. For the Christian, we must mature. After we put our faith in Christ, we are not expected to stay spiritual babies. The Scriptures challenge us to grow to be more like Jesus.

When writing to the problem-tainted church at Corinth, Paul said that their issues were rooted in a lack of spiritual development. He said, "Brothers and sisters, I could not address you as people who live by the Spirit but as people who are still worldly—mere infants in Christ" (1 CORINTHIANS 3:1).

How do we grow up? Peter urged, "Grow in the grace and knowledge of our Lord and Savior Jesus Christ" (2 PETER 3:18). We do this by meditating on the Word of God and devoting ourselves to prayer (PSALM 119:97–104; ACTS 1:14). Now is the time to grow up in our faith.

❖ *Bill Crowder*

The Best Portion of All

PSALM 73:21–28

I know what it is to be in need, and I know what it is to have plenty.
I have learned the secret of being content in any and every situation,
whether well fed or hungry, whether living in plenty or in want.

—PHILIPPIANS 4:12

When I was a boy, my brothers and I would sometimes bicker about the size of the pieces of pie Mom served us. One day Dad observed our antics then smiled at Mom as he lifted his plate: "Please just give me a piece as big as your heart." We watched in stunned silence as Mom laughed and offered him the largest portion.

If we focus on others' possessions, jealousy often results. Yet God's Word lifts our eyes to something of far greater worth than earthly possessions. The psalmist writes, "You are my portion, LORD; I have promised to obey your words. I have sought your face with all my heart" (PSALM 119:57–58). The Spirit-guided truth is that nothing matters more than keeping a strong relationship with God.

What better portion could we have than our limitless Creator? Human longing is an expansive void; one may have "everything" in the world and still be miserable. But when God is our source of happiness, we are truly content. He alone can give us the peace that matches our hearts. ❖ *James Banks*

The Mighty Finns

Now, LORD our God, deliver us from his hand,
so that all the kingdoms of the earth may know that you, LORD, are the only God

—ISAIAH 37:20

When enemy tanks and thousands of opposing infantrymen invaded Finland, things looked bleak. Assessing the murderous wave, though, an anonymous Finn wondered aloud about the enemy: "Where will we find room to bury them all?"

Some 2,600 years before Finland showed such courage in that World War II battle, an anxious Judean citizenry reacted quite differently to their own overwhelming situation. Assyrian armies had trapped the people of Jerusalem inside its walls, where things looked hopeless. Hezekiah nearly panicked. But then he prayed, "LORD Almighty, . . . you alone are God over all the kingdoms of the earth" (ISAIAH 37:16).

The Lord answered with strong words for Assyria's King Sennacherib. "Against whom have you raised your voice and lifted your eyes in pride? Against the Holy One of Israel!" (V. 23). "I will defend this city and save it!" (V. 35), said the Lord, who defeated Sennacherib and destroyed the Assyrian army (VV. 36–38).

No matter what dangers loom today, God still reigns. He longs to hear from each of us and show himself powerful.

❖ *Tim Gustafson*

Distraction

PHILIPPIANS 3:1–21

Brothers and sisters, I do not consider myself yet to have taken hold of it. But one thing I do: Forgetting what is behind and straining toward what is ahead, I press on.

—PHILIPPIANS 3:13–14

Students at a large university have a clever way of distracting opposing basketball players during free throws. They place a "curtain of distraction" behind the basket. Just prior to free-throw attempts, the students open the curtain to things like dancing unicorns or a lion wearing a tutu. Once, it was Michael Phelps wearing his gold medals while pretending to swim.

The player missed *both* free throws.

This curtain of distraction is entertaining, but there's a more serious "curtain" in our lives—and behind it are the interesting things Satan uses to distract us from our goal: Electronics that suck up our time, a friend leading us away from Jesus, or a job that tempts us to give everything to it.

Paul says it's not just good things that distract us from Christ (PHILIPPIANS 3:5–8). It can also be earlier mistakes as Satan pulls back the curtain to reveal a sin from your past.

While Satan tries to distract you, the Holy Spirit is there to remind you that your past sins have been forgiven. Keep your eyes on Jesus today!

❖ *Mike Wittmer*

Fiery Conversation

JAMES 3:2–10

Let your conversation be always full of grace, seasoned with salt,
so that you may know how to answer everyone.

—COLOSSIANS 4:6

In northern Ghana, bush fires are frequent in the dry season between December and March. I've witnessed many acres of farmland set ablaze when winds carried carelessly discarded tiny embers. All that is needed to start a devastating fire is a little spark.

That is how the apostle James describes the tongue, calling it "a world of evil among the parts of the body. It corrupts the whole body, sets the whole course of one's life on fire, and is itself set on fire by hell" (JAMES 3:6). A false statement made here or backbiting there, a vicious remark somewhere else, and relationships are destroyed. "The words of the reckless pierce like swords," says Proverbs 12:18, "but the tongue of the wise brings healing." Just as fire has both destructive and useful elements, so "the tongue has the power of life and death" (18:21).

For conversation that reflects God's presence in us and pleases Him, let it "be always full of grace" (COLOSSIANS 4:6). When expressing our opinions during disagreements, let's ask God to help us choose wholesome language that brings honor to Him.

❖ *Lawrence Darmani*

Life's Darkest Moments

1 KINGS 19:1–8

Then he lay down under the bush and fell asleep.
All at once an angel touched him and said, "Get up and eat."

—1 KINGS 19:5

Charles Whittlesey was a hero's hero. He was awarded the Medal of Honor for his bravery when his unit was trapped behind enemy lines during World War I. When the Tomb of the Unknown Soldier was dedicated in 1921, Charles was chosen to serve as pallbearer for the first soldier laid to rest there. Two weeks later, he ended his own life by stepping off a cruise ship in the Atlantic Ocean.

As happened with Elijah (1 KINGS 19:1–7), despair had set in for Charles. People frequently face situations bigger than they can handle. Sometimes it's temporary despair brought on by fatigue, as in Elijah's case. He had experienced a great victory over the prophets of Baal (18:20–40), but then he feared for his life and ran into the wilderness (19:1–3). Often, though, it's more than despair, and it's more than temporary.

God offers His presence to us in life's darkest moments. When you feel down, cry out for help—from others and from God. Perhaps He is preparing you for the strongest moment of your life.

❖ *Randy Kilgore*

The Heart of Christ

EXODUS 32:21–32

But now, please forgive their sin—
but if not, then blot me out of the book you have written.

—EXODUS 32:32

An Australian journalist who spent four hundred days in an Egyptian jail expressed mixed emotions when he was released. While admitting his relief, he said he accepted his freedom with incredible concern for friends he was leaving behind. He said he found it hard to say goodbye to fellow reporters who had been arrested and jailed with him—not knowing how much longer they would be held.

Moses also expressed great anxiety at the thought of leaving friends behind. When faced with the thought of losing the brother, sister, and nation that had worshiped a golden calf while he was meeting with God on Mount Sinai (EXODUS 32:11–14), he interceded for them. Showing how deeply he cared, he pled, "But now, please forgive their sin—but if not, then blot me out of the book you have written" (V. 32).

The apostle Paul later expressed a similar concern for family, friends, and nation. Grieving their unbelief in Jesus, Paul said he would be willing to give up his own relationship with Christ if by such love he could save his brothers and sisters (ROMANS 9:3).

❖ *Mart DeHaan*

Keep It Strong

JUDE 17–23

Keep yourselves in God's love as you wait for the mercy
of our Lord Jesus Christ to bring you to eternal life.

—JUDE 21

The great American statesman William Jennings Bryan (1860–1925) was having his portrait painted. The artist asked, "Why do you wear your hair over your ears?"

Bryan responded, "There is a romance connected with that. When I began courting Mrs. Bryan, she objected to the way my ears stood out. So to please her I let my hair grow to cover them."

"That was many years ago," the artist said. "Why don't you have your hair cut now?"

"Because," Bryan said with a wink, "the romance is still going on."

When we first came in faith to Christ, we experienced the joy of knowing our sins were forgiven. Our full hearts overflowed with love for the Lord. We longed to please Him. Do we still feel that way?

Perhaps your zeal for the Savior has begun to cool. Take to heart the words of Jude. He wrote, "Keep yourselves in God's love" (v. 21). Jesus used similar terms when He said, "Remain in my love" (JOHN 15:9–10). We nurture our connection to God when we focus on pleasing Him instead of ourselves.

Keep your love for God strong.   ❖ *David Egner*

No Greater Love

JOHN 15:1–13

Greater love has no one than this:
to lay down one's life for one's friends.

—JOHN 15:13

Bill and his wife were driving through the Rocky Mountains when a near-miss caused their car to swerve off the road and plunge into the Colorado River. After scrambling out of their sinking vehicle, they frantically treaded water in the swift current. A passerby stopped and threw a rope to them. Bill pushed his wife to where she could grab the rope—and the man pulled her out. Bill, however, was carried downstream and didn't survive. He had given his life for the woman he loved.

To give your life so another person can live is the ultimate proof of love. On the night Jesus was betrayed, He told His disciples of His intention to give His life in exchange for mankind. He told them: "Greater love has no one than this: to lay down one's life for one's friends" (JOHN 15:13). And then He set the ultimate example of self-sacrifice by going to the cross.

Jesus died in your place. He proved His love for you while making it possible to be forgiven of your sins. There is no greater love.

❖ *Dennis Fisher*

Girl in the Yellow Coat

GENESIS 2:18–25

A man shall leave his father and mother and be joined to his wife,
and they shall become one flesh.

—GENESIS 2:24 (NKJV)

I t was her yellow raincoat that first caught my attention, and quickly I became increasingly interested in this cute freshman with long, brown hair. Soon I worked up my courage, interrupted Sue as she walked along reading a letter from a guy back home, and awkwardly asked her for a date. To my surprise, she said yes.

More than four decades later, Sue and I look back and laugh at our first uncomfortable meeting on that college campus—and marvel how God put a shy guy from Ohio together with a shy girl from Michigan. Through the years, we have faced innumerable crises together as we raised our family. We've negotiated parenting four kids, and we've struggled mightily with losing one of them. Problems big and small have tested our faith, yet we've stuck together. Today we rejoice in God's design, spelled out in Genesis 2:24—to leave our parents, to be unified as man and wife, and to become united as one flesh. We cherish this amazing plan that has given us such a wonderful life together.

God's design for marriage is beautiful. So, we pray for married couples to sense how awesome it is to enjoy life together under God's blessing.

❖ *Dave Branon*

Loving God

Dear friends, since God so loved us,
we also ought to love one another.

—1 JOHN 4:11

Early in our marriage, I thought I knew the ultimate shortcut to my wife's heart. I arrived home one night with a bouquet of a dozen red roses behind my back. When I presented the flowers to Martie, she thanked me graciously, sniffed the flowers, and then took them into the kitchen. Not quite the response I had expected.

While she appreciated the gesture, she was mentally calculating the cost of an expensive bouquet of flowers—a budget breaker for a young couple in seminary! As I've discovered through the years, she is far more interested in my time and attention than in gifts.

Did you ever wonder how God wants us to show that we love Him? We get a clue when we read, "He who loves God must love his brother also" (1 JOHN 4:21 NKJV). It's that simple. One of the primary ways we show our love for God is by loving our brothers and sisters in Christ.

So watch for opportunities to care for others. It's a priceless way to demonstrate your love for the Lord.

❖ *Joe Stowell*

Nothing Hidden

HEBREWS 4:12–16

Nothing in all creation is hidden from God's sight.
Everything is uncovered and laid bare before the eyes of him
to whom we must give account.

—HEBREWS 4:13

Recently an international research company stated that there were 245 million surveillance cameras in operation worldwide, and the number is growing by fifteen percent every year. In addition, millions of people with smartphones capture images ranging from birthday parties to bank robberies. We live in a global, cameras-everywhere society.

The book of Hebrews says that in our relationship with God, we experience a far greater level of exposure and accountability than anything surveillance cameras may see. His Word, like a sharp, two-edged sword, penetrates to the deepest level of our being where it "judges the thoughts and attitudes of the heart. Nothing in all creation is hidden from God's sight. Everything is uncovered and laid bare before the eyes of him to whom we must give account" (HEBREWS 4:12–13).

But don't panic! Because Jesus experienced temptation but did not sin, we can "approach God's throne of grace with confidence, so that we may receive mercy and find grace to help us in our time of need" (VV. 15–16). Need grace? It's available 24/7.

❖ *David McCasland*

Forgiving the Offender

NUMBERS 21:4–9

So Moses made a bronze serpent, and put it on a pole; and so it was,
if a serpent had bitten anyone, when he looked at the bronze serpent, he lived.

—NUMBERS 21:9 (NKJV)

During his final pizza delivery of the night, nineteen-year-old Brady was robbed and pistol-whipped by three young men. Brady's head injury needed seventy stitches. *Fast forward five years.* Brady and one of the young men who had assaulted him became friends! Brady, a believer in Jesus, reached out to Marcellous—extending forgiveness. Marcellous credits Brady for helping him finish high school and leave gang life behind.

Brady's forgiving ways remind me of God's forgiveness. For instance, during their lengthy trek from Egypt to the Promised Land, the Israelites' behavior became offensive to Him, so He disciplined them with snakes. Soon, recognizing their offensive behavior, they cried out to Moses, "We sinned. . . . Pray that the Lord will take the snakes away" (NUMBERS 21:7).

God provided a way for the people to be healed of the snakebites—just by looking at a bronze snake on a pole (21:9). God's loving forgiveness was on full display!

Later, Jesus was lifted up on a cross so all who look to Him for spiritual healing can be forgiven (JOHN 3:14–15). Jesus forgives offenders—like us.

❖ *Tom Felten*

Gentle Witness

ACTS 1:1–11

"You will receive power when the Holy Spirit comes on you; and you will be my witnesses in Jerusalem, and in all Judea and Samaria, and to the ends of the earth."

—ACTS 1:8

Years ago, I was hospitalized following a life-threatening, thirty-eight-foot fall from a bridge. One day, the wife of the man in the next bed spoke to me. "My husband told me what happened," she said. "We believe God spared your life because He wants to use you. We've been praying for you."

I was stunned. I had grown up going to church, but I never imagined that God wanted to be involved in my life. Her words pointed me to a Savior I had heard of but didn't know—and marked the beginning of my coming to Christ. I cherish the memory of those words from a gentle witness who cared enough to say something to a stranger about the God whose love is real. Her caring words offered purpose and promise.

Jesus challenged His disciples—and us—to tell others about God's love: "You will be my witnesses in Jerusalem, and in all Judea and Samaria, and to the ends of the earth" (ACTS 1:8).

Through the Holy Spirit our words can have the power to make an eternal difference in someone's life.

❖ *Bill Crowder*

Happily Ever After?

[Her] beauty should not come from outward adornment . . .
Rather, it should be that of your inner self, the unfading beauty
of a gentle and quiet spirit, which is of great worth in God's sight.

—1 PETER 3:3–4

There's no guarantee that if you are married you will live happily ever after. Things go wrong—sometimes terribly wrong. Even with the best of intentions, we may find ourselves in a house full of resentment, hostility, unrest, and misery. There is no heartache quite like the heartache of an unhappy marriage.

Yet a difficult marriage can be the setting in which God can deal with "the hidden person of the heart" (1 PETER 3:4 NKJV). Our own heart! Instead of focusing only on what is wrong with our wife, we need to ask the Lord to confront the evil in us. He will begin to do so—gently, gradually, graciously. We can then see ourselves as we are—and not as the perfect, self-controlled person we imagine ourselves to be. We will come to see how much *we* need the Savior's forgiveness and the Spirit's help to do what is right and loving (VV. 1–12).

Our growth may change our wife, or it may not. But with God's help, *we* can change. Although all our marriage ills may not be cured, God's grace can make *us* well.

❖ *David Roper*

In the Driver's Seat

MATTHEW 5:13–16

In the same way, let your light shine before others,
that they may see your good deeds and glorify your Father in heaven.

—MATTHEW 5:16

I enjoy the story of the stressed-out woman who was tailgating a man on a busy boulevard. When he slowed to a stop at a yellow light, the woman hit the horn, cussing and screaming in frustration and gesturing angrily. Still in mid-rant, she heard a tap on her window. It was a police officer, who ordered her to exit the car. He took her to the police station and placed her in a holding cell.

An hour later, the officer returned and said, "I'm sorry, Ma'am. This has been a big mistake. When I saw how you were acting and then saw your 'What Would Jesus Do?' license plate holder and your 'Follow Me to Sunday School' bumper sticker, I assumed the car was stolen!"

Satan wants to see Christians who don't act like they belong to Jesus. If he can get us to live like the ungodly, he knows we will dishonor the name of Christ in the process.

Here's a better way: "Let your light shine before others, that they may see your good deeds and glorify your Father in heaven."

❖ *Joe Stowell*

Eye Level to a Bull Dog

ISAIAH 42:1–7

"I, the LORD, have called you in righteousness; . . . to open eyes that are blind,
to free captives from prison and to release from the dungeon those who sit in darkness."

—ISAIAH 42:6–7

My son and his wife have a one hundred twenty-pound American bulldog with a powerful body and fearsome face. Yet until we became friends, "Buddy" wasn't sure he could trust me. As long as I was on my feet, he'd keep his distance. But if I'd get down on the ground, Buddy's mood would change. Sensing I was no longer a threat, he'd playfully come running like a freight train, pounce on me, and want me to scratch his muscular neck.

Maybe what Buddy needed from me is a glimmer of what our God gave us by coming down to our level and living among us in the person of Christ. From the day our first parents sinned and hid from the Lord's presence in the garden of Eden, our tendency has been to be afraid of coming to a high and holy God on His terms (JOHN 3:20).

So, as Isaiah predicted, God showed how low He was willing to go to bring us to himself. By adopting the form of a lowly servant, our Creator lived and died to disarm our wrongs. How can we still be afraid to trust Him?

❖ *Mart DeHaan*

What Do the Experts Say?

JOHN 5:31–40

These are the very Scriptures that testify about me,
yet you refuse to come to me to have life.

—JOHN 5:39–40

Boston *Globe* columnist Jeff Jacoby writes of the "uncanny ability of experts to get things hopelessly, cataclysmically wrong." A quick glance at history shows he's right. The great inventor Thomas Edison, for instance, once declared that talking movies would never replace silent films. And in 1928, Henry Ford declared, "People are becoming too intelligent ever to have another war." Countless other predictions by "experts" have missed the mark badly.

Only one Person is completely reliable. The religious leaders of Jesus's day claimed to have the truth. They thought they knew what the promised Messiah would be like. But Jesus cautioned them, "You study the Scriptures diligently because you think that in them you have eternal life." Then He pointed out how they were missing the heart of the matter. "These are the very Scriptures that testify about me, yet you refuse to come to me to have life" (JOHN 5:39–40).

No matter what scary predictions we hear, don't be alarmed. Our confidence remains in the One at the very heart of the Scriptures. He has a firm grip on us and on our future.

❖ *Tim Gustafson*

Blended Together

As each part does its own special work, it helps the other parts grow.

—EPHESIANS 4:16 (NLT)

My wife, Janet, bought me a new Dreadnought D-35 guitar for my birthday. Originally developed in the early 1900s, the Dreadnought is known for its bold and loud tone. The back of the D-35 is unique. Because of the shortage of wide pieces of high quality rosewood, the craftsmen innovatively fit three smaller pieces of wood together, which resulted in a richer tone.

God's workmanship is a lot like that innovative guitar design. Jesus takes fragments and blends them together to bring Him praise. He recruited tax collectors, Jewish revolutionaries, fishermen, and others to be His followers. And down through the centuries Christ continues to call out people from varied walks of life. The apostle Paul tells us, "He makes the whole body fit together perfectly. As each part does its own special work, it helps the other parts grow, so that the whole body is healthy and growing and full of love" (EPHESIANS 4:16 NLT).

In the Master's hand many kinds of people are fit together and are being built into something with great potential for praise to God and service for others.

❖ *Dennis Fisher*

Cutting a Trail

PROVERBS 4:1–7

Listen, my sons, to a father's instruction; pay attention and gain understanding.

—PROVERBS 4:1

The Native Americans of Michigan were the state's first highway route engineers. With few exceptions, Michigan's major highways follow the trails they cut through the wilderness hundreds of years ago. A trail was twelve to eighteen inches wide, and the people followed single file. Later, packhorses followed these trails, widening them. Then came wagons, and the trails became dirt roads—and eventually, highways.

In a similar way, Solomon followed the trail of his father and in turn paved the way for his sons and grandsons. He did this by encouraging his sons to heed his instructions just as he had followed the sound teaching of his father (PROVERBS 4:4–5). So this father, giving his sons good practical and spiritual counsel, was passing on what he had learned from the boys' grandfather, David. The younger generation of believers often learns best about God from the family.

Our physical and spiritual children watch the path we're taking. As God's men, let's make certain we cut a righteous, wise, and clear trail—an ongoing legacy to God's glory.

❖ *David Egner*

Ponder Your Path

Above all else, guard your heart, for everything you do flows from it.
Keep your mouth free of perversity; keep corrupt talk far from your lips.
Let your eyes look straight ahead; fix your gaze directly before you.
Give careful thought to the paths for your feet and be steadfast in all your ways.

—PROVERBS 4:23–26

A forty-seven-year-old Austrian man gave away his entire $4.7 million fortune after concluding that his wealth and lavish spending were keeping him from real happiness. Karl Rabeder told the London *Daily Telegraph*, "I was working as a slave for things I did not wish for or need. I realized how horrible, soulless, and without feeling the 'five-star' lifestyle is." His money now funds his charities to help people in Latin America.

Proverbs 4 urges us to consider carefully our own road in life. The passage contrasts the free, unhindered path of the just with the dark, confused way of the wicked (V. 19). "Above all else, guard your heart, for everything you do flows from it" (V. 23). "Give careful thought to the paths for your feet and be steadfast in all your ways" (V. 26). Each verse encourages us to evaluate where we are in life.

Seek grace today to embrace His Word and follow Him wholeheartedly.

❖ *David McCasland*

Press On

PHILIPPIANS 3:12–21

I press on toward the goal to win the prize
for which God has called me heavenward in Christ Jesus.

—PHILIPPIANS 3:14

One of my favorite TV programs is *The Amazing Race*. In this show, ten couples go to a foreign country where they must race—via trains, buses, cabs, bikes, and feet—from one point to another to get their next instructions. The goal is to get to a designated finishing point first. The prize? A million bucks!

Writing to the church at Philippi, Paul compared the Christian life to a race, admitting that he had not arrived at the finish line. "Brothers and sisters, I do not consider myself yet to have taken hold of it. But one thing I do: Forgetting what is behind and straining toward what is ahead. I press on toward the goal to win the prize" (3:13–14). Paul did not allow his past failures to weigh him down, nor did he let his present successes make him complacent. He pressed on toward the goal of becoming more like Jesus.

We're running this race too. Let's "press on" toward the ultimate goal of becoming more Christlike as we race for the ultimate reward of enjoying Him forever.

❖ *Marvin Williams*

Ordinances of Heaven

PSALM 19:1–7

"This is what the LORD says: 'If I have not made my covenant with day and night and established the laws of heaven and earth, then I will reject the descendants of Jacob and David my servant and will not choose one of his sons to rule.'"

—JEREMIAH 33:25–26

Mark your calendar now if you want to see the next celestial convergence of Venus, Jupiter, and the moon. On November 18, 2052, you'll be able to peer through the evening darkness as those solar system neighbors "gather" in a tiny area of the sky. That remarkable juxtaposition of reflective spheres last sparkled the night sky on December 1, 2008.

Astronomic predictability, such as this and the return of Halley's Comet (July 28, 2061), prove the orderliness of the universe. If no fixed set of laws governed the movement of celestial bodies, such predictions could not be made.

Can we see God's hand in these cosmic certainties? Look at Jeremiah 33:25–26. God has in view the covenantal relationship between himself and His people, and He uses a scientific fact in the analogy. God suggests that His fixed universal laws, "the ordinances of heaven and earth (V. 25, NKJV)," have the same certainty as His promises to His covenant people.

So mark your calendar, and be amazed by God's unchanging control.

❖ *Dave Branon*

Gentle Influence

COLOSSIANS 3:12–17

Therefore, as God's chosen people, holy and dearly loved,
clothe yourselves with compassion, kindness, humility, gentleness and patience.

—COLOSSIANS 3:12

A few years before he became the 26th US president (1901–1909), Theodore Roosevelt got word that his oldest son, Theodore Jr., was ill. While his son would recover, the cause of Ted's illness hit Roosevelt hard. Doctors told him that *he* was the cause. Ted was suffering from "nervous exhaustion," having been pressed unmercifully by Theodore to become the "fighter" hero-type he himself had not been as a child. The elder Roosevelt made a promise never again to "press Ted either in body or mind."

The father was true to his word. From then on he paid close attention to how he treated his son—the same son who would one day bravely lead the landing of Allied soldiers on Utah Beach in World War II.

God has entrusted each of us with influence in the lives of others. We have a deep responsibility in those relationships. For this very reason, followers of Christ are urged to be patient and gentle with one another (COLOSSIANS 3:12). Since Jesus came in humility, how can we withhold such kindness from one another?

❖ *Randy Kilgore*

You're at War

For our struggle is not against flesh and blood, but against the rulers, against the authorities, against the powers of this dark world and against the spiritual forces of evil in the heavenly realms.

—EPHESIANS 6:12

Neville Chamberlain was duped in the months before World War II. As British prime minister, he appeased Hitler and acquiesced to his demands—thinking Hitler simply wanted to regain Germany's rightful land.

Soon Chamberlain realized Hitler's word meant nothing. When German tanks rolled into Poland, England had to declare war.

Sometimes I wonder whether I'm a spiritual Chamberlain, unaware that I'm at war. Consider Jude 1:9: "Michael was arguing with the devil [about] Moses' body" (NET) *What?* Michael and Satan tussled over Moses's dead body? Now flip to the story of Moses, which simply says, "the LORD buried him . . . but to this day no one knows the exact place" (DEUTERONOMY 34:6 GNT). Apparently that simple statement, "the LORD buried him," conceals a lot of angelic activity.

I don't know why Satan wanted Moses's body. But Satan was apparently at war with the Israelites during their trek in the desert—and they didn't realize it. How would the Israelites have responded if they knew their desert trials were part of a larger war?

Be on guard, you're at war.

❖ *Mike Wittmer*

EPHESIANS 2:10–22

In him the whole building is joined together
and rises to become a holy temple in the Lord

—EPHESIANS 2:21

It was only scrap wood, but Charles Hooper saw much more than that. Salvaging old timbers from a long-abandoned corncrib, he sketched some simple plans, felled a few oak and poplar trees, and painstakingly squared them with his grandfather's broadax. Piece by piece, he fit together the old lumber with the new.

Today you can see Charles and Shirley Hooper's postcard-perfect log cabin, tucked away in the trees of northwestern Tennessee. The structure stands as tribute to Charles's vision, skill, and patience.

Paul told the church at Ephesus that Jesus was creating something new by bringing together Jewish and non-Jewish believers "by the blood of Christ" (2:13). This new structure was "built on the foundation of the apostles and prophets, Christ Jesus himself as the chief cornerstone. In him the whole building is joined together and rises to become a holy temple in the Lord" (VV. 20–21).

The work continues. God takes the brokenness of our lives, artfully fits us together with other broken and rescued people, and patiently chips away our rough edges. He loves His work, you know.

❖ *Tim Gustafson*

When Not to Rejoice

EZEKIEL 25:1–7; MATTHEW 5:43–48

Do not gloat when your enemy falls;
when they stumble, do not let your heart rejoice.

—PROVERBS 24:17

The Akan people of Ghana have a proverb: "The lizard is not as mad with the boys who threw stones at it as with the boys who stood by and rejoiced over its fate!" Rejoicing at someone's downfall is like participating in the cause of that downfall.

That was the attitude of the Ammonites, who maliciously rejoiced when the temple in Jerusalem "was desecrated and over the land of Israel when it was laid waste and over the people of Judah when they went into exile" (EZEKIEL 25:3). For spitefully celebrating Israel's misfortunes, the Ammonites experienced God's displeasure, which resulted in grim consequences (VV. 4–7).

Proverbs warns us: "Do not gloat when your enemy falls; when they stumble, do not let your heart rejoice" (24:17). Instead, Jesus tells us that we show His love in action when we "love [our] enemies and pray for those who persecute [us]" (MATTHEW 5:44). By so doing, we imitate the perfect love of our Lord (5:48).

❖ *Lawrence Darmani*

The Fox and the Egg

PSALM 84

Lord Almighty, blessed is the one who trusts in you.

—PSALM 84:12

I was sitting by the window, staring out through fir and spruce trees to the mountains beyond, lost in thought. I looked down and saw a fox staring up at me—as still as a stone.

Days before, I had seen her at the edge of the woods, looking nervously over her shoulder at me. I went to the kitchen for an egg and rolled it toward the place I had last seen her. Each day I put another egg on the lawn, and each day she ventured out of the trees, picked it up, and darted back into the woods.

Now she had come to my door for an egg, convinced that I meant her no harm.

This incident reminded my wife of David's invitation: "Taste and see that the Lord is good" (PSALM 34:8). How do we start doing that? By taking in His Word. As we read and reflect on His compassion and lovingkindness, we learn that He can be trusted (84:12). We lose our dread of getting closer to Him. Our fear becomes a healthy respect.

Taste and see that the Lord is good!

❖ *David Roper*

Eager to Listen

JAMES 1:19–21

My dear brothers and sisters, take note of this:
Everyone should be quick to listen, slow to speak and slow to become angry.

—JAMES 1:19

A stepdad, trying to bond with his son, took him on a fishing trip. The boy, who preferred video games and being inside, hated it. However, instead of telling his stepdad directly, he handed him a note saying he wanted to go home. The man glanced at the note, stuck it in his pocket, and kept fishing.

When they returned home days later, the boy complained to his mother. She paused and said to him, "Son, what you don't realize is that your stepdad can't read."

Communication breaks down when we can't understand what others are saying. Usually, that means we aren't listening. James stressed, "My dear brothers and sisters, take note of this: Everyone should be quick to listen, slow to speak and slow to become angry" (JAMES 1:19).

In other words, we must focus on what the other person is saying—without debating or getting defensive.

"Fools find no pleasure in understanding but delight in airing their own opinions" said the wise man in Proverbs 18:2. But when we listen, we show others we care about them. We show them the love God shows us.

❖ *Jeff Olson*

Giving in to Jesus

JAMES 4:6–10

In the same way, count yourselves dead to sin
but alive to God in Christ Jesus.

—ROMANS 6:11

They call it "The Devil's Footprint." It's a foot-shaped impression in the granite on a hill beside a church in Ipswich, Massachusetts. According to local legend the "footprint" happened one day in 1740, when evangelist George Whitefield preached so powerfully that the devil leaped from the church steeple—landing on the rock on his way out of town.

Although it's only a legend, the story calls to mind an encouraging truth from God's Word: "Resist the devil, and he will flee from you" (JAMES 4:7).

With the help of God's strength, we can stand against our adversary and resist temptation. "Sin shall no longer be your master" (ROMANS 6:14) because of God's loving grace through Jesus Christ. As we run to Jesus when temptation comes, He enables us to stand in His strength.

As we submit to our Savior, yielding our wills to Him in the moment and walking in obedience to God's Word, He helps us. When we give in to Him instead of giving in to temptation, He is able to fight our battles. In Him we can overcome.

❖ *James Banks*

Simplify
MATTHEW 6:25–34

"Therefore do not worry about tomorrow, for tomorrow will worry about itself.
Each day has enough trouble of its own."

—MATTHEW 6:34

In a radio interview, a basketball superstar was asked about his knack for making the game-winning shot in crucial situations. The reporter asked how he was able to be so calm in such pressure-packed moments. His answer was that he tried to simplify the situation. "You only have to make one shot," the player replied. One shot. That is the essence of simplifying a difficult situation. Focus only on what is in front of you. Simplify.

Recognizing that the challenges of life can be both overwhelming and suffocating, Jesus urged us to uncomplicate things. He said, "Do not worry about tomorrow, for tomorrow will worry about itself" (MATTHEW 6:34). Worry doesn't accomplish anything positive; it just adds to the sense that we are drowning in our troubles. We must take things as they come—one day at a time—and trust Him for the wisdom to respond properly.

If you feel overwhelmed by life, do what you can today and then entrust the rest to Him. Simplify. As Jesus said, "Each day has enough trouble of its own."

❖ *Bill Crowder*

Comforted to Comfort

2 CORINTHIANS 1:3–11

[God] comforts us in all our troubles, so that we can comfort those in any trouble with the comfort we ourselves receive from God.

—2 CORINTHIANS 1:4

While speaking to a group of Christian athletes, I asked them how they normally responded to hardships. Their responses included fear, anger, self-pity, aggression, despair, abusive behavior, apathy, and turning to God. I encouraged them to trust that God would comfort them and then use them to comfort others.

Just as I encouraged those athletes, Paul encouraged a group of believers in a town called Corinth. He reminded them that afflictions were inevitable for the follower of Jesus. Many were being persecuted, imprisoned, and oppressed—all because of their relationship with Jesus. Paul wanted the Corinthians to know that in the midst of their trouble God was their source of help. Then Paul gave one of the reasons God allowed suffering and brought divine comfort—so the Corinthians might have the empathy to enter into other people's sorrow and comfort them (2 CORINTHIANS 1:4).

When we suffer, God will bring comfort to us through His Word, by the Holy Spirit, and through fellow believers. God does not comfort us so that we'll be comfortable; we are comforted by God so that we might be comforters.

❖ *Marvin Williams*

He Calls the Stars by Name

PSALM 147:1–9

He determines the number of the stars
and calls them each by name.

—PSALM 147:4

On a plateau high above the Atacama Desert in Chile, one of the world's largest radio telescopes gives astronomers a view of the universe never seen before. In an Associated Press article, Luis Andres Henao spoke of scientists "looking for clues about the dawn of the cosmos—from the coldest gases and dust where galaxies are formed and stars are born to the energy produced by the Big Bang."

The Bible celebrates the mighty power and infinite understanding of God who "determines the number of the stars" and "calls them each by name" (PSALM 147:4). The Creator of the universe is a loving heavenly Father who also "heals the brokenhearted and binds up their wounds" (V. 3). "The LORD sustains the humble" (V. 6) and "delights in those who fear him, who put their hope in his unfailing love" (V. 11).

Above it all, "He gave his one and only Son, that whoever believes in him shall not perish but have eternal life" (JOHN 3:16).

Our hope for today and forever lies in the loving mercy of God, who calls each star by name.

❖ *David McCasland*

Collision Course

2 SAMUEL 12:1–15

But if you fail to do this, you will be sinning against the Lord;
and you may be sure that your sin will find you out.

—NUMBERS 32:23

My wife and I were driving on an expressway when we saw a driver turn left into a median turnaround intended for emergency vehicles only. He was planning to make a U-turn and head back the other way.

Looking to his right, the driver waited for an opening in oncoming traffic. He failed to notice the police car backing up toward him on his left. Finally seeing an opening in traffic, the U-turn driver pulled out and rammed into the back of the police car.

It's not unusual for us to think we can get away with doing something wrong. After King David committed adultery with Bathsheba, he was focused on "getting away with it." His actions "displeased the Lord" (2 SAMUEL 11:27), so when Nathan exposed David's grievous sin, the king was remorseful. He confessed, repented, and received God's forgiveness. But the consequences of his sin never departed from his household (12:10).

Remember, "your sin will find you out" (NUMBERS 32:23). Turn yourself in to God. Don't hide. Instead, seek His gracious forgiveness.

❖ *Dennis Fisher*

Living with Expectation

So Peter and the other disciple started for the tomb.
Both were running, but the other disciple outran Peter and reached the tomb first.

—JOHN 20:3–4

When the dark day of Jesus's crucifixion drew to a close, it seemed that the most wonderful of all lives had come to an end. Christ had astounded the crowds and His followers with the wisdom of His teaching and the wonder of His miracles. But Jesus chose not to save himself from the cross, and His life was over. It seemed that nothing more could be expected of this man.

Hope returned, however, on that first resurrection morning. A painting by Eugene Burnand portrays Peter and John running to the tomb. Shortly after dawn, Mary Magdalene had told them she and her friends had found the tomb empty. In Burnand's painting, the faces of Peter and John show contending emotions of anguish and relief, of sorrow and surprise, of despair and wonder as they race toward the tomb. Their gaze is eagerly fixed forward, turning the viewer's attention to the sepulcher. What did they find? An empty tomb—the Savior was alive!

Christ still lives! Let's look beyond the empty tomb to the One who can fill our lives with the power of His resurrection!

❖ *David Egner*

Learning from the Redwoods

ISAIAH 65:17–66:2

No longer will they build houses and others live in them or plant and others eat.
For as the days of a tree, so will be the days of my people;
my chosen ones will long enjoy the work of their hands.

—ISAIAH 65:22

North America's Pacific Coast Redwoods are some of the biggest trees in the world. The tallest on record, Hyperion, soars 380 feet into the air.

During a visit to California's Muir Woods National Park, I was surprised and overwhelmed by the enormity of those redwoods.

The memory of what I felt at the base of some of the tallest and oldest trees in the world has left me with lingering thoughts about their origin. Those redwoods, like the family tree of our own humanity, are rooted in a Creator who is infinitely and eternally greater than His creation.

The prophet Isaiah caught a glimpse of this God. In a vision that mingled the wonders of a Messianic kingdom with the promise of a new heaven and earth, he describes One who makes the skies His throne and the earth His footstool (ISAIAH 66:1).

Isaiah saw a great God who wants His people to "be glad and rejoice forever in what I will create" (65:18). In response, let's bow before Him in humble adoration (66:2).

❖ *Mart DeHaan*

Cave Man
PSALM 142

Listen to my cry, for I am in desperate need;
rescue me from those who pursue me, for they are too strong for me.

—PSALM 142:6

David was stuck in a cave (PSALM 142). He was running from King Saul, who wanted to kill him (1 SAMUEL 22:1). Hemmed in by circumstances and smothered by danger, he turned to God for help.

• David was frightened, so he poured out his complaint to God (PSALM 142:2).
• He felt alone and uncared for, so he cried out to God (VV. 1, 4–5).
• His situation was desperate, so he pleaded for rescue (V. 6).

What cave surrounds you? A cave of despair brought on by grief or illness? A cave of difficulties caused by poor decisions? Are you stuck in a cave of questions or doubts that rob you of joy and confidence?

Here's what David did when trapped in his cave: He asked God for mercy, he sought refuge in Him, and he promised to use his eventual freedom as a way to praise God. In the end, he looked forward to the comfort of fellow believers.

Complaint followed by faith. Desperation followed by praise. Loneliness followed by fellowship. We can learn a lot from a cave man.

❖ *Dave Branon*

Grace That Motivates

TITUS 3:4–8

*This is a trustworthy saying. And I want you to stress these things, so that those
who have trusted in God may be careful to devote themselves to doing what is good.
These things are excellent and profitable for everyone.*

—TITUS 3:8

Nothing moved him anymore. Although he ran one of the top skateboard teams in the world and dove headlong into every pleasure he chose, Ryan Ries felt empty.

One night he nearly died from a cocaine overdose. The next morning Ryan found a Gideon Bible in his hotel room and began reading it. In time, God's grace seeped into Ryan's broken, convicted heart, and he placed his faith in Jesus. Today, he and his wife help others find real life while also breaking free from addictions and unhealthy lifestyles.

Paul knew he needed to help the believers in the church on Crete break free from an unhealthy, degenerate culture (TITUS 1:12–13). So he instructed his "true son in our common faith" Titus to appoint godly, strong elders "in every town" on the island (TITUS 1:4–5) so people could be reminded that God's *mercy* (TITUS 3:5) and *grace* (TITUS 3:7) brings salvation.

Paul wrote that God "saved us, not because of righteous things we had done," but because of His mercy and grace (TITUS 3:5). Today, we strive to help others find real life in Him.

❖ *Tom Felten*

Reason to Smile

*Therefore encourage one another and build each other up,
just as in fact you are doing.*

—1 THESSALONIANS 5:11

In the workplace, words of encouragement matter. How employees talk to one another has a bearing on customer satisfaction, company profits, and co-worker appreciation. Studies show that members of the most effective work groups give one another six times more affirmation than disapproval, disagreement, or sarcasm. Least productive teams use nearly three negative comments for every helpful word.

Paul learned by experience about the value of words in shaping relationships and outcomes. Before meeting Christ on the road to Damascus, his words and actions terrorized followers of Jesus. But by the time he wrote his letter to the Thessalonians, he had become a great encourager because of God's work in his heart. By his own example he urged his readers to cheer one another on.

Paul reminded his readers where encouragement comes from. He saw that entrusting ourselves to God, who loved us enough to die for us, gives us reason to comfort, forgive, inspire, and lovingly challenge one another (1 THESSALONIANS 5:10–11). Encourage others. Give them a taste of the goodness of God.

❖ *Mart DeHaan*

Leap the Wall

ROMANS 12:14–21

> *If your enemy is hungry, give him food to eat;*
> *if he is thirsty, give him water to drink.*

—PROVERBS 25:21

Sgt. Richard Kirkland was a Confederate soldier in the US Civil War (1861–1865). When the Union's failed charge at Marye's Heights during the Battle of Fredericksburg left wounded soldiers abandoned in no-man's land, Kirkland got permission to help them. Collecting canteens, he leaped a stone wall and bent over the first soldier to lend assistance. At great personal risk, the "Angel of Marye's Heights" extended the mercy of Christ to enemy soldiers.

While few of us will face an enemy on the battlefield, people who suffer can be found all around us—struggling against loneliness, loss, health issues, and sin. Their cries, muted by our many distractions, plead for mercy and comfort, for hope and help.

The apostle Paul said, "If your enemy is hungry, feed him; if he is thirsty, give him something to drink" (ROMANS 12:20). "Do not be overcome by evil," he instructed us, "but overcome evil with good" (V. 21).

Paul's challenge compels us to emulate Sgt. Kirkland. Today is the day for us to "leap the wall" of safety to lend comfort from God to those in need.

❖ *Randy Kilgore*

A New Career?

MATTHEW 4:18–22

Immediately they left the boat and their father and followed him.

—MATTHEW 4:22

For some guys, an annual fishing trip is the highlight of their calendar. They stay in cozy cabins and spend long days fishing just for the fun of it.

You can be sure it wasn't that way for the fisherman disciples. They weren't on vacation when they met Jesus. Fishing was their career.

Our careers often demand much of our time and attention. But Jesus has an interesting way of interrupting our business-as-usual agenda. In fact, He invites us to join His business.

Notice the sequence of His statement to the fishermen: "Follow Me, and I will make you fishers of men" (MATTHEW 4:19 NKJV). He calls us first to follow Him, and then He makes something of our lives. He leads us to prioritize so we see the needs of people and their eternity as the goal of all our endeavors.

And while God may not require you to give up your career, following Him will guarantee that you will never see your career in the same way again. Where you "fish" is not important. But if you follow, you must fish.

❖ *Joe Stowell*

He Found Me

LUKE 19:1–10

"For the Son of Man came to seek and to save the lost."

—LUKE 19:10

The film *Amazing Grace* was set in the late 1700s. It tells the story of William Wilberforce, a British politician driven by his faith in Christ to commit his money and energy to abolishing the slave trade in England. In one scene, Wilberforce's butler finds him praying. The butler asks, "You found God, Sir?" Wilberforce responds, "I think He found me."

The Bible pictures us as wayward sheep. It says, "We all, like sheep, have gone astray, each of us has turned to our own way" (ISAIAH 53:6). Paul put it this way: "There is no one righteous, not even one; there is no one who understands; there is no one who seeks God" (ROMANS 3:10–12). That's why Jesus came. We would never seek Him, so He came seeking us. "For the Son of Man came to seek and to save the lost" (LUKE 19:10).

Wilberforce was right. Jesus came to find us, for we could never have found Him if left to ourselves. Our Lord loves us so much that He pursues us and desires to make us His own. Has He "found" you?

❖ *Bill Crowder*

Pulling Together

*Let us consider how we may spur one another on
toward love and good deeds.*

—HEBREWS 10:24

Why do more than five million people a year pay money to run several miles over an obstacle course where they must ascend vertical walls, slog through mud, and climb up inside a vertical pipe with water pouring down on them? Some see it as a personal challenge to push their limit of endurance or conquer their fears. For others, the attraction is teamwork where competitors help and support each other.

The Bible urges us to pursue teamwork as a model of living out our faith in Jesus. "Let us consider how we may spur one another on toward love and good deeds, not giving up meeting together, as some are in the habit of doing, but encouraging one another" (HEBREWS 10:24–25).

Our goal is not to "finish first" in the race of faith but to reach out in tangible ways of encouragement by setting an example and lending a helping hand along the way.

The day will come when we complete our life on earth. Until then, let's spur each other on, be ready to help, and keep pulling together every day.

❖ *David McCasland*

Multiplied Generosity

2 CORINTHIANS 8:1–9

Since you excel in everything—in faith, in speech, in knowledge, in complete earnestness and in the love we have kindled in you—see that you also excel in this grace of giving.

—2 CORINTHIANS 8:7

Cheryl pulled up to deliver her next pizza, surprised to find herself outside a church. Cheryl carried the pepperoni pizza inside, where she was met by the pastor.

"Is it fair to say life hasn't been easy for you?" the pastor asked her. Cheryl agreed it hadn't. With that, he brought out an offering the church members collected. He poured over $750 into Cheryl's delivery bag as a tip! Unbeknownst to Cheryl, the pastor had asked the pizza shop to send their most financially strapped driver.

When the first Christians in Jerusalem faced poverty, a church rushed to their aid. Though in need themselves, the Macedonian Christians gave sacrificially (2 CORINTHIANS 8:1–4). Paul cited their generosity as an example for us to follow. When we help meet another's need, we reflect Jesus, who gave away His riches to meet our own spiritual poverty (V. 9).

Cheryl told all her customers about the church's kindness, and following its example, donated the rest of the day's tips to others. An act of generosity multiplied. And Christ was glorified.

❖ *Sheridan Voysey*

The Hollywood Hills Cross

1 CORINTHIANS 1:18–31

May I never boast except in the cross of our Lord Jesus Christ,
through which the world has been crucified to me, and I to the world.

—GALATIANS 6:14

One of the most recognizable images in the US is the "HOLLYWOOD" sign in Southern California. It's hard for visitors to miss the sign anchored in the foothills nearby.

Less well known in the Hollywood hills is another easily recognized symbol—one with eternal significance. Known as the Hollywood Pilgrimage Memorial Monument, this thirty-two-foot cross looks out over the city. The cross was placed there in memory of Christine Wetherill Stevenson, a wealthy heiress. In the 1920s she established the Pilgrimage Theatre, which was the venue for *The Pilgrimage Play,* a drama about Christ.

While movies come and go—their relevance being temporary at best—the cross reminds us of a drama eternal in scope. The work of Christ is a story of the loving God who pursues us and invites us to accept His offer of complete forgiveness. The high drama of Jesus's death is rooted in history. His resurrection conquered death and has an eternal impact for all of us. The cross will never lose its meaning and power.

❖ *Dennis Fisher*

True Confessions

PSALM 51:1–13

Surely I was sinful at birth, sinful from the time my mother conceived me.

—PSALM 51:5

I love coconut. I always have! So, after an exhausting day in second grade, I found a bag of shredded coconut in the cupboard and devoured the whole thing. When my mother went into the kitchen later to bake—you guessed it, a coconut cake—I heard, "Who ate the coconut?!"

I knew I was in trouble, but my escape plan was simple—a quick, easy lie: "Not me!"

My cover-up plan was doomed to failure, and later that evening I finally confessed.

No one had to teach me to lie. As the psalmist David admits, "I was . . . sinful from the time my mother conceived me" (PSALM 51:5). But in his sin David knew where to go—to the God of abundant mercy who will cleanse us from our sin (VV. 1–2).

Still today, He is waiting for us to confess our faults and embrace the forgiveness and cleansing that He readily offers.

Remember, a refreshing plunge into God's mercy awaits you on the other side of confessed sin!

❖ *Joe Stowell*

Yikes! A Checkup

PROVERBS 4:20–27

Test me, LORD, and try me, examine my heart and my mind.

—PSALM 26:2

Given a choice, I would not voluntarily visit my doctor for a physical exam. I'm inclined to assume that everything is okay and not bother him about it. But every year—into the office I go!

And given a choice, many of us are a little afraid of spiritual checkups as well. After all, if we check our spirit too closely, we might have to change a habit or two. We might need something like an "attitude-ectomy."

Can we get over our reluctance and undergo a spiritual checkup—using Proverbs 4:20–27 as a checklist.

- Ears (v. 20): Are we hearing God's Word clearly? Are we doing what those words tell us?
- Eyes (vv. 21, 25): Are we keeping our eyes on truths that will guide us toward righteousness?
- Heart (v. 23): Are we protecting our heart from evil?
- Tongue (v. 24): Is our mouth clean and pure?
- Feet (v. 26): Are we walking straight toward God's truth without wavering?

How did you do? Are there areas where you need to take action? Regular checkups will help to restore your spiritual vitality.

❖ *Dave Branon*

Wisdom's Call

PROVERBS 8:10–21

Wisdom is more precious than rubies,
and nothing you desire can compare with her.

—PROVERBS 8:11

Noted British journalist Malcolm Muggeridge came to faith in Christ at age sixty. On his seventy-fifth birthday he offered twenty-five insightful observations about life. One said, "I never met a rich man who was happy, but I have only very occasionally met a poor man who did not want to become a rich man."

Most of us would agree that money can't make us happy, but we might like to have more so we can be sure. King Solomon's net worth was an estimated two trillion US dollars, but he knew money had great limitations. Proverbs 8 is based on his experience and offers "Wisdom's Call" to us. He said, "Choose my instruction instead of silver, knowledge rather than choice gold, for wisdom is more precious than rubies, and nothing you desire can compare with her" (VV. 10–11).

Wisdom says, "My fruit is better than fine gold; . . . I walk in the way of righteousness, along the paths of justice, bestowing a rich inheritance on those who love me and making their treasuries full" (VV. 19–21).

These are true riches indeed!

❖ *David McCasland*

Wise Old Jake

LUKE 2:46–52

Jesus grew in wisdom and stature, and in favor with God and man.

—LUKE 2:52

I'll never forget Jake. His legs seemed too thin and spindly to hold him against the current of the river. His patched and discolored waders looked older than he was—which was saying something.

I watched as he worked his way upstream to a patch of quiet water. He was fishing the same water I had fished earlier in the day, but he was catching trout where I had caught none. Here was a man who could teach me a thing or two. All I had to do was ask.

We gain insight when we listen to those who have gone before and know more than we do. We can learn from others when we humble ourselves and acknowledge how little we know. Willingness to learn is a mark of the truly wise.

Consider our Lord as a young boy, "sitting among the teachers, listening to them and asking them questions" (LUKE 2:46). Proverbs 1:5 says that "a wise man will hear and increase learning, and a man of understanding will attain wise counsel" (NKJV). We can learn from people who've spent their lives seeking God's wisdom.

❖ *David Roper*

Even small children are known by their actions,
so is their conduct really pure and upright?

—PROVERBS 20:11

One night a clergyman was walking to church when a thief pulled a gun on him and demanded his money or his life. When he reached in his pocket to hand over his wallet, the robber saw his clerical collar and said: "I see you are a priest. Never mind, you can go." The clergyman, surprised by the robber's unexpected act of piety, offered him a candy bar. The robber said, "No thank you. I don't eat candy during Lent."

The man had given up candy as a supposed sacrifice for Lent, but his lifestyle of stealing showed his real character! According to the writer of Proverbs, conduct is the best indicator of character. If someone says he is a godly person, his or her words can be proven only by consistent actions (20:11). Appearances and words are deceiving; behavior is the best judge of character.

As followers of Jesus, we demonstrate our love for Him by what we do, not just by what we say. May our devotion to God, because of His love for us, be revealed in our actions today.

❖ *Marvin Williams*

God of Life

LORD my God, you are very great;
you are clothed with splendor and majesty.

—PSALM 104:1

A few winters ago, my hometown experienced an unusually long blast of bone-chilling temperatures. For two weeks straight, the thermometer dipped well below the sub-zero degree mark (-20 C; -5 F).

On one particularly bitter cold morning, the sound of chirping birds broke the silence. Dozens, if not hundreds, sang their hearts out. I could have sworn the little creatures were crying out to their Creator to please warm things up!

Bird experts tell us that most birdsongs we hear during late winter mornings are from male birds, attempting to attract mates and claim their territories. Their chirping reminded me that God fine-tuned His creation to sustain and flourish life—because He is a God of life.

In a psalm that marvels at God's flourishing earth, the author begins, "Let all that I am praise the LORD" (PSALM 104:1 NLT).

From singing and nesting birds to a vast ocean "teeming with creatures beyond number" (V. 25), we see reasons to praise the Creator for the lengths He's gone to ensure that all of life thrives.

❖ *Jeff Olson*

A Treasure to Be Shared

2 CORINTHIANS 4:1–7

We have this treasure in jars of clay to show that this
all-surpassing power is from God and not from us.

—2 CORINTHIANS 4:7

In March 1974, Chinese farmers were digging a well when they made a surprising discovery: Buried under the dry ground of central China was the Terracotta Army—life-size terracotta sculptures that dated back to the third century BC. In this extraordinary find were some 8,000 soldiers, 150 cavalry horses, and 130 chariots drawn by 520 horses. The Terracotta Army has become one of the most popular tourist sites in China, attracting over a million visitors annually. This amazing treasure lay hidden for centuries but is now being shared with the world.

The apostle Paul wrote that followers of Christ have a treasure inside them that is to be shared with the world: "We now have this light shining in our hearts, but we ourselves are like fragile clay jars containing this great treasure" (2 CORINTHIANS 4:7 NLT). The treasure inside us is the message of Christ and His love.

By God's love and grace people of every nation can be welcomed into His family. May we, through His Spirit's working, share that treasure with someone today.

❖ *Bill Crowder*

Surprise Interview

ACTS 26:9–15

"And the King will say, 'I tell you the truth, when you did it to one of the least of these my brothers and sisters, you were doing it to me!'"

—MATTHEW 25:40 (NLT)

On a crowded London commuter train, an early morning rider shoved and insulted a fellow passenger. It was the kind of unfortunate and mindless moment that usually remains unresolved. But later that day, the unexpected happened. The person who had acted so poorly on the train walked into a job interview only to discover that the person who greeted him for the interview was the person he had mistreated earlier that day.

Saul also ran into someone he never expected to see. While raging against a group called the Way (ACTS 9:1–2), he was stopped by a blinding light. Then a voice said, "Saul, Saul, why do you persecute me?" (V. 4). Saul asked, "Who are you, Lord?" The One speaking to him replied, "I am Jesus, whom you are persecuting" (V. 5).

Years earlier Jesus had said that how we treat the hungry, the thirsty, the stranger, and the prisoner reflects our relationship to Him (MATTHEW 25:35–36). Who would have dreamed that when someone insults us, or when we help or hurt another, the One who loves us takes it personally?

❖ *Mart DeHaan*

Not My Kind

GALATIANS 3:19–29

There is neither Jew nor Gentile, neither slave nor free,
nor is there male and female, for you are all one in Christ Jesus.

—GALATIANS 3:28

In the Star Wars trilogy there's a scene that reminds me of some church people I know. At an establishment somewhere in a remote corner of the galaxy, grotesque-looking creatures socialize over food and music. When Luke Skywalker enters with his two droids, C-3PO and R2-D2 (who are more "normal" than anyone else there), he is surprisingly turned away with a curt rebuff: "We don't serve their kind here!"

That strange scene captures the malady we all struggle with in our relationships. We are always more comfortable with people who are just like us.

Those of us who follow Christ shouldn't have "they're not my kind" in our vocabulary. As Paul reminds us, in Him "there is neither Jew nor Gentile, neither slave nor free, nor is there male and female; for you are all one in Christ Jesus" (GALATIANS 3:28). So, whether others are different in attitude, perspective, race, class, political slant, or social standing, it should make no difference to those of us who call ourselves by Jesus's name.

Find someone who is "not your kind" and share Jesus's love with him or her today!

❖ *Joe Stowell*

Trouble at the Top

MALACHI 1:6–14

"Oh, that one of you would shut the temple doors,so that you would not light useless fires on my altar! I am not pleased with you," says the LORD Almighty, "and I will accept no offering from your hands."

—MALACHI 1:10

Leadership has its privileges, but more important—it comes with huge responsibilities.

Through the years, I've observed the lives of many Christian leaders. I've noticed that they don't always demonstrate godly traits.

When God removes His hand of blessing because a leader engages in ungodly activity, everyone suffers. That's why it's so important for every Christian in a leadership position to strive daily to keep his heart attuned to God and His Word.

In Israel in 500 BC, there arose leadership issues that God dealt with directly. Apparently, the priests who were supposed to be serving God weren't. They dishonored the Lord by offering defiled sacrifices (MALACHI 1:7–8). So God removed His blessing from the priests. He could not accept their sacrifices (V. 10). Imagine the difficulties this brought on the people.

Are you a leader? Stay close to God. Obey His Word. Worship Him "in the Spirit and in truth" (JOHN 4:24). Don't risk losing the Lord's blessing by causing trouble at the top.

❖ *Dave Branon*

Getting Nautical

LUKE 8:22–25

You rule over the surging sea;
when its waves mount up, you still them.

—PSALM 89:9

The Sea of Galilee was known for its sudden and violent storms. One evening, Jesus suggested that He and His disciples cross the large inland lake by boat (LUKE 8:22). As they made their way, a strong storm moved in. Fierce waves threatened to sink their vessel.

The disciples were understandably scared—fearful of drowning. But not Jesus—He was snoozing in the back of the boat (LUKE 8:23). After the disciples awakened Him, Jesus stood up (maybe even stretched a bit) and ordered the wind and the waves to calm down. And they did (LUKE 8:24).

Shocked, the disciples didn't know what to fear more—Jesus or the storm. "Who is this man?" they wondered out loud. "Even the wind and waves obey him!" (LUKE 8:25 TLB). Centuries earlier, the psalmist asked, "Where is there anyone as mighty as you, O Lord? . . . You rule the oceans. You subdue their storm-tossed waves" (PSALM 89:8–9 NLT).

May God's power and authority—two things that amazed the disciples and inspired an ancient poet—reassure us when life starts to get "nautical." He is greater than anything we will ever face.

❖ *Jeff Olson*

Not Even a Nod

LUKE 17:11–19

One of them, when he saw he was healed,
came back, praising God in a loud voice.

—LUKE 17:15

Traffic was bad and everyone was cranky on that hot afternoon. I noticed a car with two young men waiting to enter traffic from a fast-food restaurant driveway. I thought it was nice when the driver ahead of me let them in.

But when the "nice" driver ahead of me didn't get a nod or even a thank you wave, he turned ugly. He shouted at the driver he had let in, raced forward as if to ram into his car, and honked his horn as he continued to vent his anger.

Who was "more wrong"? Did the young driver's ingratitude justify the "nice" driver's angry response? Was he owed a thank you?

Certainly the ten lepers Jesus healed in the Luke 17 story owed gratitude to Him. How could only one return to say thank you? If the King of Kings can get only a one in ten response of thanks, how can we expect more from others?

May the grace of God be seen in us even when our kind acts go unappreciated.

❖ *Randy Kilgore*

Misplaced Trust

PSALM 20

Some trust in chariots and some in horses,
but we trust in the name of the LORD our God.

—PSALM 20:7

I like watching birds, an activity I developed while growing up in a forest village in Ghana. Recently I observed the behavior of some crows. Flying toward a mostly leafless tree, they decided to take a rest. But instead of settling on the sturdy branches, they landed on dry and weak limbs, which quickly gave way. They flapped their way out of danger—only to repeat the useless effort. Apparently their bird-sense didn't tell them solid branches were more trustworthy and secure.

How about us? Where do we place our trust? David observes in Psalm 20:7: "Some trust in chariots and some in horses, but we trust in the name of the LORD our God." Chariots and horses represent material and human assets. While useful in daily life, these don't give us security in times of trouble. If we place our trust in things or possessions or wealth, we'll find that they give way beneath us.

Those who trust in things can be "brought to their knees and fall," but those who trust in God will "rise up and stand firm" (V. 8).

❖ *Lawrence Darmani*

What about the Box?

JOHN 6:1–14

Then Jesus declared, "I am the bread of life. Whoever comes to me will never go hungry, and whoever believes in me will never be thirsty."

—JOHN 6:35

One time, I ordered a twenty-eight-ounce steak at a restaurant. Big mistake. I had the remainder boxed up to take home. I looked forward to another feast.

As I left the restaurant, a homeless man approached me, asking for money. At first I refused. But struck by sudden guilt, I gave him five dollars and blessed him in Jesus's name. I was happy to go on my way, boxed-up steak in hand, until he asked, "What about the box?" I have to admit, I had a hard time parting with my steak.

One of my favorite New Testament stories is about the little boy who brown-bagged it to a revival service (JOHN 6:1–14). He was willing to give his lunch of five barley loaves and two small fish to Jesus. I think he may have known that Jesus could do something extraordinary with his lunch. And He did. He fed thousands of hungry people.

Jesus is still looking for a folks like us who are willing to commit out-of-the-ordinary, intentional acts of selfless sacrifice so He can turn our offering into His glory.

❖ *Joe Stowell*

Write Your Epitaph

2 TIMOTHY 4:1–8

*I have remained faithful. The prize is not just for me
but for all who eagerly look forward to his appearing.*

—2 TIMOTHY 4:7-8 (NLT)

A famous epitaph in the Boothill Graveyard in Tombstone, Arizona, reads, "HERE LIES LESTER MOORE, FOUR SLUGS FROM A 44, NO LES NO MORE." The Wells, Fargo & Co. station agent died in an Old West gun battle with another man in the late 1800s.

Some eighteen centuries earlier, Paul wrote his own "epitaph." In an apparent final letter written prior to his martyrdom in Rome, the apostle told his protégé Timothy: "I have fought the good fight, I have finished the race, I have kept the faith" (2 TIMOTHY 4:7-8). Paul's summation of his life must have been a challenge and encouragement to Timothy, just as it is to us today.

One day, if you and I were to write our own epitaph, may we find that these two words best described our time on earth: *offering,* (V. 6); *faithful* (V. 7).

Paul wrote, "The prize is not just for me but for all who eagerly look forward to his appearing" (2 TIMOTHY 4:8 NLT). Far better than a well-worded epitaph, our living, loving Lord gives us the hope and strength we need to live for Him today!

❖ *Tom Felten*

What on Earth?

MATTHEW 17:24–27

Whatever you have learned or received or heard from me, or seen in me—
put it into practice. And the God of peace will be with you.

—PHILIPPIANS 4:9

When Andrew Cheatle lost his cell phone at the beach, he thought it was gone forever. About a week later, however, fisherman Glen Kerley called him. He had pulled Cheatle's phone, still functional after it dried, out of a twenty-five-pound cod.

Life—and the Bible—have lots of odd stories. One day tax collectors came to Peter demanding, "Doesn't your teacher pay the temple tax?" (MATTHEW 17:24). This became a teaching moment. Jesus wanted Peter to understand His role as king. Taxes weren't collected from the children of the king, so the Lord said neither He nor His children owed any temple tax (VV. 25–26).

Yet Jesus wanted to be careful not to "cause offense" (V. 27), so He told Peter to go fishing, and Peter found a coin in the mouth of the first fish he caught.

What is Jesus doing here? He is the rightful King—and when we accept His role as Lord in our lives, we become His children.

Life will still throw its various demands at us, but Jesus will provide for us. In both kingdoms.

❖ *Tim Gustafson*

God in the Details

MATTHEW 10:29–31

The LORD is good to all; he has compassion on all he has made.

—PSALM 145:9

When my chocolate Labrador retriever puppy was three months old, I took him to the veterinarian's office for his shots and checkup. As our vet carefully looked him over, she noticed a small white marking in his fur on his left hind paw. She smiled and said to him, "That's where God held you when He dipped you in chocolate."

I couldn't help but laugh, but she had unintentionally made a great point. God cares deeply about His creation.

Jesus tells us in Matthew 10:30 that "even the very hairs of your head are all numbered." God takes infinite interest in the most intimate details of our lives. No concern is too trivial to bring before Him. He cares that much!

God not only created us but He also sustains and keeps us. Perhaps you've heard the line: "the devil is in the details." It's far better to understand that God is in them, watching over even the things that escape our notice. Our wise and caring heavenly Father holds us—along with all of creation—in His strong and loving hands!

❖ *James Banks*

Play in Pain

LAMENTATIONS 3:1–3, 25–33

Though he brings grief, he will show compassion, so great is his unfailing love.

—LAMENTATIONS 3:32

During his nineteen-year career, Baseball Hall of Fame catcher Gary Carter (1954–2012) drew strength and endurance from his faith in God to compete. In a *Wall Street Journal* article shortly after Carter died of brain cancer, writer Andrew Klavan told how Carter had influenced his life.

Klavan had sunk to a low point in his life. His mind dwelt on suicide. Then he heard Carter interviewed after a game. His team, the New York Mets, had won, and the aging catcher had helped by running hard at a critical point in the game. When Carter was asked how he could do that with his aching knees, he replied, "Sometimes you just have to play in pain." That simple statement helped draw Klavan out of his depression. "I can do that!" he declared. Encouraged, he found hope—and later became a believer in Christ.

We may face difficulties, but we don't have to sink into self-pity. The same God who allows our suffering also showers us with His compassion (LAMENTATIONS 3:32). With God's love lifting us up, we can—if we have to—"play" in pain.

❖ *David Egner*

One Step Closer

ROMANS 13:10–14

Do this, understanding the present time: The hour has already come for you to wake up from your slumber, because our salvation is nearer now than when we first believed.

—ROMANS 13:11

Some years ago a friend and I set out to climb California's Mount Whitney. At 14,505 feet, it is the tallest mountain in the contiguous United States. Whitney is not a technical climb but rather a long, exhausting walk—eleven miles of relentless ascent.

The climb, though hard-going, was exhilarating, with stunning vistas, beautiful blue lakes, and lush meadows along the way. But the trail grew long and exhausting, a test for legs and lungs. I thought of turning back as the day wore on and the trail seemed to stretch endlessly before us.

Occasionally, however, I caught a glimpse of the summit and realized that each step was bringing me one step closer. If I just kept walking, I would get there. That was the thought that kept me going.

Paul assures us, "Our salvation is nearer now than when we first believed" (ROMANS 13:11). Every day brings us one day closer to that great day when we shall "summit" and see our Savior's face. That's the thought that can keep us going.

❖ *David Roper*

The Cost of Fighting

JAMES 4:1–10

What causes fights and quarrels among you?
Don't they come from your desires that battle within you?

—JAMES 4:1

During a documentary on World War I, the narrator said that if Britain's casualties in "the war to end all wars" were marched four abreast past London's war monument, the processional would take seven days to complete. This staggering word picture set my mind spinning at the awful cost of war. Both soldiers and civilians pay the ultimate price, multiplied exponentially by the grief of the survivors. War is costly.

When believers go to war with one another, the cost is also high. James wrote, "What causes fights and quarrels among you? Don't they come from your desires that battle within you?" (JAMES 4:1). In our own selfish pursuits, we sometimes battle without considering the price exacted on our witness to the world or our relationships with one another. Perhaps that is why James preceded these words with the challenge, "Now the fruit of righteousness is sown in peace by those who make peace" (3:18 NKJV).

If we are to represent the Prince of Peace in our world, believers need to stop fighting with one another and practice peace.

❖ *Bill Crowder*

Herd Instinct

JOHN 10:14–30

My sheep listen to my voice; I know them, and they follow me.

—JOHN 10:27

Near Gevas in eastern Turkey, while shepherds ate breakfast, one of their sheep jumped off a forty-five-foot cliff to its death. Then, as the stunned shepherds looked on, the rest of the flock followed. In all, 1,500 sheep mindlessly went over the cliff. The only good news was that the last 1,000 were cushioned in their fall by the growing woolly pile of those who jumped first. According to *The Washington Post*, 450 sheep died.

The Bible often refers to human beings as sheep (PSALM 100:3; ISAIAH 53:6; MATTHEW 9:36). Easily distracted and susceptible to group influence, we would rather follow the crowd than the wisdom of the Shepherd.

I'm glad the Bible also describes sheep in a positive way. Jesus said, "I am the good shepherd. . . . My sheep listen to my voice; I know them, and they follow me" (JOHN 10:14, 27).

So the big question for us is this: Who are we following? One another? Self-centered shepherds? Or the voice and direction of the Good Shepherd?

Make it a daily question: Am I listening for the voice of the Good Shepherd?

❖ *Mart DeHaan*

Titanic II

*This is what the L*ORD *says: "Cursed is the one who trusts in man, who draws strength from mere flesh and whose heart turns away from the L*ORD.*"*

—JEREMIAH 17:5

Mark Wilkinson purchased a sixteen-foot boat for fishing and recreation, and he christened it *Titanic II* after the ill-fated luxury ship that hit an iceberg and sank in April 1912. *Titanic II*'s maiden voyage out of a harbor in Dorset, England, went well. But when Wilkinson headed back, the boat started taking on water. Soon he was clinging to a rail waiting for rescue. Wilkinson reportedly said, "It's all a bit embarrassing, and I got pretty fed up with people asking me if I had hit an iceberg."

The story of *Titanic II* is quite ironic. But it also makes me think of the original *Titanic* and the danger of misplaced trust. The ocean liner was believed to be unsinkable! Many put their trust in that, but how wrong they were! Jeremiah reminds us: "Cursed is the one who trusts in man, who draws strength from mere flesh and whose heart turns away from the LORD" (JEREMIAH 17:5).

Our security is not in people or things. So, let's forsake false confidences and turn to God. We should never put our ultimate trust in something other than Him.

❖ *Dennis Fisher*

It's the Real Deal

1 PETER 1:3–12

With the help of Silas, whom I regard as a faithful brother, I have written to you briefly, encouraging you and testifying that this is the true grace of God. Stand fast in it.

—1 PETER 5:12

One of the coolest things hanging on the wall in my home office is a Certificate of Authenticity. It has on it the logo of US Space Shuttle flight 110, which was launched in April 2002. Aboard the *Atlantis* on that flight was mission specialist Rex Walheim, who took an article from *Our Daily Bread* titled "Seeing God's Glory." Lt. Col. Walheim sent me the certificate to prove that this devotional page actually visited outer space.

If I were to show that article to someone and say, "This flew on the Space Shuttle," I could be doubted. But when Walheim sent me the Certificate of Authenticity, he provided verification.

Simon Peter created a Certificate of Authenticity for his message about the grace of God. In 1 Peter 5, he wrote, "I have written to you briefly, encouraging you and testifying that this [letter] is the true grace of God" (V. 12). Peter was assuring his readers that his messages—themes of hope and courage and even suffering—were the real deal.

Looking for evidence of God's grace? Read 1 Peter. Be confident; you can trust his teaching.

❖ *Dave Branon*

A Good Name

PROVERBS 10:2–15

A good name is more desirable than great riches;
to be esteemed is better than silver or gold.

—PROVERBS 22:1

Charles Ponzi's name will be forever associated with financial fraud. In early 1920 he began offering investors a fifty-percent return on their money in forty days and a one hundred-percent return in ninety days. Money poured in. Ponzi used money from new investors to pay prior investors and fund his lavish lifestyle. By the time his fraud was discovered in August, investors had lost twenty million dollars and five banks had failed. Ponzi spent three years in prison, was later deported to Italy, and died penniless in Brazil in 1949 at age sixty-six.

Proverbs frequently contrasts the reputations of wise and foolish people: "The name of the righteous is used in blessings, but the name of the wicked will rot. Whoever walks in integrity walks securely, but whoever takes crooked paths will be found out" (PROVERBS 10:7, 9). Solomon sums it up by saying, "A good name is more desirable than great riches; to be esteemed is better than silver or gold" (22:1).

We seek a good name, not to honor ourselves but to glorify Christ our Lord whose name is above all names.

❖ *David McCasland*

Not a Sprint

2 CORINTHIANS 11:16–12:10

> *I have labored and toiled and have often gone without sleep; I have known hunger*
> *and thirst and have often gone without food; I have been cold and naked.*
>
> —2 CORINTHIANS 11:27

In 1983, a sixty-one-year-old potato farmer named Cliff Young showed up for a grueling, weeklong ultramarathon from Sydney, Australia, to Melbourne—in overalls and work boots. He started off slowly and soon was miles behind. But at night, as the other runners slept, Cliff took a quick nap and kept going. Five days and five nights later he came in first—and set a course record!

Like Cliff, the apostle Paul wasn't the most orthodox champion. He confessed to being the worst of sinners, and he suffered from a humbling "thorn in [his] flesh" (1 TIMOTHY 1:15; 2 CORINTHIANS 12:7). His enemies added to his struggles, beating him with whips and stones (2 CORINTHIANS 11:25).

But Paul was unashamed of his weakness, saying, "the power of Chris can work through me. For when I am weak, then I am strong" (2 CORINTHIANS 12:9–10 NLT).

Remember the steady pace of Cliff Young and the apostle Paul as you run *your* race. It's a marathon, not a sprint, so "let us run with endurance the race God has set before us" (HEBREWS 12:1–2 NLT).

❖ *Mike Wittmer*

Always on Duty

ACTS 20:22–32

Remember your leaders, who spoke the word of God to you.
Consider the outcome of their way of life and imitate their faith.

—HEBREWS 13:7

As my kids were discarding their trash at the local mall food court, my older son was almost run into by a man clearly on a mission. My younger son jokingly remarked, "Maybe he stole something." Seeing this as a teachable moment, I said, "That's what the Bible calls judging." He asked with a smile: "Why are you always 'pastoring' me?" After I finished laughing, I told my sons I could never take a vacation from shepherding them.

Paul told the Ephesian elders that they could never take a vacation from shepherding God's people (ACTS 20). He was convinced that false teachers would try to ravage the church (V. 29), and the elders needed to protect the group from them. Caring for God's people includes feeding them spiritually, leading them gently, and warning them firmly.

Church leaders have a big responsibility to watch over our souls, for they will give an account to the Lord for their work among us. Let's bring them joy by responding to their faithful, godly leadership with obedience and submission (HEBREWS 13:17).

❖ *Marvin Williams*

Almighty Power

2 CHRONICLES 16:6–13

For the eyes of the LORD range throughout the earth to strengthen those whose hearts are fully committed to him. You have done a foolish thing, and from now on you will be at war.

—2 CHRONICLES 16:9

Boxing and strongman competitions have a unique aspect to them. In the events, the athletes compete individually for the purpose of demonstrating their superior strength. It's like arm wrestling—you do it to prove that you are the strongest person in the room.

One aspect of God's glory is His almighty power. But how does He show His strength? He doesn't do it by rearranging the galaxies before our very eyes or changing the color of the sun on a whim. Instead, in His love and compassion for needy people like ourselves, God has chosen to "strengthen those whose hearts are fully committed to him" (2 CHRONICLES 16:9).

The pattern is consistent throughout Scripture. From the dividing of the Red Sea, to the miraculous virgin birth, and ultimately to the power of the resurrection, our Almighty God has chosen to demonstrate His strength to bless, preserve, and protect His people.

Be assured that He delights in showing himself strong in the challenges of our life. And when He proves His power on our behalf, let's remember to give Him the glory!

❖ *Joe Stowell*

Our Jealous God

2 CORINTHIANS 11:1–4

Do not worship any other god, for the LORD,
whose name is Jealous, is a jealous God.

—EXODUS 34:14

A University of California researcher used a stuffed dog to show that animals are capable of jealousy. Professor Christine Harris asked dog owners to show affection for a stuffed animal in the presence of their pet. She found that three-fourths of the dogs responded with apparent envy.

In a dog, jealousy seems heartwarming. In people, it can lead to less admirable results. Yet, as Moses and Paul remind us, there is also another jealousy—one that beautifully reflects the heart of God.

When Paul wrote to the church at Corinth, he said he was "jealous for you with a godly jealousy" (2 CORINTHIANS 11:2). He didn't want them to be "led astray from [their] sincere and pure devotion to Christ" (V. 3). Such jealousy reflects the heart of God in the Ten Commandments, "I, the LORD your God, am a jealous God" (EXODUS 20:5).

God's jealousy is not like our self-centered love. His heart expresses His protective zeal for those who are His. How could we ask for anything more than a God who is so zealous—and jealous—for our happiness?

❖ *Mart DeHaan*

Initial Point

*Jesus answered, "It is written: 'Man shall not live on bread alone,
but on every word that comes from the mouth of God.'"*

—MATTHEW 4:4

If you drive south of our home in Boise, Idaho, you'll see a volcanic butte that rises out of the sagebrush on the east side of the road. This is the initial point from which the state of Idaho was surveyed.

In 1867, four years after Idaho was organized as a territory, Lafayette Cartee, the surveyor general, commissioned Peter Bell to survey the new territory. Bell took a sledge and drove a brass post into a little knob on the summit of that butte, declaring it to be the initial point from which he began his survey.

We may read many books, but the Word of God is our "initial point," the fixed reference point. John Wesley read widely, but he always referred to himself as "a man of one book." Nothing can compare to the Book of books, the Word of God. When we allow the Bible to be our guide in all of life, we can say with the psalmist, "How sweet are your words to my taste, sweeter than honey to my mouth!" (PSALM 119:103).

❖ *David Roper*

Getting Focused

I press on.

—PHILIPPIANS 3:14

I enjoy playing golf, so I occasionally watch instructional videos. One video, however, left me disappointed. The teacher presented a golf swing that had eight steps and a dozen sub-points. Too much information!

Years of playing golf have taught me this: The more thoughts you have as you swing, the less likely you are to be successful. You must simplify your thought process and focus on what matters most—making solid contact. Eight steps and twelve sub-points is too complicated!

In golf and in life, we must focus on what matters most.

In Philippians 3, Paul describes how that relates to the Christian. He wanted to focus on what mattered most. He said, "One thing I do: Forgetting what is behind and straining toward what is ahead, I press on toward the goal to win the prize for which God has called me heavenward in Christ Jesus" (VV. 13–14).

"One thing." It's vital for the child of God to stay focused, and there is no better point of focus in the universe than Jesus Christ himself. Is He what matters most to you?

❖ *Bill Crowder*

Help with a Home Run

1 PETER 4:7–11

Each of you should use whatever gift you have received to serve others,
as faithful stewards of God's grace in its various forms.

—1 PETER 4:10

Sara Tucholsky, a softball player for Western Oregon University, hit a home run in a game against Central Washington. But she nearly didn't get credit for it. As she rounded first base in excitement, she missed it! Wheeling around to step on first, she injured her knee. By rule, she had to touch all four bases for the home run to count. Her teammates could not assist her.

Then Mallory Holtman, the first baseman for the opposing team, spoke up. "Would it be okay if we carried her around?" After conferring, the umpires said yes. So Mallory and another teammate made a chair of their hands and carted Sara around the bases. By the time they were through carrying her, many were crying at this selfless act of compassion, and Sara was awarded her home run.

Likewise, when fellow Christians stumble and fall, we can follow the example of these ballplayers. Reach out. Lift them up and carry them along. What an opportunity to "serve others, as faithful stewards of God's grace" (1 PETER 4:10).

❖ *David Egner*

Hold On!

*I am coming soon. Hold on to what you have,
so that no one will take your crown.*

—REVELATION 3:11

A cowboy friend of mine who grew up on a ranch in Texas has a number of colorful sayings. One of my favorites is "It don't take much water to make good coffee." And when someone ropes a steer too big to handle or is in some kind of trouble, my friend will shout, "Hold everything you've got!" meaning "Help is on the way! Don't let go!"

In chapters two and three of the book of Revelation we find letters "to the seven churches in the province of Asia" (REVELATION 1:4). These messages from Jesus are filled with encouragement, rebuke, and challenge, and they speak to us today just as they did to the first-century recipients.

Twice in these letters we find the phrase, "Hold on to what you have." Both Thyatira and Philadelphia got this message. In the midst of great trials and opposition, these believers clung to God's promises and persevered in faith.

When our circumstances are harsh and sorrows outnumber joys, Jesus shouts to us, "Hold everything you've got! Help is on the way!" And with that promise, we can hold on in faith and rejoice.

❖ *David McCasland*

A Risk for the Savior

PHILIPPIANS 2:25–30

So then, welcome him in the Lord with great joy
and honor people like him, because he almost died for the work of Christ.
He risked his life to make up for the help you yourselves could not give me.

—PHILIPPIANS 2:29–30

Desmond Doss irritated his drill instructor and fellow soldiers in the Army. A pacifist by conviction, he refused to carry a weapon into battle, so his peers doubted his courage. Trained as a medic, the young Christian had no qualms about facing combat, but his goal was to save lives.

Doubts about Doss changed, however, when his unit faced combat. During the World War II Battle of Okinawa, he ducked under machine gun fire to pull the wounded to safety. He prayed, "Lord, give me the strength to save just one more wounded soldier." Eventually he rescued more than seventy injured soldiers. Later, Doss was awarded the Medal of Honor. His story was told in the movie *Hacksaw Ridge*.

Scripture tells of another Christian who took great risks to help others. Of Epaphroditus, Paul wrote, "Honor people like him, because he almost died for the work of Christ. He risked his life" (PHILIPPIANS 2:29–30).

Still today, believers around the world risk their lives for the cause of Christ. Let's pray for God's protection for them.

❖ *Dennis Fisher*

From Failure to Success

ACTS 12:24–13:13

I can do all this through him who gives me strength.

—PHILIPPIANS 4:13

Thomas Edison was working in his laboratory at two o'clock one morning when an assistant came in and noticed that the inventor was smiling broadly. "Have you solved the problem," he asked. "No," replied Edison. "That experiment didn't work at all. Now I can start over again." Edison could have such a confident attitude because he knew that each failure brought him a little closer to success.

This is not a new idea. In New Testament days John Mark had joined Paul and Barnabas on their first missionary journey to Cyprus and Perga, but then he deserted them. It seemed as if he had failed. But he was willing to try again, and he became a valuable asset to Barnabas on a later trip to Cyprus. When Paul was in a Roman dungeon, he wanted Mark, whom he called "helpful" (2 TIMOTHY 4:11).

Have you faced a personal defeat recently? If so, don't view it as final. Learn from it and move ahead. Trust God to give you strength. Use that temporary setback as one more step toward success.

❖ *Dave Branon*

Waiting to Cheer

EPHESIANS 3:14–21

To know this love that surpasses knowledge—
that you may be filled to the measure of all the fullness of God.

—EPHESIANS 3:19

In his first Little League baseball game, a player I was coaching got hit in the face with a ball. He wasn't hurt but was understandably shaken. For the rest of the season, he was afraid of the ball. Game after game, he bravely kept batting, but he just couldn't hit the ball.

In our final game, we were hopelessly behind when he stepped up to the plate. *Thwack!* To our surprise, he hit the ball sharply! Everyone—teammates and parents alike—cheered loudly. I was jumping up and down! We all loved this kid and cheered him on.

I imagine that the Lord cheers us on in our lives as well. He loves us deeply and desires that we may "know this love that surpasses knowledge" (EPHESIANS 3:19).

If others think of the Lord as unloving, we have the privilege of telling them of His deep love for us—and them. Imagine their joy when they hear that God loves them so much that He sent Jesus to die on the cross for their sin. And that He wants to cheer them on!

❖ *Randy Kilgore*

Finishers

I have fought the good fight,
I have finished the race, I have kept the faith.

—2 TIMOTHY 4:7

When I was a kid, I dreamed of becoming a black belt in karate. Several years ago, I began training and came close to fulfilling that goal. However, two belts away from my goal, I quit. Two reasons: my teacher changed styles in the middle of my training, and I got so busy that I could not devote adequate time for training.

Almost every week, I am nagged by the thought that God wants me to be a finisher in all aspects of my life—but especially in my service for Him.

In Paul's final farewell (2 TIMOTHY 4:7), he used imagery-rich words to talk about finishing his service for Christ. He described his life and ministry in terms of a fight: "I have fought the good fight." Then he used the imagery of a race as synonymous with his ministry: "I have finished the race, I have kept the faith." Paul affirmed that by God's grace he had finished all that God had given him to do.

As followers of Jesus, let's strive to be finishers, persevering in our service for Jesus Christ.

❖ *Marvin Williams*

Monkey in the Yard

2 KINGS 19:29–37

Dear friends, do not believe every spirit, but test the spirits to see whether they are from God, because many false prophets have gone out into the world.

—1 JOHN 4:1

"Listen!" my wife said to me over the phone. "There's a monkey in our yard!" She held up the phone so I could hear. It sounded like a monkey—but in Michigan?

Later, my father-in-law explained: "That's a barred owl." Reality was not what it had seemed.

When King Sennacherib's armies had Judah's King Hezekiah trapped inside Jerusalem's walls, the Assyrians thought victory was theirs. The Assyrian field commander used smooth words and pretended to speak for God, the Lord had His hand on His people. "Have I come to attack and destroy this place without word from the LORD?" the commander asked (2 KINGS 18:25).

That *sounded* right, but Isaiah told the Israelites the true words of the Lord. "[Sennacherib] will not enter this city or shoot an arrow here," God said. "I will defend this city and save it" (19:32–34; ISAIAH 37:35). That very night "the angel of the LORD" destroyed the Assyrians (V. 35).

We must listen for God's voice. He speaks through His Word. He guides us with His Spirit. What He says is what is reality.

❖ *Tim Gustafson*

Showing Grace

COLOSSIANS 4:2–6

Let your conversation be always full of grace,
seasoned with salt, so that you may know how to answer everyone.

—COLOSSIANS 4:6

Since the Masters Tournament began in 1934, only three golfers have won it two years in a row (Jack Nicklaus, Nick Faldo, and Tiger Woods). On April 10, 2016, Jordan Spieth was poised to become the fourth. But he faltered on the last nine holes and finished in a tie for second. Despite his disappointing loss, Spieth was gracious toward champion Danny Willett, congratulating him on his victory and on the birth of his first child, something "more important than golf."

Writing in *The New York Times*, Karen Krouse said, "It takes grace to see the big picture so soon . . . and watch someone else have his photograph taken." Krouse continued, "Spieth's ball-striking was off all week, but his character emerged unscathed."

Paul urged followers of Jesus to "be wise in the way you act toward outsiders; make the most of every opportunity. Let your conversation be always full of grace, seasoned with salt, so that you may know how to answer everyone" (COLOSSIANS 4:5–6).

It is our privilege and calling to demonstrate it in every situation of life—win or lose.

❖ *David McCasland*

Make Way

ISAIAH 40:3–5

A voice of one calling: "In the wilderness prepare the way for the LORD;
make straight in the desert a highway for our God."

—ISAIAH 40:3

General Dwight Eisenhower was known for his courageous leadership during World War II. His battle-tested skill equipped the troops to reclaim Europe. In 1952, he was elected president.

While in Europe, Eisenhower had experienced the danger and difficulty of navigating the twisting roads. As president, for the sake of US national security, he commissioned the construction of what is now the nation's interstate highway system.

In ancient times, conquering kings gained access to newly acquired territories through highways built for their troops. Isaiah had this in mind when he declared, "Make straight in the desert a highway for our God" (ISAIAH 40:3). And John the Baptist called people to repentance to "prepare the way" (MARK 1:3) into their hearts for the arrival of King Jesus.

What preparation needs to be done to allow Jesus unhindered access to your own heart? Are there rough places of bitterness that need the bulldozer of forgiveness? Are there valleys of complaining that need to be filled with contentment? Let's prepare the way for the King!

❖ *Joe Stowell*

Tough Trees

We . . . glory in our sufferings, because we know that suffering produces
perseverance; perseverance, character; and character, hope.

—ROMANS 5:3–4

Bristlecone pines are the world's oldest living trees—some estimated to be 3,000 to 4,000 years old. In 1957, scientist Edmund Schulman found one he named "Methuselah." It is nearly 5,000 years old! It was an old tree when the Egyptians were building the pyramids.

Bristlecones grow atop the mountains of the western United States at elevations of 10,000 to 11,000 feet. They've survived some of the harshest living conditions on earth: arctic temperatures, fierce winds, thin air, and little rainfall.

Their brutal environment is one of the reasons they've survived. Hardship has produced extraordinary strength and staying power.

Paul taught that perseverance produces character (ROMANS 5:3–4). Adversity is part of the process God uses to produce good results in our lives. It leaves us dependent on Him.

So we should pray not just for relief from our affliction but also for the grace to turn it into greater openness to God and His will. Then we can be at peace in the place where God has planted us.

❖ *David Roper*

Doing What He Says

DEUTERONOMY 5:28–33

Walk in obedience to all that the LORD your God has commanded you,
so that you may live and prosper and prolong your days in the land that you will possess.

—DEUTERONOMY 5:33

I gave clear instructions to the builder who was installing an underground water tank for me. When I inspected the project, however, I was annoyed that he hadn't carried out my instructions. His excuse was as irritating as his failure to follow my directives.

As I watched him redo the work, a guilty conviction swept over me: How many times have I needed to redo things in my life in obedience to the Lord?

Like the ancient Israelites, who frequently failed to do what God asked them to do, we too often go our own way. Yet obedience is a desired result of our deepening relationship with God. Moses told the people, "Walk in obedience to all that the LORD your God has commanded you" (DEUTERONOMY 5:32–33). Long after Moses, Jesus urged His disciples to trust Him and to love one another.

This is still the kind of surrender that leads to our well-being. As the Spirit helps us to obey, it is good to remember that He "works in [us] to will and to act in order to fulfill his good purpose" (PHILIPPIANS 2:13).

❖ *Lawrence Darmani*

Reborn Identity

2 CORINTHIANS 5:14–21

If anyone is in Christ, the new creation has come:
The old has gone, the new is here!

—2 CORINTHIANS 5:17

One of my favorite movies is *The Bourne Identity*. The main character, Jason Bourne, suffers from a severe amnesia that leaves him haunted, frustrated, and confused.

A lot of us live like Jason Bourne. Our stories are not as dramatic, but the issues are the same: Who am I, and does anyone care? We run from relationship to relationship, social event to social event, job to job, or even church to church, trying to "find ourselves."

But there's good news for "identity seekers." We can have a secure identity in a relationship with Jesus.

Although God made us in His image (GENESIS 1:27), sin ravaged our souls and denied us the joy of a relationship with our Creator. Our identity as His precious creation was damaged—until Jesus came to rescue us and reclaim His created ones for His own (SEE ROMANS 5:12–19). When we trust Christ for salvation, we gain the privileged status of being "in Him." He takes all that is old and makes it new.

Once you realize that you are a new creation, your identity crisis will be over.

❖ *Joe Stowell*

Friendship

1 SAMUEL 23:14–18

A friend loves at all times,
and a brother is born for a time of adversity.

—PROVERBS 17:17

Friendship is one of life's greatest gifts. True friends seek a special kind of good for their friends: the highest good, which is that they might know God and love Him with all of their heart, soul, and mind. German pastor and martyr Dietrich Bonhoeffer (1906–1945) said, "The aim of friendship is exclusively determined by what God's will is for the other person."

Jonathan, David's friend, is a sterling example of true friendship. David was in exile, hiding in the Desert of Ziph when he learned that "Saul had come out to take his life" (1 SAMUEL 23:15). Jonathan went to Horesh to find David. The significance of this scene lies in Jonathan's intent: He helped David "find strength in God" (V. 16).

That is the essence of Christian friendship—sowing in others the words of eternal life, leaving them with reminders of God's wisdom.

Pray for your friends and ask God to give you a word at the appropriate time to help them find renewed strength in our God and His Word.

❖ *David Roper*

Ant Safari
PROVERBS 6:6–11

Go to the ant, you sluggard;
consider its ways and be wise!

—PROVERBS 6:6

In his book *Adventures Among Ants: A Global Safari with a Cast of Trillions,* Mark Moffett reflects on his early childhood fascination with ants—an interest that didn't die as he grew older. Moffett's preoccupation led to his earning a doctorate at Harvard and then embarking on worldwide travel as an expert on the subject. His study has given him marvelous insights about these industrious creatures.

Long before Moffett discovered the wonders of the ant world, the Scriptures remarked on the ingenuity and work ethic of these tiny insects. Ants are held up by wise King Solomon as an example of industry for those who tend to be lazy: "Go to the ant, you sluggard; consider its ways and be wise! It has no commander, no overseer or ruler, yet it stores its provisions in the summer and gathers its food at harvest" (PROVERBS 6:6–8).

The marvels of God's creation are beautifully illustrated as God uses His creatures to instruct us. God built spiritual lessons into nature itself, and we can learn from creatures even as tiny as an ant.

❖ *Dennis Fisher*

Stop Painting Your Bucket

COLOSSIANS 2:1–10

In Christ you have been brought to fullness.
He is the head over every power and authority.

—COLOSSIANS 2:10

A friend who worked for a Christian organization was a perfectionist. One day he finished some repair work on a backhoe and began preparing to paint its large metal bucket. But before he hit the button on the spray gun, his boss yelled, "Don't paint the bucket!" He knew the fresh paint would scrape off as soon as the bucket dug into rocky soil.

It bothered him that he couldn't *finish the job*. He tried to figure out why he felt it was so important to paint the bucket. Then it came to him. He went to his boss and said, "By saying 'Don't paint the bucket,' you were really saying I shouldn't find my value in my perfectionism. My value doesn't lie in my work, but in Jesus." His boss exclaimed, "Yes, you got it!"

The only thing that can ever satisfy is Jesus. He's the fullness of God; and if you're a believer, you've been "brought to fullness" in Him (COLOSSIANS 2:9–10). We can't add one bit of worth to what we already are in Christ. And it's a sin to try.

Don't paint that bucket!   ❖ *Mike Wittmer*

The Problem with Pride

PROVERBS 16:16–22

Pride goes before destruction,
a haughty spirit before a fall.

—PROVERBS 16:18

People who achieve extraordinary levels of fame while they are still alive are often called "a legend in their own time." A friend who played professional baseball says he met many athletes who were only "a legend in their own mind." Pride has a way of distorting how we see ourselves while humility offers a realistic perspective.

The writer of Proverbs said, "Pride goes before destruction, a haughty spirit before a fall" (16:18). Viewing ourselves in the mirror of self-importance reflects a distorted image. Self-elevation positions us for a fall.

The solution to arrogance is true, godly humility. "Better to be lowly in spirit along with the oppressed than to share plunder with the proud" (V. 19).

Jesus told His disciples, "Whoever wants to become great among you must be your servant, and whoever wants to be first must be your slave" (MATTHEW 20:26).

There is nothing wrong with receiving accolades for achievement and success. The challenge is to stay focused on the One who calls us to follow Him saying, "for I am gentle and humble in heart" (11:29).

❖ *David McCasland*

Be Coachable

PHILIPPIANS 4:10–19

I am not saying this because I am in need,
for I have learned to be content whatever the circumstances.

—PHILIPPIANS 4:11

Case Seymour, a successful soccer coach, notes that everyone on his team hates the 10-by-100 drill that ends practice. Before the players can leave the field, they must run 100 yards 10 times at full speed. The players hate it— until the day of the game. Then they find that they can play at full capacity for the entire match. Their effort has been rewarded.

The apostle Paul used metaphors of training and competition in his letters. While he was a missionary to the Gentiles, he submitted to the instructions and drills of God amid great suffering and hardship. Twice in Philippians 4, he said, "I have learned" (VV. 11–12). For him, and for each of us, following Jesus is a life-long learning process. We grow in faith as we allow God through His Word and the Holy Spirit to empower us to serve Him.

Through hardship, Paul learned to serve God well—and so can we. It's not pleasant, but it is rewarding! The more teachable we are, the more mature we will become. As members of Christ's team, let's be coachable.

❖ *David Egner*

Gone the Sun

ISAIAH 60:17–22

Your sun will never set again, and your moon will wane no more;
*the L*ORD *will be your everlasting light, and your days of sorrow will end.*

—ISAIAH 60:20

During the US Civil War, General Daniel Butterfield wanted a new melody for "lights out." So, without any musical training, he composed one in his head.

While there are no official lyrics to the hauntingly familiar strains of "Taps," here is a commonly accepted version of one verse:

Day is done, gone the sun,
From the hills, from the lake, from the sky;
All is well, safely rest, God is nigh.

What a comforting lyric as faithful members of the military are laid to rest! And what hope in the acknowledgment that God is near, even—especially—in death!

At a time when death and evil reigned, the prophet Isaiah anticipated a day when death itself would die. "Your sun will never set again," he wrote to Israel. "The LORD will be your everlasting light" (60:20).

For those who follow Jesus, the strains of "Taps" are not a funeral dirge but a song of hope. "Your days of sorrow will end" (V. 20). All is well. God is nigh.

❖ *Tim Gustafson*

Keep Climbing

1 THESSALONIANS 4:1–12

*Encourage one another daily, as long as it is called "Today,"
so that none of you may be hardened by sin's deceitfulness.*

—HEBREWS 3:13

Richard needed a push, and he got one. He was rock climbing with his friend Kevin, who was the belayer (the one who secures the rope). Exhausted and ready to quit, Richard asked Kevin to lower him to the ground. But Kevin urged him on, saying he had come too far to quit. Dangling in mid-air, Richard decided to keep trying. Amazingly, he was able to reconnect with the rock and complete the climb because of his friend's encouragement.

In the early church, followers of Jesus encouraged one another to continue to follow their Lord and to show compassion. In a culture riddled with immorality, they appealed to one another to live pure lives (ROMANS 12:1; 1 THESSALONIANS 4:1). Believers encouraged one another daily, as God prompted them (ACTS 13:15). They urged each other to intercede for the body (ROMANS 15:30), to help people stay connected to the church (HEBREWS 10:25), and to love others (1 THESSALONIANS 4:10).

Through His death and resurrection, Jesus has connected us to one another. We have the responsibility and privilege to encourage fellow believers to finish the climb.

❖ *Marvin Williams*

Complete Access

In him and through faith in him
we may approach God with freedom and confidence.

—EPHESIANS 3:12

A few years ago, a friend invited me to join him as a spectator at a pro golf tournament. Being a first-timer, I had no idea what to expect. When we arrived, we got a few nice freebies, but what topped it all was getting access to a VIP tent—complete with free food. I couldn't have gained entry to the hospitality tent on my own though. The key was my friend; it was only through him that I had complete access.

Left to ourselves, we would all be hopelessly separated from God. But Jesus, who took our penalty, offers us His life and access to God. The apostle Paul wrote, "[God's] intent was that now, through the church, the manifold wisdom of God should be made known" (EPHESIANS 3:10). Jesus made a way for us to come to God the Father. "Through faith in [Christ] we may approach God with freedom and confidence" (V. 12).

When we put our trust in Jesus, we receive the greatest access of all—access to the God who loves us and desires relationship with us.

❖ *Bill Crowder*

Finding Focus

COLOSSIANS 2:6–15

So then, just as you received Christ Jesus as Lord,
continue to live your lives in him, rooted and built up in him,
strengthened in the faith as you were taught, and overflowing with thankfulness.

—COLOSSIANS 2:6–7

In 1977, Chris Bonington and Doug Scott became the first mountain climbers to summit an infamous peak known as The Ogre in Pakistan. During their descent, however, Doug slipped and broke both of his legs. Chris also had a mishap resulting in several broken ribs. Doug, who crawled for twelve days over rocks, snow, and ice to make it back down the mountain, said he did so by focusing on "one feature at a time. To think about the whole thing was a bit mind-boggling." Amazingly, both men survived.

The focus Chris and Doug displayed reminds me of the focus Paul encouraged the Colossians to maintain in their spiritual ascent—a call to stay strong and not fall. The apostle, writing from prison, told the new believers at Colossae to persist in their faith in Jesus. "As you received Christ Jesus as Lord, continue to live your lives in him," he wrote. Your faith will grow "as you were taught" (COLOSSIANS 2:6–7).

Are you distracted or discouraged today? Remember what Jesus has done, and find all you need in Him to press on!

❖ *Tom Felten*

Follow Me

"Come, follow me," Jesus said, "and I will send you out to fish for people."
At once they left their nets and followed him.

—MARK 1:17–18

When the US launched its space program in 1958, seven men were chosen to become the first astronauts. Imagine the excitement of Scott Carpenter, Gordon Cooper, John Glenn, Gus Grissom, Walter Schirra, Alan Shepard, and Deke Slayton. They were selected to go where no one had ever gone before.

They knew they would face unforeseen dangers and challenges. Each realized that the thrill of being chosen was tempered with the fear of the unknown.

Imagine another set of men who were chosen for an important mission: the twelve men Jesus chose to be His disciples. These men left behind their occupations and families to dedicate themselves to this radical new teacher. They didn't know what kind of political, religious, or financial challenges they would face. Yet they followed Jesus.

Jesus asks the same of us today. He asks us to follow Him, love Him, obey Him, and tell others about Him. Like the apostles, we don't know what our commitment to Jesus might bring.

Lord, help us to follow you faithfully and to trust you completely with our future.

❖ *Dave Branon*

Jesus's Heart

MARK 5:1–20

When he saw the crowds, he had compassion on them,
because they were harassed and helpless, like sheep without a shepherd.

—MATTHEW 9:36

We were in line at the ice cream store when I noticed him. His face bore the marks of too many fights—a crooked nose and some scars. His clothes were rumpled, though clean. I stepped between him and my children.

The first time he spoke, I didn't hear him clearly and just nodded in acknowledgement, scarcely making eye contact. Because my wife wasn't with me, he thought I was a single parent and gently said, "It's hard raising them alone, isn't it?" I turned to look at him. Only then did I notice his children, and I listened as he told me how long his wife had been gone. His soft words contrasted with his hard exterior.

I was duly chastened. I had failed to see beyond outward appearances. Jesus encountered people whose appearance could have turned Him away, including the demon-possessed man in Mark 5:1–20. Yet He saw the heart-needs and met them.

Jesus never fails to see us with love, even though we have scars of sin and a rumpled nature. May God help us to mirror Jesus's heart of love.

❖ *Randy Kilgore*

Outrunning Cheetahs
ISAIAH 40:6–11, 28–31

The grass withers and the flowers fall, because the breath of the LORD blows on them.
Surely the people are grass. But those who hope in the LORD will renew their strength.
They will soar on wings like eagles; they will run and not grow weary,
they will walk and not be faint.

—ISAIAH 40:7, 31

The majestic African cheetah is known for reaching speeds of seventy miles per hour in short bursts, but it doesn't do so well over distances. A BBC news item reports that four members of a Kenyan village actually outran two cheetahs in a four-mile footrace.

Two large cheetahs had been feeding on village goats, so the men came up with a plan. They waited until the hottest part of the day and then chased the cats, tracking them down when the animals couldn't run any farther. The exhausted cheetahs were safely captured and turned over to authorities for relocation.

Can we see ourselves in the cheetah? Our strengths might seem impressive, but they are short-lived. As the prophet Isaiah reminds us, we are like wildflowers that soon wither (40:6–8).

At the end of ourselves, our God offers comfort. A surprise rises up to meet those who wait on the Lord. He can renew our strength. By His Spirit He can enable us to rise up on "wings like eagles" or to "run and not be weary" (V. 31).

❖ *Mart DeHaan*

Shine Like Stars

PHILIPPIANS 2:14–18

Do everything without grumbling or arguing, so that you may become blameless and pure,
"children of God without fault in a warped and crooked generation."
Then you will shine among them like stars in the sky.

—PHILIPPIANS 2:14–15

I'm not exactly what you'd call a stargazer, but I've learned enough to point out constellations such as the Big Dipper, Orion's Belt, or Aquarius. And I'll never forget the time locating the North Star saved me from spending the night lost in a cold, wet swamp. I used that beacon to find my way out of the inky darkness.

I often find myself awestruck by the enormity of the star-filled sky. But when I consider the night sky through the lens of Scripture, I find myself invited by our Maker to be a part of something as big and bright as the stars themselves.

The apostle Paul wrote that God calls us to "shine among [unbelievers] like stars in the sky as you hold firmly to the word of life" (PHILIPPIANS 2:15–16). As we do, those living in darkness will see the light and be drawn to the "word of life"—Jesus himself.

The next time you gaze up at a brilliantly lit night sky, remember that the One who hung those bright lights calls you to shine as beacons of hope and life for a dark and dying world.

❖ *Jeff Olson*

Always Listening

NEHEMIAH 2:1–9

The LORD is near to all who call on him,
to all who call on him in truth.

—PSALM 145:18

D ad had hearing damage, so he wore hearing aids. One afternoon, Mom and I were talking longer than he thought necessary, so he responded playfully, "Whenever I want peace and quiet, all I have to do is this." He turned off both hearing aids, folded his hands behind his head, and closed his eyes in a serene smile.

We laughed. To Dad, the conversation was over!

How different God is from us! He always wants to hear His children. This is underscored in a short prayer of Nehemiah. A servant to the king of Persia, Nehemiah was visibly sad in the king's presence. When the king asked why, Nehemiah said the city of his ancestors lay in ruins. Nehemiah recounts, "The king said to me, 'What is it you want?' Then I prayed to the God of heaven, and I answered the king" (NEHEMIAH 2:4–5).

Nehemiah's prayer lasted only a moment, but God heard it—and his request to rebuild Jerusalem was approved.

Isn't it comforting to know that God cares enough to listen to all of our prayers—short or long?

❖ *James Banks*

COLOSSIANS 1:24–29

To this end I strenuously contend with all the energy
Christ so powerfully works in me.

—COLOSSIANS 1:29

I love going to Chicago's Wrigley Field for a baseball game—sitting in the stands, downing a great hot dog, and cheering the Cubs on to victory!

Unfortunately, Christianity has become a lot like professional sports. As a friend of mine has observed, there are nine guys on the baseball field doing all the work and thousands in the stands just watching. And as you probably know, that's not God's game plan for His people. He wants us to climb out of the stands, get out on the field, and join the team.

If you are wondering what good you can do on the field, wonder no more. You have gifts you can contribute. God has given each of us spiritual gifts that can help advance His kingdom. Whether it's teaching, encouraging, serving, showing hospitality, or extending mercy, each ability can yield great dividends. Let's follow the example of Paul, who tirelessly served on God's field for the joy of being used by Him (COLOSSIANS 1:28–29).

Believe me, it's far more rewarding to be on the field than to sit in the stands.

❖ *Joe Stowell*

The Real Hero

He must become greater; I must become less.

—JOHN 3:30

Louis B. Neumiller was known for his humility, integrity, and commitment to quality. As president of the Caterpillar Tractor Company from 1941 until 1954, he led the manufacturer of earth-moving equipment through the challenges of World War II into global expansion. His leadership style has been described as "success without fanfare." His mark of greatness, someone noted, was that he "let his company become a hero instead of himself."

We see the same quality of selflessness in John the Baptist, the dynamic preacher who paved the way for the Messiah. When John's followers became concerned that Jesus was baptizing people and crowds were following Him, John replied: "You yourselves can testify that I said, 'I am not the Messiah but am sent ahead of him.' . . . He must become greater; I must become less" (JOHN 3:28, 30).

As followers of Christ, are we lifting Him up or seeking honor for ourselves? Rather than being disappointed when our contribution is unnoticed, we should be glad because our highest privilege is to magnify the Lord. He's the hero!

Honoring Him is the mark of greatness.

❖ *David McCasland*

Opening Doors

MATTHEW 28:16–20

Therefore go and make disciples of all nations,
baptizing them in the name of the Father and of the Son and of the Holy Spirit.

—MATTHEW 28:19

Charlie Sifford is an important name in American sports. He became the first African American playing member of the Professional Golfers Association (PGA) Tour, joining a sport that until 1961 had a "whites only" clause in its by-laws. Enduring racial injustice and harassment, Sifford earned his place at the game's highest level. In 2004 he was the first African American inducted into the World Golf Hall of Fame. Charlie Sifford opened the doors of pro golf for players of all ethnicities.

Opening doors is also a theme at the heart of the gospel. Jesus said, "Go and make disciples of all nations, baptizing them in the name of the Father and of the Son and of the Holy Spirit" (MATTHEW 28:19).

The word *nations* (V. 19) is from the Greek word *ethnos*, which is the source of the word *ethnic*. In other words, "Go and make disciples of all ethnicities." Jesus's work on the cross opened the way to God for everyone.

Because of the gospel, we can open the door for someone who never dreamed they would be welcomed personally into the house and family of God.

❖ *Bill Crowder*

When God Thunders

PSALM 81:6–10

In your distress you called and I rescued you, I answered you out of a thundercloud;
I tested you at the waters of Meribah.

—PSALM 81:7

Thunder rolls across the Sawtooth Mountains, crashing and echoing through the peaks and canyons, shaking the ground with celestial sonic booms. My old dog cuts and runs. I stand amazed and delighted.

The storm reminds me of the "secret place of thunder" from which God answered His people (PSALM 81:7 NKJV). Israel cried out from the straw pits of Egypt. In time, God's salvation rolled over the land in peals of thunder (EXODUS 9:13–34).

Another psalm speaks of the storm that overshadowed Israel as they passed through the Red Sea (PSALM 77:16–20). Its thunder spelled doom for the Egyptians but deliverance to God's people.

When Jesus foretold His death in John 12:28–29, He called on His Father to glorify His name. A voice thundered from heaven saying, "I have glorified it, and will glorify it again."

Are you in trouble? Cry out to God. You may not hear the thunder roll, but it will reverberate through the heavens as He answers you in "the secret place of thunder." God will speak comfort to your heart and deliver you from your fears.

❖ *David Roper*

"Goodbye"

NUMBERS 11:1–10

Now the people complained about their hardships in the hearing of the LORD,
and when he heard them his anger was aroused. Then fire from the LORD
burned among them and consumed some of the outskirts of the camp.

—NUMBERS 11:1

When Max Lucado participated in a half-Ironman triathlon, he experienced the negative power of complaint. He said, "After the 1.2-mile swim and the 56-mile bike ride, I didn't have much energy left for the 13.1-mile run. Neither did the fellow jogging next to me. He said, 'This stinks. This race is the dumbest decision I've ever made.' I said, 'Goodbye.'" Max knew that if he listened too long, he would start agreeing with him. So he said goodbye and kept running.

Among the Israelites, too many people listened too long to complaints and began to agree with them. This displeased God. He had delivered the Israelites from slavery and agreed to live in their midst, but they still complained. Beyond the hardship of the desert, they were dissatisfied with God's provision of manna. Because complaining poisons the heart with ingratitude and can be a contagion, God had to judge it.

Let's rehearse the faithfulness and goodness of God and say "goodbye" to complaining and ingratitude.

❖ *Marvin Williams*

Deep Roots

Then he opened their minds so they could understand the Scriptures.

—LUKE 24:45

The sequoia tree is among the world's largest and most enduring organisms. It can grow to 300 feet in height, weigh over 2.5 million pounds, and live for 3,000 years. But the majestic sequoia owes much of its size and longevity to what lies below the surface. A twelve- to fourteen-foot-deep matting of roots, spreading over as much as an acre of earth, firmly grounds this behemoth.

A sequoia's expansive root system, however, is small compared to the national history, religion, and anticipation that undergirded the life of Jesus. He told a group of religious leaders that the Scriptures they loved and trusted told His story (JOHN 5:39). In the synagogue He opened the scroll of Isaiah, read a description of Israel's Messiah, and said, "Today this scripture is fulfilled in your hearing" (LUKE 4:21).

Later, after His resurrection, Jesus helped His disciples understand how the words of Moses and the prophets showed why it was necessary for Him to suffer, die, and rise from the dead (24:46).

What grandeur—to see Jesus rooted in the history and Scriptures of a nation! How extensively our own lives are rooted in our need of Him!

❖ *Mart DeHaan*

Little Nicks—Big Trouble

GALATIANS 5:16–26

"A little yeast works through the whole batch of dough."

—GALATIANS 5:9

We couldn't figure it out. My son and I had purchased an old powerboat for fishing and couldn't make it run properly. We were unable to get the boat up to speed, and it shuddered when we tried to go faster. We adjusted the carburetor and changed the fuel filter, but that didn't solve the problem.

When we took the boat out of the water, my son found something. One of the propeller fins had a 3/4-inch nick in it. *That can't be it*, I thought. *That nick is too small.* But when we installed a new propeller, what a difference it made! We had been slowed down by a tiny nick.

A similar problem can happen in our Christian lives. Sinful practices like those described in Galatians 5:16–21 have their roots in the seemingly insignificant thoughts of the heart (MATTHEW 5:28; 15:18–19). If we ignore or tolerate "little" sins, they'll eventually grow, corrupting our thoughts and actions—even harming people around us. Just as a little yeast leavens a whole lump of dough (GALATIANS 5:9), so a "little" sin can weaken our service for Christ.

Remember, little nicks can cause big trouble.

❖ *David Egner*

Surviving in the Wilderness

EXODUS 17:1–7

For we also have had the good news proclaimed to us, just as they did;
but the message they heard was of no value to them,
because they did not share the faith of those who obeyed.

—HEBREWS 4:2

In the 1960s, the Kingston Trio released a song called "Desert Pete." The ballad tells of a thirsty cowboy crossing the desert. He finds a hand pump, which has a note on it from Desert Pete, who urges the reader: "Don't drink the water in this jar; use it to prime the pump."

The thirsty cowboy does as the note instructs and receives an abundance of cold, satisfying water from the pump. Had he not acted in faith, he would have had only a jar of warm water to drink.

This reminds me of Israel's journey through the wilderness. When their thirst became overwhelming (EXODUS 17:1–7), Moses sought the Lord, who told him to strike the rock of Horeb. Moses believed and obeyed, and water gushed from the stone.

Sadly, Israel would not consistently follow Moses's example of faith. The author of Hebrews reports that the Israelites "did not share the faith of those who obeyed" (HEBREWS 4:2).

When by faith we believe the promises of God's Word, we can experience rivers of living water and grace for our daily needs.

❖ *Dennis Fisher*

Praying with Boldness

PSALM 6

> *Let us then approach God's throne of grace with confidence,*
> *so that we may receive mercy and find grace to help us in our time of need.*

—HEBREWS 4:16

Have you ever found it tough to pray? That can happen when we're reluctant to tell God how we're really feeling—fearful of being disrespectful of our heavenly Father.

The book of Psalms can help us pray more openly. There we realize that David was not afraid to be completely open and honest with the Lord. He cried out: "LORD, do not rebuke me in your anger" (PSALM 6:1). "Have mercy on me, LORD, for I am faint" (6:2). "Why, LORD, do you stand far off?" (10:1). "Do not turn a deaf ear to me" (28:1). "My thoughts trouble me and I am distraught" (55:2).

David was saying to God: "Help me!" "Listen to me!" "Don't be mad at me!" "Where are You?" David boldly went to God and told Him what was on his mind. Of course, God expects us to come to Him with a clean heart, and we need to approach Him with reverence—but we don't have to be afraid to tell God what we're thinking.

Next time you talk with your heavenly Father—tell it straight. He'll listen, and He'll understand.

❖ *Dave Branon*

Example That Encourages

Now that I, your Lord and Teacher, have washed your feet,
you also should wash one another's feet.
I have set you an example that you should do as I have done for you.

—JOHN 13:14–15

In the late 1800s a group of European pastors attended Dwight L. Moody's Bible conference in Massachusetts. Following their custom, they put their shoes outside their room before they slept, expecting them to be cleaned by hotel workers. When Moody saw the shoes, he recognized the custom. So he collected the shoes and cleaned them himself. A friend who made an unexpected visit to his room revealed what Moody had done. Word spread, and the next few nights others took turns doing the cleaning.

Moody's leadership style of humility inspired others to follow his example. The apostle Paul reminded Timothy to "be strong in the grace that is in Christ Jesus. And the things you have heard me say in the presence of many witnesses entrust to reliable people who will also be qualified to teach others" (2 TIMOTHY 2:1–2). Recalling that our strength is a result of God's grace keeps us humble. Then in humility we pass on God's truth by being an example that encourages and inspires others to follow.

❖ *Albert Lee*

Remember the Sacrifice

1 CORINTHIANS 11:23–34

And when he had given thanks, he broke it and said,
"This is my body, which is for you; do this in remembrance of me."

—1 CORINTHIANS 11:24

Every Memorial Day in the United States, we remember those who have died in the service of our country. A place where such remembrances carry a deep and emotional significance is Arlington National Cemetery near Washington, DC. Because of the deaths of aging war veterans and the ongoing conflicts around the world, there are currently about twenty-five military funerals there every day.

This is particularly difficult for The Old Guard—members of the 3rd US Infantry Regiment who serve at Arlington. It is their task to bear the bodies of the fallen and honor their sacrifice. They are reminded of the price of liberty every day.

Believers in Christ have been given the Lord's Supper as a reminder of what our freedom from sin cost Jesus. As we partake of the bread and the cup, we fulfill His command to "do this in remembrance of me" (1 CORINTHIANS 11:24). But in this sober celebration there is joy. We need not leave our remembrances at the Lord's Table. Living for the Savior can show the world we will never forget the sacrifice He has made for us.

❖ *Bill Crowder*

Internet Brain

ROMANS 12:1–8

Do not conform to the pattern of this world, but be transformed by the renewing of your mind.
Then you will be able to test and approve what God's will is—
his good, pleasing and perfect will.

—ROMANS 12:2

In Nicholas Carr's book *The Shallows: What the Internet Is Doing to Our Brains*, he writes, "[The media] supply the stuff of thought, but they also shape the process of thought. And what the Net seems to be doing is chipping away my capacity for concentration and contemplation. Whether I'm online or not, my mind now expects to take in information the way the Net distributes it: in a swiftly moving stream of particles."

I like J. B. Phillips's paraphrase of Paul's message to the Christians in Rome: "Don't let the world around you squeeze you into its own mould, but let God re-mould your minds from within, so that you may prove in practice that the plan of God for you is good, meets all his demands and moves towards the goal of true maturity" (ROMANS 12:2). How relevant this is as we find our thoughts and the way our minds process material affected by our world.

As a tide of information bombards us, let's ask God to help us focus on Him and to shape our thinking through His presence in our lives.

❖ *David McCasland*

Always an Upgrade

COLOSSIANS 3:12–17

Therefore, as God's chosen people, holy and dearly loved,
clothe yourselves with compassion, kindness, humility, gentleness and patience.

—COLOSSIANS 3:12, 14

When I'm about to leave the house, sometimes my wife, Martie, stops me and says, "You can't go to the office dressed like that!" It's usually something about the tie not matching the jacket or the color of the slacks being out of sync with the sport coat. Though being questioned about my fashion choices may feel like an affront to my good taste, I realize that her correcting influence is always an upgrade.

Scripture often calls us to "put on" attitudes and actions that match our identity in Christ. We can make Jesus known by wearing attitudes and actions that reveal His presence in our lives. The apostle Paul advised us to set the fashion standard by modeling the wardrobe of Jesus's compassion, kindness, humility, gentleness, patience, and forgiveness (COLOSSIANS 3:12–13). Also, he added, "over all these virtues put on love" (V. 14).

Clothing ourselves in Jesus's likeness begins with spending time with Him. If you hear Him say, "You can't go out like that!" let Him lovingly take you back to the closet so He can clothe you with His likeness. It's always an upgrade!

❖ *Joe Stowell*

Keep Running!

Let us run with perseverance the race marked out for us.

—HEBREWS 12:1

You may have heard the story of John Stephen Akhwari, the marathon runner from Tanzania who finished last at the 1968 Olympics in Mexico City. No last-place finisher in a marathon ever finished quite so last.

Injured along the way, he hobbled into the stadium more than an hour after the other runners had completed the race. Only a few spectators were left in the stands when Akhwari finally crossed the finish line. When asked why he continued to run despite the pain, Akhwari replied, "My country did not send me to Mexico City to start the race. They sent me here to finish."

Akhwari's attitude should be our attitude. There is a "race marked out for us" (HEBREWS 12:1), and we are to keep running until we reach the finish line.

We're never too old to serve God. We must keep growing and serving to the end of our days. To idle away our last years is to rob the church of the choicest gifts God has given us to share. There is still much to be done.

So let's keep running "with perseverance." Let's finish the course—and finish strong.

❖ *David Roper*

God's Radiant Beauty

ROMANS 1:18–25

For since the creation of the world God's invisible qualities—
his eternal power and divine nature—have been clearly seen,
being understood from what has been made, so that people are without excuse.

—ROMANS 1:20

Lord Howe Island is a small paradise of white sands and crystal waters off Australia's east coast. When I visited some years ago, I was struck by its beauty. In its lagoon I found coral reefs full of bright orange clownfish and yellow-striped butterfly fish that rushed to kiss my hand. Overwhelmed by such splendor, I couldn't help but worship God.

The apostle Paul gives the reason for my response. Creation at its best reveals something of God's nature (ROMANS 1:20). The wonders of Lord Howe Island were giving me a glimpse of His own power and beauty.

When the prophet Ezekiel encountered God, he was shown a radiant Being seated on a blue throne surrounded by glorious colors (EZEKIEL 1:25–28). When God reveals himself, He is found to be not only good and powerful but beautiful too. Creation reflects this beauty the way a piece of art reflects its artist.

May earth's crystal waters and shimmering creatures point us to the One standing behind them. He is more powerful and beautiful than anything in this world.

❖ *Sheridan Voysey*

Einstein and Jesus

When Jesus spoke again to the people, he said, "I am the light of the world. Whoever follows me will never walk in darkness, but will have the light of life."

—JOHN 8:12

We remember Albert Einstein as the genius who changed the way we see the world. Through his "Special Theory of Relativity" he reasoned that since everything in the universe is in motion, all knowledge is a matter of perspective. He said the speed of light is the constant by which we can measure space, time, or physical mass.

Long before Einstein, Jesus talked about the role of light in understanding our world, but from a different perspective. To support His claim to be the Light of the World (JOHN 8:12), Jesus healed a man who was born blind (9:6). When the Pharisees accused Christ of being a sinner, this grateful man said, "Whether He is a sinner or not, I do not know. One thing I do know. I was blind, but now I see" (V. 25).

While Einstein's ideas are difficult to test, Jesus's claims can be tested. When we can spend time with Jesus in the Gospels and invite Him into our daily routine, we can see for ourselves how He changes our perspective on everything.

❖ *Mart DeHaan*

The Power of Soft Answers

PROVERBS 15:1–4

A gentle answer turns away wrath, but a harsh word stirs up anger.

—PROVERBS 15:1

When my car broke down on a Boston-area Interstate at 2 a.m. I had the car towed to a repair shop.

Unfortunately, the shop also doubled as a parking lot during Red Sox baseball games. So, when I arrived after work the next day to pick up my car, it was hemmed in by thirty vehicles of Fenway Park patrons!

Let's just say I was less than Christlike in my reaction. I ranted and raved. Then, realizing they weren't about to budge for this rude customer, I gave up. As I stormed toward the glass doors, I struggled to get them open. My anger increased when the station workers laughed at me.

I had barely made it out when I realized how unlike Christ I had been. Chastened, I rapped on the locked doors and mouthed "I'm sorry" to the staff inside. They were stunned! They let me back in, and I meekly told them that Christians shouldn't behave as I had. Minutes later, they were shifting cars to free up mine. I learned that soft rather than harsh words can change circumstances (PROVERBS 15:1).

❖ *Randy Kilgore*

Let's Celebrate

Praise him with timbrel and dancing, praise him with the strings and pipe.

—PSALM 150:4

After Ghana's Asamoah Gyan scored a goal against Germany in the 2014 World Cup, he and his teammates did a coordinated dance step. When Germany's Miroslav Klose scored a few minutes later, he did a running front flip. "Soccer celebrations are so appealing because they reveal players' personalities, values, and passions," says Clint Mathis, who scored for the US at the 2002 World Cup.

In Psalm 150:6, the psalmist invites "everything that has breath" to celebrate and praise the Lord in many different ways. He suggests that we use trumpets and harps, stringed instruments and pipes, cymbals and dancing. He encourages us to creatively and passionately celebrate, honor, and adore the Lord. Because the Lord is great and has performed mighty acts on behalf of His people, He is worthy of all praise. "Let everything that has breath praise the LORD," the psalmist declares (V. 6).

Although we may celebrate the Lord in different ways, our praise to God always needs to be meaningful. When we think about the Lord's mighty acts toward us, we cannot help but celebrate Him through our praise and worship.

❖ *Marvin Williams*

The Real Jesus

MATTHEW 16:13–20

Simon Peter answered, "You are the Messiah, the Son of the living God."

—MATTHEW 16:16

Who is Jesus? Some make it impossible to recognize Him as the Jesus of the Bible. Certain groups add to what the Bible says about Him, while others diminish Him to simple humanity. Some would like to make Him disappear altogether.

This reminds me of Thomas Jefferson, who was the primary author of the US Declaration of Independence. He went through the New Testament Gospels with scissors and cut out all references to Jesus's deity and all things supernatural. This is known as *The Jefferson Bible*.

When Jesus asked His twelve disciples what people were saying about who He was, some answers were Elijah, Jeremiah, and John the Baptist, but these answers were all inadequate. Peter was correct when he said, "You are the Messiah, the Son of the living God" (MATTHEW 16:16).

Don't be deceived by fuzzy, watered down, or false descriptions of Jesus that you read, see, or hear about. Stick to the Bible and the truth of history. When people try to minimize your Savior's identity, tell them in no uncertain terms who the real Jesus is!

❖ *David Egner*

God's Front Porch

Praise him, sun and moon; praise him, all you shining stars.

—PSALM 148:3

In 1972 NASA astronaut Gene Cernan, the commander of Apollo 17, became the last human to walk on the moon. When asked later what it was like to stand on the moon's surface, Cernan responded, "Looking back to see the Earth in all of its fullness and beauty was like looking out from God's front porch."

We don't have to go to the moon to know there's a Creator. Looking into the vast night sky as he stood on Earth's surface, the psalmist David was convinced. He wrote, "LORD, our Lord, how majestic is your name in all the earth! . . . When I consider your heavens, the work of your fingers, the moon and the stars, which you set in place" (PSALM 8:1, 3).

David wrote that the "heavens" tell persuasively of their Creator: "They have no speech, they use no words; no sound is heard from them. Yet their voice goes out into all the earth" (PSALM 19:2–4).

On the next clear night, look up and "listen" to what the stars have to say about the Creator-God who set them in place.

❖ *Jeff Olson*

The Land of "What Is"

PSALM 46:1–7

Brothers and sisters, we do not want you to be uninformed about those who sleep in death, so that you do not grieve like the rest of mankind, who have no hope.

—1 THESSALONIANS 4:13

Even all these years after losing our seventeen-year-old daughter Melissa in a car accident on June 6, 2002, I sometimes find myself entering the world of "What If." It's easy, in grief, to reimagine the events of that tragic spring evening and think of factors that—if rearranged—would have had Mell arriving safely home.

In reality, though, the land of "What If" is not a good place to be. It is a place of regret, second-guessing, and hopelessness. While the grief is real, life is better and God is honored if we dwell in the world of "What Is."

In that world, we can find hope, encouragement, and comfort. We have the sure hope (1 THESSALONIANS 4:13)—the assurance—that because Melissa loved Jesus she is in a place that is "better by far" (PHILIPPIANS 1:23). We have the helpful presence of the God of all comfort (2 CORINTHIANS 1:3). We have God's "ever-present help in trouble" (PSALM 46:1). And we have the encouragement of fellow believers.

When we face hard times, our greatest help comes from trusting God, our hope in the land of "What Is."

❖ *Dave Branon*

Shocking Honesty

In the same way, you husbands must give honor to your wives.
Treat your wife with understanding as you live together.
She may be weaker than you are, but she is your equal partner in God's gift of new life.
Treat her as you should so your prayers will not be hindered.

—1 PETER 3:/ (NLT)

When the minister asked one of his elders to lead the congregation in prayer, the man shocked everyone. "I'm sorry, Pastor," he said, "but I've been arguing with my wife all the way to church, and I'm in no condition to pray." The next moment was *awkward*. The minister prayed. The service moved on. Later, the pastor vowed never to ask anyone to pray publicly without first asking privately.

That elder demonstrated astonishing honesty when hypocrisy would have been easier. But there is a larger lesson here. God is a loving Father. If I as a husband do not respect and honor my wife—a cherished daughter of God—why would her heavenly Father hear my prayers?

The apostle Peter instructed husbands to treat their wives with respect and as equal heirs in Christ "so your prayers will not be hindered" (1 PETER 3:7). Our relationships affect our prayer life.

What might God do through us when we pray and learn to love each other as we love ourselves?

❖ *Tim Gustafson*

Pass It On

PSALM 78:1–8

We will not hide them from their descendants;
we will tell the next generation the praiseworthy deeds of the LORD,
his power, and the wonders he has done.

—PSALM 78:4

I enjoy watching relay races. The physical strength, speed, skill, and endurance required of the athletes amaze me. But one crucial point of the race always makes me anxious: Passing the baton. One moment of delay and the race could be lost.

In a sense, Christians are in a relay race, carrying the baton of faith and the knowledge of the Lord and of His Word. We must pass this baton from one generation to another. In Psalm 78, Asaph declares: "I will utter . . . things from of old—things we have heard and known, things our ancestors have told us. . . . We will tell the next generation the praiseworthy deeds of the LORD" (VV. 2–4).

Similarly, Moses said to the Israelites: "Do not forget the things your eyes have seen or let them fade from your heart as long as you live. Teach them to your children" (DEUTERONOMY 4:9).

For generations to come, we are called to pass along "the praises of him who called [us] out of darkness into his wonderful light" (1 PETER 2:9).

❖ *Lawrence Darmani*

Test Match

How long, Lord, will you look on?
Rescue me from their ravages, my precious life from these lions.

—PSALM 35:17

A test match in cricket can be grueling. Competitors play from 11 a.m. to 6 p.m. with lunch and tea breaks, but the games can last up to five days. It's a test of endurance as well as skill.

The tests we face in life are sometimes intensified for a similar reason—they feel unending. The long search for a job, an unbroken season of loneliness, or a lengthy battle with illness is made even more difficult because you wonder if it will ever end.

Perhaps that's why the psalmist cried out, "How long, Lord, will you look on? Rescue me from their ravages, my precious life from these lions" (PSALM 35:17). Bible commentaries say this was speaking of the long period in David's life when he was pursued by Saul—a time of trial that lasted several years.

Yet, in the end, David sang, "The LORD be exalted, who delights in the well-being of his servant" (V. 27). His testing drove him to deeper trust in God—a trust that we can also experience in our own long seasons of testing, hardship, or loss.

❖ *Bill Crowder*

Quiet Conversations

PSALM 116:5–9

Praise the LORD, my soul, and forget not all his benefits.

—PSALM 103:2

Do you ever talk to yourself? Sometimes when I'm working on a project—usually under the hood of a car—I find it helpful to think aloud, working through my options on the best way to make the repair. If someone catches me in my "conversation," it can be a little embarrassing—even though talking to ourselves is something most of us do every day.

The psalmists often talked to themselves in the Psalms. The author of Psalm 116 is no exception. In verse 7 he writes, "Return to your rest, my soul, for the LORD has been good to you." Reminding himself of God's kindness and faithfulness in the past was a practical comfort and help to him in the present. We see "conversations" like this frequently in the Psalms. In Psalm 103:1 David tells himself, "Praise the LORD, my soul; all my inmost being, praise his holy name." And in Psalm 62:5 he affirms, "Yes, my soul, find rest in God; my hope comes from him."

It's good to remind ourselves of God's faithfulness and the hope we have in Him. We can follow the example of the psalmist and spend some time naming the many ways God has been good to us. As we do, we can be encouraged.

❖ *James Banks*

Broken to Be Made New

PSALM 119:71–75

I know, LORD, that your laws are righteous, and that in faithfulness you have afflicted me.

—PSALM 119:75

During World War II my dad served with the US Army in the South Pacific.

Even in the midst of war, Dad rejected religion, saying, "I don't need a crutch." Yet the day came when his attitude toward spiritual things would change. Mom had gone into labor with their third child, and my brother and I went to bed with the excitement of soon seeing our new brother or sister. When I got out of bed the next morning, I excitedly asked Dad, "Is it a boy or a girl?" He replied, "It was a little girl, but she was born dead." We cried together that morning.

For the first time, Dad took his broken heart to Jesus in prayer. Although his daughter would always be irreplaceable, at that moment he felt an overwhelming sense of peace and comfort from God. He began to pray to the One who was healing his broken heart. His faith grew through the years, and he even became a leader in his church.

Jesus is the source of new spiritual life! When we're broken, He can make us new and whole (PSALM 119:75).

❖ *Dennis Fisher*

Mayday! Mayday! Mayday!

PSALM 86:1–13

When I am in distress, I call to you, because you answer me.

—PSALM 86:7

The international distress signal "Mayday" is always repeated three times in a row—"Mayday-Mayday-Mayday"—so the situation will be clearly understood as a life-threatening emergency. The word was created in 1923 by Frederick Stanley Mockford, a senior radio officer at London's Croydon Airport. That now-closed facility once had many flights to and from Le Bourget Airport in Paris. According to the National Maritime Museum, Mockford coined "Mayday" from the French word *m'aidez,* which means "help me."

Throughout King David's life, he faced life-threatening situations for which there seemed to be no way out. Yet, we read in Psalm 86 that during his darkest hours, David's confidence was in the Lord. He sent out this Mayday: "Hear my prayer, LORD; listen to my cry for mercy. When I am in distress, I call to you, because you answer me" (VV. 6–7).

The most difficult situations we face can become doorways to a deeper relationship with our Lord. This begins when we call on Him to help us in our trouble, knowing that He will answer.

❖ *David McCasland*

Whitewater Experiences

1 CHRONICLES 28:9–20

David also said to Solomon his son, "Be strong and courageous, and do the work. Do not be afraid or discouraged, for the LORD God, my God, is with you. He will not fail you or forsake you."

—1 CHRONICLES 28:20

I was enjoying the start of my first whitewater rafting experience—until I heard the roar of the rapids up ahead. Joy was replaced with uncertainty. Riding through the whitewater was a first-rate, white-knuckle experience! Then suddenly it was over. I was safe—at least until the next set of rapids.

Transitions in our lives are like whitewater. The inevitable leaps from one season of life to the next—college to career, singleness to marriage, career to retirement, marriage to widowhood—are all marked by uncertainty and insecurity.

In one of the most significant transitions in Old Testament history, Solomon assumed the throne from his father David. I'm sure he was filled with "white-knuckle" uncertainty about the future. His father's advice? "Be strong and courageous . . . for the LORD God, my God, is with you" (1 CHRONICLES 28:20).

You'll face tough transitions in life. But with God in your raft you're not alone. He's taken lots of others through before. Smooth waters are just ahead.

❖ *Joe Stowell*

Selfish Servants

ACTS 4:1–21

"What are we going to do with these men?" they asked.
Everyone living in Jerusalem knows they have
performed a notable sign, and we cannot deny it."

—ACTS 4:16

The lighthouse keepers had survived harsh, lonely conditions on a meager salary, endured the loud foghorn, and rescued sailors. But they also resisted efforts to install a new lens that would have doubled their station's light. Why? They had a financial arrangement with the maker of the old lens, and they didn't want to lose the cash—even if it would have saved lives.

They seem similar to religious leaders who opposed Peter and John. These priests and teachers did help people, but they also earned a nice income for their services—an income they would lose if Judaism was replaced by the gospel.

So they challenged the disciples' healing of a disabled person. When Peter asked why he was being questioned for healing a crippled man (ACTS 4:9), the leaders agreed that what they did was miraculous. "But to stop this thing from spreading any further among the people, we must warn them to speak no longer to anyone in this name" (ACTS 4:16–17).

Hard questions for us: Is my service helping or hurting? If necessary, will I step aside for the good of someone else?

❖ *Mike Wittmer*

Eagle Flight

ISAIAH 40:29–31

He gives strength to the weary and increases the power of the weak.

—ISAIAH 40:29

I was watching an eagle in flight when for no apparent reason it began spiraling upward. With its powerful wings, the great bird soared ever higher, dissolved into a tiny dot, and then disappeared.

Its flight reminded me of Isaiah's uplifting words: "Those who hope in the LORD will renew their strength. They will soar on wings like eagles" (40:30–31).

Life's heartbreaks and tragedies can put an end to our resilience, our endurance, our nerve, and bring us to our knees. But if we put our hope in the Lord, He renews our strength. The key to our endurance lies in the exchange of our limited resources for God's limitless strength. And it is ours for the asking.

With God's strength we can "run and not grow weary" (V. 31) even when days become hectic and demanding. With His strength we can "walk and not be faint," even though tedious, dull routine makes the way seem dreary and long.

Oh, what an exchange—God's infinite strength for our finite weakness!

❖ *David Roper*

Back from the Dead

EPHESIANS 2:1–10

God . . . made us alive with Christ even when we were dead in transgressions—
it is by grace you have been saved.

—EPHESIANS 2:4–5

Can a man be officially alive after being declared legally dead? That question became international news when a man from Ohio showed up in good health after being reported missing more than twenty-five years earlier. At the time of his disappearance he had been unemployed, addicted, and hopelessly behind in child support payments. So he went into hiding. On his return, however, he discovered how hard it is to come back from the dead. When the man went to court to reverse the ruling that had declared him legally dead, the judge turned down his request, citing a three-year time limit for changing a death ruling.

That unusual request of a human court turns out to be a common experience for God. Paul's letter to the Ephesians tells us that though we were spiritually dead, God "made us alive together with Christ" (EPHESIANS 2:5). Our sin required the suffering, death, and resurrection of God's Son (VV. 4–7).

Having been declared alive in Christ, we are called to live in gratitude for the immeasurable mercy and life given to us.

❖ *Mart DeHaan*

Roll 'em Up

But someone will say, "You have faith; I have deeds."
Show me your faith without deeds, and I will show you my faith by my deeds.

—JAMES 2:18

When fast-food pioneer Dave Thomas died in 2002, he left behind more than just thousands of Wendy's restaurants. He also left the legacy of a practical, hard-working man who was respected for his down-to-earth values.

Among the pieces of good advice that outlived the smiling entrepreneur is his view of what Christians should be doing with their lives. Thomas, who as a youngster was influenced for Christ by his grandmother, said that believers should be "roll-up-your-shirtsleeves" Christians.

In his book *Well Done*, Thomas said, "Roll-up-your-shirtsleeves Christians see Christianity as faith and action. They still make the time to talk with God through prayer, study Scripture with devotion, be super-active in their church, and take their ministry to others to spread the Good Word."

That statement has more meat in it than a Wendy's triple burger. Thomas knew about hard work in the restaurant business, and he knew it is vital in the spiritual world too. That's what James 2:17 says.

Let's roll up our sleeves and get to work. There's plenty to do.

❖ *Dave Branon*

Defeat or Victory?

1 JOHN 5:1–13

Everyone born of God overcomes the world.
This is the victory that has overcome the world, even our faith.

—1 JOHN 5:4

Each year on June 18 the great Battle of Waterloo is recalled in what is now Belgium. On that day in 1815, Napoleon's French army was defeated by a multinational force commanded by the Duke of Wellington. Since then, the phrase "to meet your Waterloo" has come to mean "to be defeated by someone who is too strong for you or by a problem that is too difficult for you."

When it comes to our spiritual lives, some people feel that ultimate failure is inevitable, and it's only a matter of time until each of us will "meet our Waterloo." But John refuted that pessimistic view when he wrote to followers of Jesus: "Everyone born of God overcomes the world. This is the victory that has overcome the world, even our faith" (1 JOHN 5:4).

John weaves this theme of spiritual victory throughout his first letter as he urges us not to love the things this world offers, which will soon fade away (2:15–17). Instead, we are to love and please God, "And this is what he promised us—eternal life" (2:25).

❖ *David McCasland*

Carried
GALATIANS 2:11–21

I have been crucified with Christ and I no longer live, but Christ lives in me.
The life I now live in the body, I live by faith in the Son of God,
who loved me and gave himself for me.

—GALATIANS 2:20

In June 2014, Hunter Gandee strapped his seven-year-old brother Braden on his back and walked forty miles. The duo faced the energy-sapping trio of heat, rain, and muscle fatigue. So why take the grueling trek? Fourteen-year-old Hunter wanted to raise awareness of cerebral palsy by doing that they called the Cerebral Palsy Swagger. Due to the effects of the muscular malady, young Braden can't walk without assistance.

At the thirty-mile mark, the two guys were exhausted and ready to quit. But they credit prayer as one of the things that helped them reach their goal. Hunter carried his fifty-pound brother the entire way.

When a group of people called Judaizers forgot that Christ alone carries us to salvation, Paul stepped in. They wanted to add circumcision to the message of salvation, but Paul told them that Jesus alone carries us from death to life (GALATIANS 1:2; 2:11, 16).

When we trust in Jesus for our salvation, Jesus does the work. He *carries* us.

❖ *Tom Felten*

The Core of the Problem

ROMANS 3:10–18

For I know that good itself does not dwell in me, that is, in my sinful nature.
For I have the desire to do what is good, but I cannot carry it out.

—ROMANS 7:18

One of my favorite television cartoons as a boy was *Tom Terrific*. When Tom faced a challenge, he would work through the matter with his faithful sidekick Mighty Manfred, the Wonder Dog. Usually, those problems found their source in Tom's archenemy, Crabby Appleton. To this day, I remember how this villain was described on the show. He was "Crabby Appleton—rotten to the core."

We all share Crabby Appleton's primary problem: apart from Christ, we're all rotten to the core. The apostle Paul described us this way: "There is no one righteous, not even one" (ROMANS 3:10). None of us are capable of living up to God's perfect standard of holiness. Because we are separated from a holy God, He sent His Son Jesus to die on the cross for the punishment we deserve and then rise again. Now we can be "justified freely by his grace" through faith in Him (V. 24).

Jesus Christ has come to people who are rotten to the core, and He makes us "a new creation" by faith in Him (2 CORINTHIANS 5:17). In His goodness, He has fixed our problem completely.

❖ *Bill Crowder*

Prayer Malfunction

This is his command: to believe in the name of his Son, Jesus Christ,
and to love one another as he commanded us.

—1 JOHN 3:23

In a box of my father's old tools I found an ancient hand drill. I could barely get the wheel to turn. The gears were clogged with dirt, and the pieces that hold the drill bit in place were missing. But I wanted to see if I could get it to work.

I began by wiping the dirt off the gears and oiled them. With some effort the gears began to turn smoothly. Then I saw a cap at the top of the handle. Unscrewing it, I discovered the missing parts for the drill bit. I placed them in the drill, inserted a bit, and easily bored a neat hole in a piece of wood.

Working with that old drill taught me something about prayer. Jesus said we will receive from God what we ask of Him (MATTHEW 7:7–8). But there are conditions. For example, John said we must obey God and do what pleases Him (1 JOHN 3:22). If we don't meet God's conditions, our prayers will be ineffective—just like that old drill.

If your prayer-life is malfunctioning, make sure you're meeting the conditions. Then have confidence that your prayers will be effective.

❖ *David Egner*

Delivering the Dirt

JUNE 22

PROVERBS 26:20–28

Without wood a fire goes out;
without a gossip a quarrel dies down.

—PROVERBS 26:20

Christian industrialist and inventor R. G. LeTourneau is known for his enormous earth-moving machines. One of his products was known simply by the name, "Model G." A prospective buyer, hoping to stump a salesman, asked, "What does the 'G' stand for?"

"I guess the G stands for gossip," was the salesman's quick reply. "Because, like gossip, this machine moves a lot of dirt, and moves it fast!"

The Proverbs have a lot to say about gossip: Those who gossip are untrustworthy (11:13) and should be avoided (20:19). Gossip separates the closest of friends (16:28) and keeps relational strife boiling (18:8). It pours fuel on the coals of conflict, feeding the flames of hurt and misunderstanding (26:21–22).

The Hebrew word for "gossip" or "talebearing" actually means "whispering that is damaging." Gossip leaves behind a wide swath of destruction and is never a victimless crime. Someone is always hurt. So here's a word to men who want to be wise: "Without a gossip a quarrel dies down" (PROVERBS 26:20). Let's leave the dirt-moving to big machines. Put the shovels away and push for gossip-free relationships!

❖ *Joe Stowell*

We're Safe

Praise be to the God and Father of our Lord Jesus Christ!
In his great mercy he has given us new birth into a living hope
through the resurrection of Jesus Christ from the dead, and into an inheritance
that can never perish, spoil or fade. This inheritance is kept in heaven for you.

—1 PETER 1:3–4

The United States Bullion Depository in Fort Knox, Kentucky, is a fortified building that stores 5,000 tons of gold bullion and other precious items entrusted to the federal government. Fort Knox is protected by a twenty-two-ton door and layers of physical security: including unmarked Apache helicopters. Fort Knox is considered one of the safest places on earth.

There's another place that's safer, and it's filled with something more precious than gold: Heaven holds our gift of eternal life. Peter encouraged believers in Christ to praise God because we have "a living hope"—a confident expectation that grows and gains strength the more we learn about Jesus (1 PETER 1:3). Our hope is based on the resurrected Christ. His gift of eternal life will never come to ruin. No matter what harm may come to us, God is guarding our souls. Our inheritance is safe.

Like a safe within a safe, our salvation is protected by God and we're secure.

❖ *Marvin Williams*

The Discus Thrower

1 PETER 5:6–10

The God of all grace, who called you to his eternal glory in Christ,
after you have suffered a little while, will himself
restore you and make you strong, firm and steadfast.

—1 PETER 5:10

A story attributed to John Eldredge describes a nineteenth-century Scottish athlete. This man constructed an iron throwing discus based on a description he read in a book. Unaware that the discus used in official competition was made of wood with an outer rim of iron, he built his of solid metal. It weighed three or four times more than normal.

The man marked out the record distance in a field and trained day and night for years to match it. Then he took his iron discus to England for his first competition.

When he arrived at the event, he easily set a new record with a real discus—a record that stood for many years. This man trained under a heavy burden and became better for it.

When we are given a burden to bear, our goal should be to bear it in Jesus's strength and for His sake. God can use that burden to make us "strong, firm and steadfast" as 1 Peter 5:10 says.

Our burdens can make us better than we ever imagined—when we bear it in our Savior's name.

❖ *David Roper*

Whopper or Adventures?

But you remain the same, and your years will never end.

—PSALM 102:27

My grandfather loved to tell stories. Papaw had two kinds of tales. "Whoppers" were stories with a whiff of truth but that changed with each new telling. "Adventures" were stories that really happened, and the facts never changed when retold. One day he told a story that seemed too far-fetched to be true. "Whopper," I declared, but Grandfather insisted it was true. Although his telling never varied, I simply couldn't believe it; it was that unusual.

Then one day while listening to a radio program, I heard the announcer tell a story that confirmed the truth of my grandfather's tale. His "whopper" suddenly became an "adventure." This moment of remembrance made him even more trustworthy in my eyes.

When the psalmist wrote about the unchanging nature of God (102:27), he was offering this same comfort—the trustworthiness of God—to us. The idea is repeated in Hebrews 13:8 with these words, "Jesus Christ is the same yesterday and today and forever." This can lift our hearts above our trials to remind us that an unchanging, trustworthy God rules over the chaos of a changing world.

❖ *Randy Kilgore*

Doubts and Faith

JOHN 20:24–31

Thomas said to him, "My Lord and my God!"

—JOHN 20:28

Can a Christian who has occasional doubts about faith ever be effective in serving the Lord? Some people think mature and growing Christians never question their beliefs. But just as we have experiences that can build our faith, so we can also have experiences that cause us to temporarily doubt.

The disciple Thomas had initial doubts about reports of Jesus's resurrection. He said, "Unless I see the nail marks in his hands, . . . I will not believe" (JOHN 20:25). Christ showed Thomas the evidence he asked for. Amazed at seeing the risen Savior, Thomas exclaimed: "My Lord and my God!" (20:28). After this incident, the New Testament says very little about Thomas.

Some early church traditions, however, suggest Thomas went as a missionary to India where he preached the gospel, worked miracles, and planted churches. A number of these churches in India still have active congregations that trace their founding back to Thomas.

A time of doubt doesn't have to become a life pattern. Renew your faith in the reality of God's presence. You can still accomplish great things for Him.

❖ *Dennis Fisher*

Mysterious Ways

In him we were also chosen, having been predestined according to the plan of him who works out everything in conformity with the purpose of his will.

—EPHESIANS 1:11

Jacob DeShazer served the US Army Air Corps in World War II as a bombardier in the squadron of General Jimmy Doolittle. While participating in Doolittle's raid on Tokyo in 1942, DeShazer and his crew ran out of fuel and bailed out over China. He was taken to a Japanese prison camp where he trusted Jesus as his Savior. After his release, he became a missionary to Japan.

One day DeShazer handed a tract with his story in it to a man named Mitsuo Fuchida. He didn't know that Mitsuo was on his way to a trial for his wartime role as the commander of Japanese forces that attacked Pearl Harbor. Fuchida read the pamphlet and got a Bible. He soon became a Christian and an evangelist to his people. Eventually, DeShazer and Fuchida met again and became friends.

It's amazing how God can take two men who were mortal enemies, bring them together, and lead them to himself. Nothing—not even a world war—can stop God from working "everything in conformity with the purpose of his will" (EPHESIANS 1:11).

❖ *Dave Branon*

Leadership Notes

PHILEMON 8–18

I prefer to appeal to you on the basis of love. It is as none other than Paul—
an old man and now also a prisoner of Christ Jesus.

—PHILEMON 9

In his book *Spiritual Leadership*, J. Oswald Sanders explores the qualities and the importance of tact and diplomacy. "Combining these two words," Sanders says, "the idea emerges of skill in reconciling opposing viewpoints without giving offense and without compromising principle."

During Paul's imprisonment in Rome, he became the spiritual mentor and close friend of a runaway slave named Onesimus, whose owner was Philemon. When Paul wrote to Philemon, a leader of the church in Colossae, asking him to receive Onesimus as a brother in Christ, he exemplified tact and diplomacy. "Although in Christ I could be bold and order you to do what you ought to do, yet I prefer to appeal to you on the basis of love. . . . [Onesimus] is very dear to me but even dearer to you, both as a fellow man and as a brother in the Lord" (PHILEMON 8–9, 16).

Paul, a respected leader of the early church, appealed to Philemon on the basis of equality, friendship, and love. He demonstrated true leadership.

❖ *David McCasland*

No Cause for Alarm

EPHESIANS 4:25–32

In your anger do not sin:
Do not let the sun go down while you are still angry.

—EPHESIANS 4:26

The sound of the alarm blaring from inside the church I was pastoring struck panic in my heart. I had arrived at church early one Sunday morning, planning to spend a little time in peace and quiet before the congregation arrived. But I forgot to disarm the burglar alarm. As I turned the key, the disruptive and annoying blasting of the alarm filled the building—and no doubt the bedrooms of sleeping neighbors.

Anger is a lot like that. In the midst of our peaceful lives, something turns a key in our spirit and triggers the alarm. And our internal peace—not to mention the tranquility of those around us—is interrupted by the disruptive force of our exploding emotions.

It's important to know why the alarm is sounding and to respond in a godly way. But one thing is sure, anger was never intended to continue unchecked.

It's no wonder Paul reminds us of the psalmist's warning: " 'In your anger do not sin': Do not sin let the sun go down while you are still angry" (EPHESIANS 4:26; PSALM 4:4).

❖ *Joe Stowell*

Rough Going

JOHN 16:19–33

"I have told you these things,
so that in me you may have peace."

—JOHN 16:33

There's a lake near our home in the mountains that is known for good fishing. It's hard to get to, but one day I discovered that it's possible to drive within a half-mile of the lake. I carefully mapped the road so I could find it again.

Several months later, I drove the road again. I came to a section that was rocky, rutted, and steep. I wondered if I had missed a turn, so I stopped and checked my map. There, penciled alongside the stretch on which I was driving, were the words: "Rough and steep. Hard going." I was on the right road.

Jesus said our life's journey will be rough going if we choose to follow Him: "In this world you will have trouble" (JOHN 16:33). So we shouldn't be surprised if our path becomes difficult, nor should we believe we've taken a wrong turn. We can "take heart" because Jesus also said that in Him we can have peace, for He has "overcome the world" (V. 33).

If you're following Christ and experiencing some bumpy times, take heart—you're on the right road!

❖ *David Roper*

No More Prejudice

My brothers and sisters, believers in our glorious
Lord Jesus Christ must not show favoritism.

—JAMES 2:1

A survey by *Newsweek* magazine contained a couple of startling statistics: 57 percent of hiring managers believe an unattractive (but qualified) job candidate would have a harder time getting hired; 64 percent of hiring managers said they believe companies should be allowed to hire people based on appearance. Both are clear examples of unacceptable prejudice.

Prejudice is not new. It had crept into the early church, and James confronted it head-on. He wrote: "My brothers and sisters, believers in our glorious Lord Jesus Christ must not show favoritism" (JAMES 2:1). James gave an example of this type of prejudice—favoring the rich and ignoring the poor (VV. 2–4). This was inconsistent with holding faith in Jesus without partiality (V. 1), betrayed the grace of God (VV. 5–7), violated the law of love (V. 8), and was sinful (V. 9). The answer to partiality is following the example of Jesus: loving your neighbor as yourself.

We fight the sin of prejudice when we let God's love for us find full expression in the way we love and treat each other.

❖ *Marvin Williams*

On Our Side

ROMANS 8:31–39

What, then, shall we say in response to these things?
If God is for us, who can be against us?

—ROMANS 8:31

A young Christian was working the night shift at an assembly plant to earn money for college. His co-workers were pretty rough, and he was laughed at for being a Christian. The harassment became more and more vulgar.

One night was worse than the others. They were laughing at him, swearing, and mocking Jesus. He was about ready to quit. Then an older man sitting at the back of the room said, "That's enough! Find someone else to pick on." They immediately backed off. Later the older fellow told the young man, "I saw you struggling, and I wanted to let you know I'm on your side."

Maybe you're standing alone against others who don't know God. It seems as if Satan is winning. The Lord may send a fellow believer to stand with you. But even if He doesn't, you can be confident that He is on your side. You can never be separated from His love and care (ROMANS 8:38–39).

With assurance you can now say, "If God is for us, who can be against us?" (V. 31).

❖ *David Egner*

Call of the Chickadees

Do not quench the Spirit.

—1 THESSALONIANS 5:19

The black-capped chickadee has a surprising level of complexity in the noises it makes for alarm calls. Chickadees use a high-frequency call to warn of danger. Depending on the situation, the "chickadee" call can cue other birds about food that is nearby or predators that are too close for comfort.

Chickadees don't sense danger from large predators such as the great horned owl, because they're not likely to prey on such a petite bird. But smaller owls, which are closer to the size of the chickadee and more of a threat, prompt sentinel chickadees to repeat their alarm sound—the chickadee's distinctive "dee" note.

A similar level of awareness might serve us well. In 1 Thessalonians, Paul didn't just condemn the evils of the world. He also focused on the matters of the heart that can do harm to us with barely a notice. "See that no one renders evil for evil to anyone, but always pursue what is good." "Do not quench the Spirit." "Test all things" (1 THESSALONIANS 5:15, 19, 21 NKJV).

With the Spirit's help, let's keep attuned to every caution in the Word about our heart.

❖ *Mart DeHaan*

NEHEMIAH 8:5–12

They read from the Book of the Law of God, making it clear and giving the meaning so that the people understood what was being read.

—NEHEMIAH 8:8

Far from home and training for World War II, American service personnel turned to humor and correspondence to cope with the challenges they faced. In one letter home a soldier described the vaccination process: "Two medical officers chased us with harpoons. They grabbed us and pinned us to the floor and stuck one in each arm."

Another soldier took a different approach. After receiving a Bible, he wrote, "I enjoy it, and I read it every night. I never realized you could learn so much from a Bible."

Long ago, Jewish exiles returned home after years of slavery in Babylon to find their problems came with them. As they struggled to rebuild Jerusalem's walls, they faced opposition. Amid their trouble, they turned to God's Word. They were surprised at what they learned when the priests read from it. They were moved to tears (NEHEMIAH 8:9) and found comfort (V. 10).

Facing trouble? The Bible is where we learn about His character, His forgiveness, and His comfort. As we read it, we'll be surprised at what God's Spirit will show us.

❖ *Tim Gustafson*

T-Ball Faith

Therefore I will give their wives to other men and their fields to new owners.
From the least to the greatest, all are greedy for gain;
prophets and priests alike, all practice deceit.

—JEREMIAH 8:10

I love T-ball. Every kid gets a taste of the fun and joy of baseball before tasting the disappointment of striking out.

A baseball is placed on a rubber tee about waist-high to the five- and six-year-old batters. Players swing until they hit the ball and then run. On my first night as a coach, the first batter hit the ball far into the outfield. Suddenly every player from every position ran to get the ball instead of staying where they were supposed to. When one of them reached it, there was nobody left in the infield for him to throw it to! All the players stood together—cheering with unrestrained exuberance!

Those who have recently come to know Jesus as Savior have an unrestrained joy that is a delight to be around. We rejoice with them, and so do the angels in heaven! (LUKE 15:7). New Christians are in love with God and excited about knowing Him.

Rejoice with those who've come to faith. God can use them to inspire you to renew your own commitment to Jesus.

❖ *Randy Kilgore*

The Restoration Business

PHILIPPIANS 3:1–8

Yet indeed I also count all things loss for the excellence of the knowledge of
Christ Jesus my Lord, for whom I have suffered the loss of all things,
and count them as rubbish, that I may gain Christ.

—PHILIPPIANS 3:8 (NKJV)

Adam Minter is in the junk business. He circles the globe researching junk. In his book *Junkyard Planet,* he chronicles the multibillion-dollar waste-recycling industry. He says entrepreneurs around the world devote themselves to locating discarded materials and repurposing them to make something new and useful.

After the apostle Paul turned his life over to the Savior, he realized that his own achievements and abilities amounted to little more than trash. But Jesus transformed it all into something new and useful. Paul said, "I also count all things loss for the excellence of the knowledge of Christ Jesus my Lord, for whom I have suffered the loss of all things, and count them as rubbish, that I may gain Christ" (PHILIPPIANS 3:7–8). After being transformed by Christ, the tangled wreckage of his angry past was transformed into the love of Christ for others (2 CORINTHIAN 5:14–17).

God has always been in the restoration business. When we turn our lives over to Him, He makes us into something new and useful for Him and others.

❖ *Dennis Fisher*

Declared Dead

As for you, you were dead in your transgressions and sins.

—EPHESIANS 2:1

As a young man, my dad was traveling with a group of friends to an out-of-town sporting event when the tires of their car slipped on the rain-soaked roads. They had an accident—a bad accident. One of his friends was paralyzed and another was killed. My dad was declared dead and taken to the morgue. His shocked and grief-stricken parents came to identify him. But my dad revived from what turned out to be a deep coma. Their mourning turned to joy.

In Ephesians 2, the apostle Paul reminds us that apart from Christ we are "dead in [our] transgressions and sins" (V. 1). But because of His great love for us, "God, who is rich in mercy, made us alive with Christ even when we were dead in transgressions" (VV. 4–5). Through Christ we have been brought from death to life.

So in every sense, we all owe our life to the Father in heaven. Through His great love, He has made it possible for us—dead in sin though we were—to have life and purpose through His Son.

❖ *Bill Crowder*

"Will We See Snakes?"

1 CHRONICLES 16:11–18, 28–36

Devote yourselves to prayer, being watchful and thankful.

—COLOSSIANS 4:2

"Will we see any snakes?"

Allan, a young neighbor boy, asked that question as we started on a hike by the river near our home.

"We never have before," I answered, "but we might! So let's ask God to keep us safe." We paused, prayed together, and kept walking.

Several minutes later my wife, Cari, suddenly took a step backward, narrowly avoiding a poisonous copperhead on the path ahead. After the snake left the trail, we paused and thanked God nothing bad had happened. Through Allan's question, God had prepared us for the encounter, and our prayer was part of His providential care.

Our brush with danger brings to mind the importance of David's words: "Look to the LORD and his strength; seek his face always" (1 CHRONICLES 16:11).

What does it mean to "seek [God's] face"? It means we turn our hearts toward Him at all times. Even if our prayers are answered differently from what we request, God is faithful. He will direct our paths with His wisdom, mercy, strength, and love. When we declare our dependence on Him, we are stepping into His strength.

❖ *James Banks*

Marking Time

No one who hopes in you will ever be put to shame,
but shame will come on those who are treacherous without cause.

—PSALM 25:3

The military command, "Mark Time, March" means to march in place without moving forward. It is an active pause in forward motion while remaining mentally prepared and expectantly waiting the next command.

In everyday language, the term *marking time* has come to mean "not doing anything important while you wait." It conveys a feeling of idle, meaningless waiting.

In contrast, the word *wait* in the Bible often means "to look eagerly for, to hope, and to expect." The psalmist, when facing great difficulties, wrote "O my God, I trust in You. . . . Indeed, let no one who waits on You be ashamed" (25:2–3 NKJV).

We often have no choice about the things we must wait for—a medical diagnosis, a job interview result, the return of a loved one—but we can decide *how* we wait. Rather than giving in to fear, we "march in place," actively seeking God's strength and direction.

"Show me Your ways, O LORD. . . . You are the God of my salvation; on You I wait all the day" (VV. 4–5 NKJV).

❖ *David McCasland*

Clinging to Hope

HEBREWS 6:13–20

God did this so that, by two unchangeable things in which it is impossible for God to lie, we who have fled to take hold of the hope set before us may be greatly encouraged.

—HEBREWS 6:18

One summer day, Dave Mull spent nearly four hours adrift and alone in Lake Michigan, clinging to the handles of a Coleman cooler. Dave's fishing boat had capsized before sinking five miles offshore, forcing him and his three companions into the deep, troubled waters. Before Dave became separated from the others, he surrendered his life jacket to one of his friends who was struggling. Eventually, the four were rescued.

While out in the middle of this huge lake, Dave knew he wasn't alone: "It's hard to explain, but I don't know when I've ever felt more in God's hand. I never lost the hope that I was going to be found."

The greatest hope we can ever cling to is centered in the promises of God, which are ultimately fulfilled in Jesus. In describing this hope, Hebrews compares it to an "anchor" for the soul that is "firm and secure" (HEBREWS 6:19). It's a hope based in a relationship with God and His Son (V. 20).

No matter the circumstances, it's the hope found in Jesus that steadies our souls. He's the One who keeps us afloat.

❖ *Jeff Olson*

Get to Know Jesus

2 PETER 1:1–11

But grow in the grace and knowledge of our Lord and Savior Jesus Christ.
To him be glory both now and forever! Amen.

—2 PETER 3:18

In his book *The Call*, Os Guinness tells a story about Arthur Burns, chairman of the US Federal Reserve Board during the 1970s. Burns, who was Jewish, became part of a Bible study held at the White House. One day, those in the group listened in surprise as Burns prayed, "O God, may the day come when all Jews will come to know Jesus." But then came a bigger surprise: He prayed for the time "when all Christians will come to know Jesus."

Burns hit on a profound truth. Even if we claim the name of Jesus Christ, that may not be evident to others. Do we have a personal relationship with Jesus? Are we striving, praying, and working to know Jesus more intimately each day?

Peter, a man who knew Jesus well, said that "the knowledge of God and of Jesus our Lord" will bring us multiplied "grace and peace" (2 PETER 1:2). And knowledge of Jesus will help us develop character traits that show the world that we are connected to Him (VV. 5–8).

Can we say, "I know Jesus better today than I did yesterday"?

❖ *Dave Branon*

Trivial Pursuits

2 PETER 1:1–4

His divine power has given us everything we need for a godly life
through our knowledge of him who called us by his own glory and goodness.

—2 PETER 1:3

I was in the library of a prestigious university, and as I walked among the bookshelves, I happened to pass by a row of cubicles set aside for study. I spied a student reading a Bugs Bunny comic book. I almost laughed out loud. Here was a young man surrounded by the wisdom of the ages, yet he was immersed in childish trivia.

Of course, all of us need an occasional respite from study, but we need to get beyond trivial pursuits. Entertaining books and clever social media can become the primary influence in our lives. But remember: We have in our hands the Word of Life—the Book that tells us how to know God and live abundantly.

If we neglect the Bible, it's not from a lack of time but a lack of heart. We must not neglect the mysteries of God's grace and love that are written on every page of the Bible. That's where we find everything we need for "a godly life" (2 PETER 1:3).

Ask God to give you a desire for His Word and a hunger to taste His goodness every day.

❖ *David Roper*

True Wealth

1 TIMOTHY 6:6–19

Command those who are rich in this present world not to be arrogant
nor to put their hope in wealth, which is so uncertain, but to put their hope in God,
who richly provides us with everything for our enjoyment.

—1 TIMOTHY 6:17

Money is a powerful force. We work for it, save it, spend it, use it to satisfy our longings, and then wish we had more. Aware of its distracting danger, Jesus taught more about money than any other topic. And, as far as we know, He never took an offering for himself. Clearly, He didn't teach about giving to fill His own pockets. Instead, Jesus warned us that trusting in wealth and using it to gain power clogs our spiritual arteries more readily than most other impediments to spiritual development.

So, what does it mean to be rich toward God? Paul tells us that those who are rich should not be conceited about their wealth, "nor to put their hope in wealth, which is so uncertain" (1 TIMOTHY 6:17). Rather, we are to "be rich in good deeds, and to be generous and willing to share" (V. 18).

Interesting! God measures wealth by the quality of our lives and our generous disbursement of wealth to bless others. That's great advice for all of us who think our security and reputation are tied up in the size of our bank account.

❖ *Joe Stowell*

Good Medicine

EPHESIANS 4:25–32

A cheerful heart is good medicine, but a crushed spirit dries up the bones.

—PROVERBS 17:22

Careless driving, rising tempers, and use of foul language among some drivers are constant sources of traffic fights in our city of Accra, Ghana. But one incident I witnessed took a different turn. A bus was almost hit by a careless taxi driver, so I expected the bus driver to get angry and yell. Instead, he smiled broadly at the guilty-looking taxi driver. The smile worked wonders. With a raised hand, the taximan apologized, smiled back, and moved on—the tension diffused.

A smile has a fascinating effect on our brain chemistry. Researchers say a smile releases brain chemicals called endorphins. This has a physiological, relaxing effect. Not only can a smile diffuse a tense situation but it can also diffuse inner tension. The Bible teaches us to "get rid of all bitterness, rage and anger, brawling and slander, along with every form of malice. Be kind and compassionate to one another" (EPHESIANS 4:31–32).

When anger or tension or bitterness threatens our relationship with others, it helps to remember that "a cheerful heart is good medicine."

❖ *Lawrence Darmani*

Running the Race

So then, dear friends, since you are looking forward to this,
make every effort to be found spotless, blameless and at peace with him.

—2 PETER 3:14

In 2015, Rob Young ran nearly 374 miles in eighty-eight hours—setting the world record for distance running without sleep. Young, who had endured abuse by his father as a child, said he ran with two goals in mind: to test the limits of human endurance and to help the world become a better place for kids.

The apostle Peter encourages us to continue running the race for Jesus—making "every effort to be found living peaceful lives that are pure and blameless in [God's] sight" (2 PETER 3:14 NLT). The race in Christ can sometimes seem to be long and taxing, but God "isn't really being slow about his promise" (V. 9 NLT)—He's simply patiently allowing us to keep following His pace, for "He does not want anyone to be destroyed, but wants everyone to repent" (V. 9 NLT).

As believers in Jesus, we run life's race to serve others: working toward helping them experience God's life and joy—now and eternally. The Lord provides the wisdom, power, and strength we need to stay in the race as we grow in Christlikeness. "To him be glory both now and forever! Amen" (V. 18).

❖ *Tom Felten*

Fishing

MATTHEW 4:18–22

"Come, follow me," Jesus said,
"and I will send you out to fish for people."

—MATTHEW 4:19

A skilled fly fisherman whips his line back and forth over his head. Then he releases the line and precisely sets the fly-like lure down on the water's surface. If he's successful, a big rainbow trout will rise, strike the lure, and the fisherman will set the hook. The battle is on!

That's one way to catch fish. Halibut fishermen use another method. They go out on the ocean and drop big baited hooks 125 to 150 feet into the water. When one of those big, flat fish goes for the bait and is hooked, he begins a long ride to the surface.

Jesus told Peter and Andrew to follow Him, and He would make them "fishers of men" (MATTHEW 4:18–19 NKJV). As followers of Christ today, we too are to be "fishing" for people in our world, using various methods to spread the good news of salvation through faith in Jesus.

Are you fishing? Have you reached out to your neighborhood and community with the good news? Keep following Jesus, and keep fishing.

❖ *David Egner*

A Hard Goodbye

A father to the fatherless, a defender of widows,
is God in his holy dwelling.

—PSALM 68:5

When our youngest son joined the Army, we knew that challenges lay ahead. We knew he would face danger and be tested physically, emotionally, and spiritually. We also knew that our home would never fully be his home again. As his departure neared, my wife and I steeled ourselves for these challenges.

Then the day came when Mark had to report. We hugged and said our goodbyes, and he walked into the recruiting station—leaving me with a moment for which I was decidedly unprepared. The pain of that hard goodbye felt unbearable. I can't remember when I have wept as hard as I did that day. The hard goodbye, and the sense of loss it delivered, cut me to the heart.

In such moments, I am thankful for a heavenly Father who knows what it is to be separated from a beloved Son. He's a God described as "a father to the fatherless, a defender of widows" (PSALM 68:5). If He cares for the orphaned and the widows in their loneliness, He'll also care for me and comfort me—even when I face a hard goodbye.

❖ *Bill Crowder*

Kossi's Courage

2 KINGS 23:12–14, 21–25

You shall have no other gods before me.

—EXODUS 20:3

As he awaited his baptism in Togo's Mono River, Kossi stooped to pick up a worn wooden carving. His family had worshiped the object for generations. Now they watched as he tossed the grotesque figure into a fire. No longer would their choicest chickens be sacrificed to this god.

In Togo, West Africa, idols represent literal gods that must be appeased with sacrifice. Idol burning and baptism make a courageous statement about a new believer's allegiance to the one true God.

As an eight-year-old, King Josiah came to power in an idol-worshiping culture. His father and grandfather had been two of the worst kings in all of Judah's sordid history. Then the high priest discovered the book of the law. When the young king heard its words, he took them to heart (2 KINGS 22:8–13). Josiah destroyed the pagan altars. In place of idol worship, he celebrated the Passover (23:21–23).

Whenever we look for answers apart from God, we pursue a false god. It would be wise to ask ourselves: What idols, literal or figurative, do we need to throw into the fire?

❖ *Tim Gustafson*

Untethered

JUDGES 6:1–32

"I said to you, 'I am the LORD your God; do not worship the gods of the Amorites, in whose land you live.' But you have not listened to me."

—JUDGES 6:10

When Nik Wallenda became the first man to walk across a tightrope stretched above Niagara Falls, the folks behind the TV network that filmed the event insisted that Wallenda wear a tether. Even if he had slipped, he would not have plummeted to his death.

Later, Wallenda said, "I had a tether but I didn't use it." Actually, he did, for the tether still supplied confidence. Would he have been as surefooted if he knew one false step could have swept him to his death?

It's great to have a backup plan in the physical world, but if you trust God, you don't need a tether. The Israelites had a *tether*. They worshiped Yahweh, but they also hedged their bets by praying to pagan gods. They assumed God would provide, but they figured it wouldn't hurt to have a Plan B.

Gideon's backup plan was to have a large army in his battle with the Midianites. But to make sure he got the point, God whittled down Gideon's army to 300 men (JUDGES 7:7). No backup plan or tether can compete with our Lord. Trust Him alone.

❖ *Mike Wittmer*

Dealing with Delay

GENESIS 45:1–8

It was not you who sent me here, but God.
He made me father to Pharaoh, lord of his entire household and ruler of all Egypt.

—GENESIS 45:8

A global computer system outage causes widespread flight cancellations, stranding hundreds of thousands of passengers. During a winter storm, multiple auto accidents close major highways. Delays can often produce anger and frustration. But as followers of Jesus, we can see a solution in Scripture: patience.

Think of Joseph, who was sold to slave traders by his jealous brothers, falsely accused by his employer's wife, and imprisoned in Egypt. "But while Joseph was there in the prison, the LORD was with him" (GENESIS 39:20–21). Years later, when Joseph interpreted Pharaoh's dreams, he was made second in command in Egypt (CHAPTER 41).

The most remarkable fruit of his patience occurred when his brothers came to buy grain during a famine. "I am your brother Joseph," he said, "the one you sold into Egypt! And now, do not be distressed and do not be angry with yourselves for selling me here, because it was to save lives that God sent me ahead of you" (45:4–5).

In our delays, brief or long, may we, like Joseph, gain patience, perspective, and peace as we trust in the Lord.

❖ *David McCasland*

God's Enduring Word

PSALM 119:89–96

Heaven and earth will pass away,
but my words will never pass away.

—MATTHEW 24:35

At the beginning of World War II, aerial bombings flattened much of Warsaw, Poland. However, most of one damaged building still stubbornly stood—the Polish headquarters for the British and Foreign Bible Society. Still legible on a surviving wall were these words: "Heaven and earth shall pass away, but my words shall not pass away" (MATTHEW 24:35 KJV).

Jesus made that statement to encourage His disciples when they asked Him about the "end of the age" (V. 3). But His words also give us courage in the midst of our embattled situation today. Standing in the rubble of our shattered dreams, we can still find confidence in God's indestructible character and promises.

The psalmist wrote: "Your word, LORD, is eternal; it stands firm in the heavens" (PSALM 119:89). But it is more than the word of the Lord; it is His very character. That is why the psalmist could also say, "Your faithfulness continues through all generations" (V. 90).

As we face tough times, because God will not abandon us, we can confidently choose hope. His enduring Word assures us of His unfailing love.

❖ *Dennis Fisher*

Correct Them

1 SAMUEL 2:12, 27–36

Why do you scorn my sacrifice and offering that I prescribed for my dwelling?
Why do you honor your sons more than me by fattening yourselves
on the choice parts of every offering made by my people Israel?

—1 SAMUEL 2:29

Therapist and mother Lori Gottlieb says that parents who are obsessed with their children's happiness may actually contribute to their becoming unhappy adults. These parents coddle their children, do not equip them to deal with the real world, and look the other way when their children do wrong.

In 1 Samuel, we read that the high priest Eli sometimes looked the other way. He failed to properly deal with his sons' behavior as grown men serving in God's temple. They were selfish, lustful, and rebellious, putting their own needs foremost. At first, Eli rebuked them, but they would not listen. Instead of removing them from service, he looked the other way. As a result of his sons' sins and because Eli honored his sons above the Lord (1 SAMUEL 2:29), the Lord warned Eli that his family would suffer judgment (V. 34; 4:17–18).

As Christian parents, we have the awesome responsibility to lovingly discipline our children (PROVERBS 13:24; 29:17; HEBREWS 12:9–11). As we impart God's wisdom to them, we can help them develop into responsible, God-fearing adults.

❖ *Marvin Williams*

Plowing Straight Lines

PHILIPPIANS 3:8–17

I press on toward the goal to win the prize
for which God has called me heavenward in Christ Jesus.

—PHILIPPIANS 3:14

I t's my first day on the tractor! Dropping the plow into the soil, I head out across the field. I look down at the gauges, squeeze the cold steel of the steering wheel, and admire the power at my disposal. At the end of the row, I look back. Instead of the ramrod straight line I expected, though, I see what looks like a slithering snake.

I know better. "Plow with your eye on the fence post," I've been told. By focusing on a point across the field, a straight line is assured. On my return, I comply. Now my line is straight. The row was messed up only when I didn't have a focus point.

Paul had similar wisdom when he wrote of having his focus on Jesus. Not only did he ignore distractions (PHILIPPIANS 3:8, 13) but he also set the focus (VV. 8, 14), noted the result (VV. 9–11), and observed the pattern it sets for others (VV. 16–17).

If we focus on Christ, we will plow a straight path and accomplish God's purpose in our lives.

❖ *Randy Kilgore*

The Pleasure Is Mine

ECCLESIASTES 2:1–11

I denied myself nothing my eyes desired; I refused my heart no pleasure.
My heart took delight in all my labor, and this was the reward for all my toil.
Yet when I surveyed all that my hands had done and what I had toiled to achieve,
everything was meaningless, a chasing after the wind; nothing was gained under the sun.

—ECCLESIASTES 2:10–11

I always look forward to summer. The warm sunshine, baseball, beaches, and barbecues are pleasures that bring joy after a long, cold winter. But pleasure-seeking isn't just seasonal. Don't we all enjoy good food, engaging conversation, and a crackling fire on cool summer evenings?

The desire for pleasure isn't wrong. God has built us for it. Paul reminds us that God "gives us richly all things to enjoy" (1 TIMOTHY 6:17 NKJV). Other passages welcome us to the healthy pleasure of food, friends, and the intimacy of a marriage relationship. But thinking that we can find ultimate pleasure in people and things is, in the final analysis, an empty pursuit.

Ultimate pleasure is not found in the short-lived thrills our world offers, but rather in the long-term joy from a deepening intimacy with our Lord.

What we are really looking for is satisfied only in a fulfilling and growing relationship with Jesus. Pursue Him and taste His delights!

❖ *Joe Stowell*

Dad's Hat

EPHESIANS 6:1–4

"Honor your father and mother,"
which is the first commandment with a promise.

—EPHESIANS 6:2

Amid the celebration, there was tragedy. It was the opening ceremonies of the 1992 Summer Olympic Games in Barcelona. One by one the teams entered the stadium and paraded around the track to the cheers of 65,000 people. But in one section of Olympic Stadium, shock and sadness fell as Peter Karnaugh, father of United States swimmer Ron Karnaugh, was stricken with a fatal heart attack.

Five days later, Ron showed up for his race wearing his dad's hat, which he carefully set aside before his competition began. It was Ron's tribute to his dad, whom he called "my best friend." The hat was one his dad had worn when they went fishing and did other things together. Wearing the hat was Ron's way of honoring his dad for standing beside him, encouraging him, and guiding him.

There are many ways to honor our fathers, as Scripture commands us to do (EPHESIANS 6:2). One way, is to show respect for the good values they taught us.

What can you do for your dad today to show him the kind of honor the Bible talks about?

❖ *Dave Branon*

ISAIAH 12

"Surely God is my salvation; I will trust and not be afraid.
The LORD, the LORD himself, is my strength and my defense; he has become my salvation."

—ISAIAH 12:2

I have an ancient leaf blower I use to clean up our patio. It sputters, rattles, smokes, emits irritating fumes, and is considered by my wife (and probably by my neighbors) to be excessively noisy.

But our old dog is utterly indifferent to the racket. When I start up the blower, she doesn't even raise her head. That's because she trusts me.

A young man who occasionally mows our yard uses a similar blower, but our dog won't tolerate his. Years ago, when she was a puppy, the boy teased her with the machine and she has never forgotten. Now when the kid enters the backyard, we have to put her in the house, because she growls, barks, and snarls at him. Same set of circumstances, but the hands that use the blower make all the difference.

Frightening circumstances are less troublesome if we trust the hands that control them. We have no reason to fear. But the hands that control the universe—God's hands—are wise and compassionate. We can trust them in spite of our circumstances and not be afraid.

❖ *David Roper*

Why He's So Special
JOHN 1:1–14

"I and the Father are one."

—JOHN 10:30

Some pretty good people have founded religions over the centuries. One religious leader spent a good portion of his life trying to find truth—an admirable quest.

Another religious leader was a teacher and a civil servant who drew up an honor code for his people—a respectable venture.

No matter how good any originators of world religions may have been, however, they cannot compare with the founder of Christianity. Here's why: They are all in the category of "good men," while Jesus is in a category by himself—the God-man.

Jesus alone is Immanuel (God with us; MATTHEW 1:23), the Savior (LUKE 2:11), and the Messiah (JOHN 1:41). Only Jesus could truthfully assert His equality with His heavenly Father: "I and the Father are one," (JOHN 10:30). Only Jesus's words are divine. His life was the only perfect one. Only Jesus's death and resurrection provide life everlasting.

Jesus is unique. He alone is worthy of our worship, adoration, and awe. He alone is the perfect Man. The divine One. The provider of salvation. Don't settle for anything—or anyone—less.

❖ *Dave Branon*

LUKE 10:29–37

*He answered, "'Love the Lord your God
with all your heart and with all your soul
and with all your strength and with all your mind'; and,
'Love your neighbor as yourself.'"*

—LUKE 10:27

It would have been simpler just to buy a new hair dryer. But determined to save a buck, I decided to fix it myself. To loosen the screw in the handle, I took out my pocket knife. As I put pressure on the knife to turn the screw, the blade folded back—on my finger.

I learned a lesson that day: I love myself. And I am urgent about meeting my needs. I wanted the bleeding stopped immediately. I instructed my first-aid team (my wife and kids) to wash my finger *gently* and then to put the bandage on in a way that would avoid having the hairs on my finger pulled up when it was removed. My thoughts, words, and actions were driven by my love for myself.

To love "your neighbor as yourself" (LUKE 10:27) requires the same urgent kind of love. It's a love that notices the need of another person and won't rest until it's been met. It's the kind of love God wants to share with your neighbors through you.

❖ *Joe Stowell*

Setting Prisoners Free

He upholds the cause of the oppressed and gives food to the hungry
The LORD sets prisoners free.

—PSALM 146:7

When my wife and I visited the National Museum of the Mighty Eighth Air Force near Savannah, Georgia, we were especially moved by the prisoner-of-war exhibit, with its re-creation of a German prisoner-of-war camp's barracks. Marlene's dad, Jim, served in the "Mighty Eighth" as they flew missions over Europe during World War II. Jim was shot down and held as a prisoner of war. As we walked through the exhibit, we recalled Jim telling about the absolute joy he and his fellow prisoners felt the day they were set free.

God's care for the oppressed and the liberation of the imprisoned are declared in Psalm 146. The psalmist describes the one who "upholds the cause of the oppressed and gives food to the hungry," who "sets prisoners free" (V. 7). This is cause for celebration. But the greatest freedom is freedom from our guilt and shame. Jesus said, "So if the Son sets you free, you will be free indeed" (JOHN 8:36).

Through Christ's sacrifice, we are set free from the prison of sin to know His joy and the freedom only forgiveness can bring.

❖ *Bill Crowder*

PHILIPPIANS 2:1–11

Let each of you look out not only for his own interests,
but also for the interests of others.

—PHILIPPIANS 2:4 (NKJV)

During the Bosnian War (1992–1996), more than 10,000 people were killed in the city of Sarajevo as gunfire and mortar rounds rained down from the surrounding hills. Steven Galloway's gripping novel *The Cellist of Sarajevo* unfolds there. The book follows three fictional characters who must decide if they will become self-absorbed in their struggle to survive or will somehow rise above their numbing circumstances to help others during great adversity.

From a prison in Rome, Paul wrote to the Christians in Philippi, saying, "Let each of you look out not only for his own interests, but also for the interests of others" (PHILIPPIANS 2:4 NKJV). Paul cited Jesus as the great example of a selfless focus on others: "Christ Jesus . . . humbled Himself and became obedient to the point of death, even the death of the cross" (VV. 5–8 NKJV). Rather than seeking sympathy from others, Jesus gave everything to rescue us from the tyranny of sin.

Our challenge as followers of Jesus is to see through His eyes and respond to the needs of others in His strength, even in our own difficult times.

❖ *David McCasland*

Have a Great Day . . . or Not

PSALM 118

*This is the day the L*ORD *has made; we will rejoice and be glad in it.*

—PSALM 118:24 (NKJV)

I was in a convenience store one day, standing in line behind a man paying for his groceries. When he was finished, the clerk sent him off with a cheery "Have a great day!"

To the clerk's surprise (and mine) the man exploded in anger. "This is one of the worst days of my life!" he shouted. "How can I have a great day?" Then out he stormed.

We all have "bad" days over which we seem to have no control. How can that be a great day? Recall these words: "This is the day the LORD has made" (PSALM 118:24 NKJV).

The Lord has made every day. He has control over everything in it—even the hard things that come my way. All events have been screened through His wisdom and love, and they are opportunities for us to grow in faith.

Now when people give me the parting admonition to have a great day, I reply, "That's beyond my control, but I can be grateful for whatever comes my way and rejoice—for this is the day the Lord has made."

❖ *David Roper*

Grateful for Everything

DEUTERONOMY 8:6–18

When you have eaten and are satisfied, praise the LORD your God
for the good land he has given you.

—DEUTERONOMY 8:10

During busy holiday times in Australia, rest stops are set up on major highways with volunteers offering free coffee. My wife, Merryn, and I grew to enjoy these stops.

On one trip, we pulled in for our coffee. An attendant handed two cups over and then asked me for two dollars. I asked why. She pointed to the small print on the sign. At this stop, only the driver got free coffee; you had to pay for passengers. Annoyed, I grumbled, paid the two dollars, and walked off. Back at the car, Merryn pointed out my error: I turned a gift into an entitlement and became ungrateful. She was right.

When the Israelites were about to enter the Promised Land, Moses urged them to be grateful (DEUTERONOMY 8:10). The land was abundant, but they could easily treat this prosperity as something they deserved (VV. 17–18). The Jews developed a practice of giving thanks for every meal, no matter how small.

I went back to the woman and apologized. A free cup of coffee was a gift I didn't deserve—and something for which to be thankful.

❖ *Sheridan Voysey*

Brother to Brother

GENESIS 33:1–11

"A new command I give you: Love one another.
As I have loved you, so you must love one another."

—JOHN 13:34

My brother and I, less than a year apart in age, were quite "competitive" growing up (translation: we fought!). Dad understood. He had brothers. Mom? Not so much.

Our story could have fit in the book of Genesis, which might well be subtitled *A Brief History of Sibling Rivalry*. Cain and Abel (GENESIS 4); Isaac and Ishmael (21:8–10); Joseph and everyone not named Benjamin (CHAPTER 37). But for brother-to-brother animosity, it's hard to beat Jacob and Esau.

Esau's twin brother had cheated him twice, so he wanted to kill Jacob (27:41). Decades later Jacob and Esau would reconcile (CHAPTER 33). But the rivalry continued on in their descendants, who became the nations of Edom and Israel. When Israel prepared to enter the Promised Land, Edom resisted (NUMBERS 20:14–21).

Happily for us, the Bible contains the story of God's redemption!

As my brother and I got older, we became close. That's the thing with God. When we respond to the forgiveness He offers through redemption, His grace can transform even sibling rivalries into brotherly love.

❖ *Tim Gustafson*

Buried Treasure

LEVITICUS 19:9–15

Open my eyes that I may see wonderful things in your law.

—PSALM 119:18

Growing up in rural Missouri where American outlaw Jesse James (1847–1882) had lived, my friends and I were convinced he had buried treasure nearby. We wandered the woods in hopes of digging it up. Often we would run into an elderly man chopping firewood. We watched this mysterious man trudge the highways looking for soda cans—his kind of treasure. Redeeming the cans for cash, he'd retire to his run-down, unpainted shack with a bottle in a brown paper bag. After his death, his family found bundles of money stashed away in his ramshackle home.

Like this man who ignored his treasure, we Christians sometimes ignore parts of Scripture. For instance, who knew Leviticus held so much buried treasure? In an efficient seven verses in chapter 19, God teaches us how to provide for the poor and disabled without stripping them of their dignity (VV. 9–10, 14), how to run our businesses ethically (VV. 11, 13, 15), and how to embed respect for Him into our daily life (V. 12).

Think of all the treasure that can be ours if we dig into our Bibles every day.

❖ *Randy Kilgore*

When We're Let Down

1 SAMUEL 17:33–50

*"All those gathered here will know that
it is not by sword or spear that the Lord saves;
for the battle is the Lord's, and he will give all of you into our hands."*

—1 SAMUEL 17:47

On August 4, 1991, the MTS *Oceanos* cruise ship ran into a terrible storm off the coast of South Africa. When the ship began to sink, the captain and his officers abandoned ship without telling anyone. Passenger Moss Hills, a British musician, noticed that something was wrong and sent out a Mayday signal. Then Moss, his wife Tracy, and other entertainers on board organized the safe evacuation of all passengers onto rescue helicopters.

Sometimes people we look to for leadership let us down. When King Saul and his officers faced the belligerent insults of the Philistine giant Goliath, they responded with fear and timidity (1 SAMUEL 17:11). But a young boy named David had faith in God, which transformed his perspective on this threat. David said to Goliath, "You come against me with sword . . . , but I come against you in the name of the Lord Almighty" (V. 45). David defeated the enemy and turned the tide of battle (V. 50).

When others let us down, God may be calling us to provide leadership in His strength and for His honor.

❖ *Dennis Fisher*

Freedom at Alcatraz

PHILEMON 4–16

I appeal to you for my son Onesimus,
who became my son while I was in chains.

—PHILEMON 10

A tour of the former federal prison on Alcatraz Island in San Francisco Bay left me with some unforgettable images. As our tour boat pulled into the dock, I could see why this maximum-security federal prison was once known as "The Rock."

Later, inside the legendary Big House, I saw row after row of cagelike cells that housed well-known inmates such as Al Capone and Robert Stroud, the "Birdman of Alcatraz."

But another image made a deeper impression. Stepping into an empty cell, I saw the name "Jesus" scrawled on a wall. In another, a Bible lay on a shelf. Together they quietly spoke of the greatest of all freedoms.

Paul knew such liberty while waiting to be executed. Regarding himself as a "prisoner of Christ" (PHILEMON 1), he used his incarceration to help other inmates discover freedom in Christ (V. 10).

Barred windows and doors represent one kind of confinement. Physical paralysis, inescapable poverty, and prolonged unemployment are others. Perhaps you endure another. None are to be desired—yet who would trade "imprisonment" with Christ for life "on the outside" without Him?

❖ *Mart DeHaan*

In All Circumstances

1 THESSALONIANS 5:16–18

Give thanks in all circumstances;
for this is God's will for you in Christ Jesus.

—1 THESSALONIANS 5:18

In our suburb we complain about the constant power outages. They hit often, plunging the neighborhood into darkness. The inconvenience is hard to bear when we cannot use basic appliances.

Our Christian neighbor often asks, "Is this something to thank God for?" She is referring to 1 Thessalonians 5:18: "Give thanks in all circumstances, for this is God's will for you in Christ Jesus." We always say, "Yes," but the half-hearted manner in which we say it is contradicted by our grumbling when the power goes off.

One day our belief in thanking God in all circumstances took on new meaning. I returned from work to find our neighbor visibly shaken. "Thank Jesus the power was off," he said. "My house would have burned down, and my family and I would have perished!"

A truck had hit an electricity pole and brought down high-tension cables right over several houses. Had there been power, fatalities would have been likely.

The difficult circumstances we face can make it hard to say, "Thanks, Lord." But we can be thankful, for every situation is an opportunity to trust Him.

❖ *Lawrence Darmani*

A Loving Father

PSALM 107:7–13

As a father has compassion on his children,
so the LORD has compassion on those who fear him.

—PSALM 103:13

The parents seemed weary from dragging two energetic preschoolers through airports, and now their final flight was delayed. As I watched the boys running around the gate area, I wondered how Mom and Dad were going to keep them settled down for our half-hour flight into Grand Rapids. When we finally boarded, I noticed that the father and one of the sons were behind me. I heard the weary dad say to his son, "Let me read one of your storybooks to you." During the entire flight, this loving father softly and patiently read to his son, keeping him calm.

In one of his psalms David declares, "As a father has compassion on his children, so the LORD has compassion on those who fear him" (PSALM 103:13). This tender word gives us a picture of how deeply our heavenly Father loves His children.

God longs for you to listen again to the story of His love for you when you are restless on your own life journey. He is always near, ready to encourage you with His Word.

❖ *Bill Crowder*

The Last Will Be First

MARK 9:33–37

For those who exalt themselves will be humbled,
and those who humble themselves will be exalted.

—MATTHEW 23:12

On a recent flight, my seat was in the middle of the plane, but I had to put my bag in an overhead compartment by the last row. I knew I would have to wait for everyone else to leave before I could retrieve my luggage.

As I settled into my seat, a thought occurred to me that seemed to be from the Lord: "It really won't hurt you to wait. It will actually do you good." I decided to enjoy the extra time after we landed, helping other passengers and assisting a flight attendant with cleaning. When I was able to retrieve my bag, I laughed when someone said she thought I worked for the airline.

That experience made me ponder Jesus's words: "Anyone who wants to be first must be the very last, and the servant of all" (MARK 9:35).

In Jesus's "upside down" kingdom, there's a place of honor for those who voluntarily set themselves aside to attend to others' needs.

Jesus came into our me-first world not "to be served, but to serve" (MATTHEW 20:28). We serve Him best by serving others.

❖ *James Banks*

Secrets Exposed

PSALM 32:1–7

Then I acknowledged my sin to you and did not cover up my iniquity.
I said, "I will confess my transgressions to the LORD." And you forgave the guilt of my sin.

—PSALM 32:5

For many years, Lake Okeechobee hid its secrets in thick waters and layers of muck. But in 2007, a drought shrank the Florida lake to its lowest level since officials began keeping records in 1932, unveiling hundreds of years of history. Raking through the bottom of the lake, archaeologists found artifacts, pottery, human bone fragments, and even boats.

After King David committed adultery with Bathsheba and planned the death of her husband, Uriah, he covered his sins. He probably went many months conducting business as usual. As long as David cloaked his sinful secrets, he experienced God's crushing finger of conviction and his strength evaporated like water in the heat of summer (PSALM 32:3–4).

When Nathan confronted David about his sin, God's conviction was so great that David confessed his sins to God and turned away from them. Immediately the Lord forgave David, and he experienced His grace (2 SAMUEL 12:13; PSALM 32:5; PSALM 51).

When we uncover our sins by confessing them to God, we are covered with His forgiveness. What an amazing feeling!

❖ *Marvin Williams*

Weighed Down

*Therefore, since we are surrounded by such a great cloud of witnesses,
let us throw off everything that hinders and the sin that so easily entangles.*

—HEBREWS 12:1

August 10, 1628, was a dark day in naval history. On that day the royal warship *Vasa* set out on her maiden voyage, but the pride of the Swedish navy sank one mile out to sea. What went wrong? The excessive load was too heavy to make her seaworthy. Excess weight pulled the *Vasa* to the bottom of the ocean.

The Christian life can also be weighed down by excess baggage.

Encouraging us in our spiritual journey, the book of Hebrews says: "Let us throw off everything that hinders and the sin that so easily entangles. And let us run with perseverance the race marked out for us, fixing our eyes on Jesus, the pioneer and perfecter of faith" (12:1–2).

Like the lavishly decorated *Vasa*, we may project to others an impressive exterior. But if on the inside we are weighed down with sin, our perseverance can be impaired. There is a remedy, however. By relying on God's guidance and the empowering of the Holy Spirit, our load can be lightened and our perseverance buoyant.

Forgiveness and grace are always available to the spiritual traveler.

❖ *Dennis Fisher*

ISAIAH 46:8–11

Remember the former things, those of long ago; I am God, and there is no other;
I am God, and there is none like me.

—ISAIAH 46:9

My wife and I don't always understand each other. For instance, it's a great mystery to her how I can continue to follow the Detroit Tigers even if they have no chance of making the playoffs. And I surely can't fathom her love of clothes shopping.

To love someone intensely doesn't mean you have to understand him or her completely. That's good news, because there's no way we can begin to grasp the deep mysteries of the God we love.

We can't always deduce why God does what He does. Yet some people look at tragedies, for instance, and turn their backs on God—assuming that their finite knowledge about the situation is better than His infinite wisdom.

If we could figure God out, where would be the awe and the majesty of the Almighty? One reason we know God to be so great is that we cannot reduce His thinking to ours.

"Who has known the mind of the Lord?" (1 CORINTHIANS 2:16). No one. Praise God! Even when we don't understand Him, we know we can trust Him.

❖ *Dave Branon*

In Every Generation
PSALM 100

For the LORD is good and his love endures forever;
his faithfulness continues through all generations.

—PSALM 100:5

It may seem surprising when children don't follow their parents' example of faith in God. Equally unexpected is a person with a deep commitment to Christ who emerges from a family where faith was not present. In every generation, each person has a choice.

Samuel was a great man of God who appointed his two sons, Joel and Abijah, as leaders over Israel (1 SAMUEL 8:1–2). Unlike their father, however, they were corrupt and "turned aside after dishonest gain" (V. 3). Yet, years later, we find Heman, Joel's son, appointed as a musician in the house of the Lord (1 CHRONICLES 6:31–33). Heman, Samuel's grandson—along with Asaph, his right-hand man and the author of many of the psalms—served the Lord by singing joyful songs (1 CHRONICLES 15:16–17).

Even though a person seems indifferent toward the faith so important to his or her parents, God is still at work. Things can change in later years, and seeds of faith may spring to life in generations to come.

"The LORD is good and his love endures forever; his faithfulness continues through all generations."

❖ *David McCasland*

Victory

2 THESSALONIANS 1:7–12

On the day he comes to be glorified in his holy people
and to be marveled at among all those who have believed.
This includes you, because you believed our testimony to you.

—2 THESSALONIANS 1:10

Have you ever heard of a Pyrrhic victory? In 279 BC King Pyrrhus of the tiny Greek state of Epirus defeated the Romans in the Battle of Asculum. Yet Pyrrhus lamented, "If we are victorious in one more battle with the Romans, we shall be utterly ruined." They won the battle, but they were about to lose the war.

Paul wrote to a group of young believers in Thessalonica who were losing ground—and battles. Defeat seemed imminent. But he also knew a greater power was at work. Paul said God would "give relief" for those being persecuted, and He would bring justice with "the glory of his might" (2 THESSALONIANS 1:7, 9).

Jesus won the ultimate victory on the cross long ago—though it might have seemed like He lost the battle. Just prior to releasing His spirit in death, Jesus said, "It is finished!" (JOHN 19:30). He had conquered sin and death!

Today, as you face your battles, remember that victory is found in the One who gives "us eternal encouragement and good hope" (2 THESSALONIANS 2:16). Jesus *is* the Victor!

❖ *Tom Felten*

Disappointing Heroes

And so, dear brothers and sisters who belong to God and are partners with those called to heaven, think carefully about this Jesus whom we declare to be God's messenger and High Priest.

—HEBREWS 3:1 (NLT)

A recent book portrays Old West gunslingers Wyatt Earp and Doc Holliday as shiftless bums. Through the years, in books and Hollywood movies, they've become heroes. Yet reputable historical accounts show they were not.

In contrast, the Bible tells us about flawed people who became real heroes. But don't lose sight of the vital source of their heroic actions. The object of their faith was *God,* who chooses flawed human beings for His remarkable purposes.

As biblical heroes go, Moses stands tall. We tend to forget that he was a murderer and a reluctant leader who once directed a rant at God: "What did I do to deserve the burden of all these people? Did I give birth to them?" (NUMBERS 11:11–12 NLT).

How very *human* of Moses! Yet Hebrews reminds us: "Moses was certainly faithful in God's house as a servant" (HEBREWS 3:5 NLT).

Real heroes point to the Hero who never disappoints. "Jesus deserves far more glory than Moses" (V. 3 NLT).

❖ *Tim Gustafson*

Register Rock

HEBREWS 11:3–40

Therefore, since we are surrounded by such a great cloud of witnesses,
let us throw off everything that hinders and the sin that so easily entangles.
And let us run with perseverance the race marked out for us.

—HEBREWS 12:1

Along the old Oregon Trail in Idaho there is a marker—a giant lava boulder known locally as Register Rock. It's located in an area that was a favorite overnight camping area for westbound immigrants traveling the trail in the nineteenth century.

Travelers often inscribed their names on the rock as a memorial to their passage. Register Rock stands as a monument to their courage and tenacity.

When I think of Register Rock, I think of other pilgrims who have passed by us on their journey. Hebrews 11 lists some of those hardy souls—Gideon, Samson, David, and Samuel.

But there are other more recent pilgrims: my mother and father, my fifth-grade Sunday school teacher Mrs. Lincoln, my youth leader John Richards, and my mentors Ray Stedman and Howard Hendricks.

The author of Hebrews reminds us to remember "pilgrims" who have gone before us, especially those "who spoke the Word of God" to us (HEBREWS 13:7). Most important, he encourages us to follow their faith.

❖ *David Roper*

The Power of Simple Words
2 PETER 1:12–21

For we did not follow cleverly devised stories when we told you about
the coming of our Lord Jesus Christ in power,
but we were eyewitnesses of his majesty.

2 PETER 1:16

Raucous laughter marked the guests in my father's hospital room: Two old truck drivers, one former country/western singer, one craftsman, two women from neighboring farms, and me.

". . . and then he got up and busted the bottle over my head," the craftsman said, finishing his story about a bar fight.

The room burst into laughter at this now-humorous memory.

Suddenly, about forty minutes into this visit, the craftsman clears his throat, turns to my dad, and gets serious. "No more drinking and bar fights for me, Howard. Those days are behind me. Now I have a different reason to live. I want to tell you about my Savior."

He then proceeded to do just that, over my father's surprisingly mild protests. If there's a sweeter, gentler way to present the gospel message, I've never heard it.

My dad listened and watched, and some years later believed in Jesus too. It was a simple testimony from an old friend living a simple life. Simple isn't naïve or stupid; it's direct and unpretentious.

Just like Jesus. And salvation.

❖ *Randy Kilgore*

Enemy Love

JONAH 3:10–4:11

"If you love those who love you, what credit is that to you?
Even sinners love those who love them."

—LUKE 6:32

When war broke out in 1950, fifteen-year-old Kim Chin-Kyung joined the South Korean army to defend his homeland. He soon found, however, that he wasn't ready for the horrors of combat. As young friends died around him, he begged God for his life and promised that if allowed to live he would learn to love his enemies.

Sixty-five years later, Dr. Kim reflected on that answered prayer. Through decades of caring for orphans and assisting in the education of North Korean and Chinese young people, he won many friends among those he once regarded as enemies.

The prophet Jonah left a different kind of legacy. Even a dramatic rescue from the belly of a big fish didn't transform his heart. Although he eventually obeyed God, Jonah said he'd rather die than watch the Lord show mercy to his enemies (JONAH 4:1–2, 8).

We are left to wonder about ourselves. Will we settle for his attitude toward those we fear and hate? Or will we ask God for the ability to love our enemies as He has shown mercy to us?

❖ *Mart DeHaan*

Turn Off the Scoreboard

Forgiving each other,
just as in Christ God forgave you.

—EPHESIANS 4:32

At his son's wedding reception, my friend Bob offered advice and encouragement to the newlyweds. In his speech he told of a football coach in a nearby town who, when his team lost a game, kept the losing score on the scoreboard all week to remind the team of their failure. While that may be a good football strategy, Bob wisely advised, it's a terrible strategy in marriage. When your spouse upsets you or fails you in some way, don't keep drawing attention to the failure. Turn off the scoreboard.

What great advice! Scripture is full of commands for us to love each other and overlook faults. We are reminded that love "keeps no record of wrongs" (1 CORINTHIANS 13:5) and that we should be ready to forgive one another "just as in Christ God forgave you" (EPHESIANS 4:32).

With God, forgiveness means that our sin is out of sight *and* out of mind. May He give us grace to extend forgiveness to those around us. At home, let's turn off the scoreboard.

❖ *Joe Stowell*

The "Underbird"

JAMES 2:1–9

Indeed, the very hairs of your head are all numbered.
Don't be afraid; you are worth more than many sparrows.

—LUKE 12:7

Charlie Brown, the comic strip character, identified with the underdog, probably because he felt like one. In one scene he was building a birdhouse when the cynical Lucy came by. "I'm building it for sparrows," Charlie told her. Lucy said, "For sparrows? Nobody builds birdhouses for sparrows." "I do," he replied. "I always stick up for the underbird."

At times Christians may overlook the "sparrows," the little people in their worlds. They may ignore those they view as less valuable.

James said we should avoid partiality (JAMES 2:1) and favoritism (V. 9). There's no excuse for disrespecting people with our attitudes and words.

Jesus didn't do this. He crossed all kinds of traditional barriers to talk with tax-collectors, sinners, non-Jews, people of mixed races, the poor, as well as the rich. He came to identify with each of us, and to pay the price on the cross for all our sins.

When a sparrow falls, the Father takes note of it. But He cares much more for people, including the "underbird." Perhaps we need a little more Charlie Brown in us.

❖ *David Egner*

Be Still

The LORD Almighty is with us; the God of Jacob is our fortress.

—PSALM 46:11

"We've created more information in the last five years than in all of human history before it, and it's coming at us all the time," observed Daniel Levitin, author of *The Organized Mind*. "In a sense," Levitin says, "we become addicted to the hyperstimulation." The constant barrage of news and knowledge can dominate our minds, making it difficult to find time to be quiet, to think, and to pray.

Psalm 46:10 says, "Be still, and know that I am God." Many people find that a "quiet time" is an essential part of each day—a time to read the Bible, pray, and focus on the goodness and greatness of God.

When we, like the writer of Psalm 46, experience the reality that "God is our refuge and strength, an ever-present help in trouble" (V. 1), it drives our fear away (V. 2), shifts our focus from the world's turmoil to God's peace, and creates a quiet confidence that our Lord is in control (V. 10).

No matter how chaotic the world may become, we can find quietness and strength in our heavenly Father's love and power.

❖ *David McCasland*

Remembering Our Father's Words

PSALM 119:89–93

I will never forget your precepts, for by them you have preserved my life.

—PSALM 119:93

Jim Davidson was climbing down Mount Rainier when he fell through a snow bridge and into a crevasse (a pitch-black, ice-walled crack in a glacier). As Jim stood bloodied and bruised in that dark ice cave, he reflected on how his father had repeatedly reminded him that he could accomplish great things if he pressed through adversity. Those words helped sustain Jim as he spent the next five hours climbing out of that dark ice cave to safety under extremely difficult circumstances.

The psalmist seemed to climb out of his own crevasse of affliction and pain by recalling his heavenly Father's words. He admitted that if God and His Word had not sustained him, he would have died in his misery (PSALM 119:92). He expressed full confidence in the Lord's eternal Word (V. 89) and in the faithfulness of His character (V. 90). The psalmist committed never to forget God's words to him because they had a central role in rescuing him.

In our darkest moments of affliction, our souls can be revived by our Father when we fill our minds with His encouraging words.

❖ *Marvin Williams*

Who Are You?

1 JOHN 2:1–11

We know that we have come to know him if we keep his commands.

—1 JOHN 2:3

Identity theft is a big problem in the age of credit cards and the internet. It's not hard for someone to retrieve your vital information and pose as you. If that were to happen, however, it would not change the essence of who you are. The thief would not steal your true identity—just some superficial information about you.

Your identity goes much deeper than your ID numbers. In reality, you are who God says you are. That alone will dictate your eternal destiny, and that alone will indicate whether you can live life to the fullest.

In 1 John 2, there are three truths that will indicate to others that we are God's children:

- We obey His commands (V. 3).
- We live as Jesus lived (V. 6).
- We avoid hatred toward others (V. 9).

Who are you? What is your identity? Do you know Jesus? Obeying His commands, living as He did, and loving others are traits we will have.

❖ *Dave Branon*

Dingo the Dog

PHILIPPIANS 2:1-4

Not looking to your own interests but each of you to the interests of the others.

—PHILIPPIANS 2:4

Harry Tupper is a fishing legend here in Idaho. There's a spot on Henry's Lake over on the east side of the state that's named for him: "Tupper's Hole."

The thing I remember most about Harry, aside from fishing prowess, was his dog, Dingo. Now there was a dog! Dingo sat alongside Harry in his boat and watched intently while he fished. When Harry hooked a trout, Dingo would bark furiously until the fish was netted and released.

Dingo's enthusiasm taught me something: It's better to get more excited about what others are doing than what we are doing.

As I read Philippians 2:4 and think about Dingo, I ask myself: Do I spend time thinking about "the interests of others"? Do I get as excited about what God is doing through a friend as I do about what He is doing through me? Do I long to see others grow in grace?

We are most like God when our thoughts for ourselves are lost in our thoughts for others. Paul said, "In humility value others above yourselves" (2:3). Is that how we live?

❖ *David Roper*

The Lost Book

2 KINGS 22:8–13

Hilkiah the high priest said to Shaphan the secretary,
"I have found the Book of the Law in the temple of the LORD."
He gave it to Shaphan, who read it.

—2 KINGS 22:8

Two US Senate staffers were cleaning out a storeroom underneath the Capitol when they spotted a partially opened door. Curious, they found a small room jammed with dusty old brochures and payroll records. A leather-bound book with gold lettering caught their attention: Senators' Compensation and Mileage. It bore the dates 1790–1881.

What a find! It was a unique record of every dollar paid to senators during the Senate's first ninety years. Plus, the book contained the handwritten signatures of Thomas Jefferson and John Adams. Said historian Richard Baker, "There is nothing that comes remotely close to it in the archives of the Senate."

I imagine that Hilkiah the high priest felt even more excitement when he discovered the long-lost "Book of the Law" in some hidden cranny in the temple (2 KINGS 22:8). King Josiah recognized its value and ordered it to be read aloud to the people (23:1–2).

What a reminder to rediscover some "dusty" parts of the Bible! Dust them off and read them. They speak volumes—and their message may be just what you need.

❖ *David Egner*

Never Alone

HEBREWS 13:1–8

Keep your lives free from the love of money and be content with what you have, because God has said, "Never will I leave you; never will I forsake you."

—HEBREWS 13:5

Having played intercollegiate soccer, I've never lost my love for "The Beautiful Game." I especially enjoy watching the English Premier League—for the skill and speed with which the game is played. Also, I love the way the fans sing in support of their beloved "sides." For instance, Liverpool has for years had "You'll Never Walk Alone" as its theme. How moving to hear 50,000 fans rise as one to sing that old standard! It's an encouragement to players and fans alike that they will see each other through to the end. Walk alone? Never.

This sentiment has meaning for everyone. We are made for community, so isolation and loneliness are painful. During tough times, our faith is vital.

The child of God never needs to fear abandonment. God has said, "Never will I leave you; never will I forsake you" (HEBREWS 13:5). This is the promise of God himself to those who are the objects of His love. He is there—and He isn't going away.

With Christ, you will never walk alone.

❖ *Bill Crowder*

Is Jesus Exclusive?

JOHN 14:1–12

Jesus answered, "I am the way and the truth and the life.
No one comes to the Father except through me."

—JOHN 14:6

Anne Graham Lotz, appearing on a popular talk program, was asked, "Are you one of those who believe that Jesus is exclusively the only way to heaven?" He added, "You know how mad that makes people!" Without blinking she replied, "Jesus is not exclusive. He died so that anyone could come to Him for salvation."

What a great response! Christianity is not an exclusive club limited to an elite few. Everyone is welcome regardless of color, class, or clout.

In spite of this wonderful reality, Christ's claim in John 14:6 to be the only way to God continues to offend. Yet Jesus is the only viable option. We are all guilty before God—sinners who cannot help ourselves. Our sin had to be dealt with. Jesus died to pay the penalty for our sins and then rose from the dead. No other religious leader offers what Jesus provides in His victory over sin and death.

The gospel of Christ is the wonderful truth that God loves us enough to take care of our biggest problem—sin. And as long as sin is the problem, the world needs Jesus!

❖ *Joe Stowell*

Below the Deck

ROMANS 16:1–16

Receive her in the Lord in a manner worthy of the saints,
and assist her in whatever business she has need of you;
for indeed she has been a helper of many and of myself also.

—ROMANS 16:2 (NKJV)

James Deitz's paintings of airplanes and their crews are on display in many aviation galleries in the United States, including the Smithsonian. One of the paintings by Deitz, titled *Unsung*, depicts a crew of four mechanics working on a dive bomber—far below the flight deck of an aircraft carrier somewhere in the Pacific during World War II. The serious-looking, grease-stained men are working tirelessly to get the plane ready to go back into battle.

We too may be performing unnoticed tasks as we support the biblical mandate to spread the gospel and train believers. Without a cadre of volunteers, no work of God could be done effectively.

As the apostle Paul closed his letter to the believers in Rome, he listed several people who receive no other mention in Scripture. For example, Paul referred to Phoebe and said that she was "a helper of many" (16:2). Phoebe and the others were essential to the life and work of the early church.

Are you working "below the flight deck"? Your service for Christ is essential.

❖ *David Egner*

What Could Go Wrong?

ACTS 9:1–19

*In a vision he has seen a man named Ananias come
and place his hands on him to restore his sight.*

—ACTS 9:12

It was an early Saturday morning in my sophomore year of high school, and I was eager to get to my job at the local bowling lanes. The evening before, I had stayed late to mop the muddy tile floors because the janitor called in sick. I hadn't told my boss about the janitor. I wanted to surprise him. After all, *What could go wrong?*

Plenty, it turns out.

Stepping in the door, I saw inches of standing water with bowling pins and boxes of paper scoresheets bobbing on top. I realized what I had done: *I had left a large faucet running overnight!* Incredibly, my boss greeted me with a huge hug and a big smile—"for trying," he said.

Saul was actively punishing and harassing Christians (ACTS 9:1–2) when he came face-to-face with Jesus on the road to Damascus (VV. 3–4), Jesus confronted him about his sinful actions. Blinded by the experience, Paul would need a Christian—Ananias—to restore his sight in an act of courage *and* grace (V. 17).

Both Saul and I received *unexpected* grace.

Let's look for ways to be the face of grace in life-changing encounters with others.

❖ *Randy Kilgore*

Do It Now!

HEBREWS 3:7–15

But encourage one another daily, as long as it is called "Today,"
so that none of you may be hardened by sin's deceitfulness.

—HEBREWS 3:13

Several years ago, a friend took me to a motivational seminar where the leaders guided us toward understanding our unique identity and purpose in life. Then they passed along some helpful methods for effective living. One motto has stayed with me: "Do it now." They said it takes as much energy to avoid a task as it does to do it. Procrastination saps power; completion gives relief.

A spiritual application can be seen in Hebrews 3, a passage that calls us to obey the Lord. "Today, if you will hear his voice, do not harden your hearts as you did in the rebellion, . . . but encourage one another daily, as long as it is called 'Today,' so that none of you may be hardened by sin's deceitfulness" (VV. 7–8, 13). We don't know how long it would have taken the Israelites to reach the Promised Land if they had obeyed God, but their forty-year journey resulted from their unwilling hearts. An entire generation missed the adventure of a lifetime (VV. 8–11).

When we know how the Lord wants us to live, say "Yes!" No debate, no delay. Do it now.

❖ *David McCasland*

Fishing Where They Ain't

LUKE 7:34–48

When one of the Pharisees invited Jesus to have dinner with him,
he went to the Pharisee's house and reclined at the table.

—LUKE 7:36

I have a good friend I fish with who sits on the tailgate of his truck and scans the river for fifteen minutes or more, looking for rising fish. "No use fishing where they ain't," he says. This makes me think of another question: "Do I fish for souls where they ain't?"

It was said of Jesus that He was "a friend of tax collectors and sinners" (LUKE 7:34). As Christians, we are to be unlike the world in our behavior, but squarely in it as He was. If I have only Christian friends, I may be fishing for souls "where they ain't."

Being with nonbelievers is the first step in "fishing." Then comes love—a heart-kindness that sees beneath the surface of their off-hand remarks and listens for the deeper cry of the soul.

Such love is not a natural instinct. It comes solely from God. And so we pray: *"Lord, when I am with nonbelievers today, may I become aware of the cheerless voice, the weary countenance, or the downcast eyes. May I listen to others, show your compassion, and speak your truth today."*

❖ *David Roper*

Sleepless in Heaven

PSALM 121

He will not let your foot slip—
he who watches over you will not slumber.

—PSALM 121:3

One of the most dangerous aspects of flying is the landing. As the aircraft gets closer to land, the air traffic is more congested, the weather on the ground may be far worse than the weather at 30,000 feet, and the runways may not be clear of other planes. Pilots rely on the air-traffic controller to coordinate all the details so every plane can arrive without incident.

Imagine, then, the panic when the pilot of an airliner full of passengers radioed the tower and got no answer. It was eventually discovered that the air-traffic controller was in fact there but sound asleep. The good news is that the plane landed safely.

Even better news is that God, the ultimate traffic controller, neither slumbers nor sleeps. We know that from God's heavenly vantage point, our "help comes from the LORD, . . . He will not let your foot slip—he who watches over you will not slumber" (PSALM 121:2–3).

Count on it—God knows the impending dangers and will tirelessly direct the traffic of your life for your good and His glory (ROMANS 8:28).

❧ *Joe Stowell*

Dying for Justice

DEUTERONOMY 24:14–22

*Remember that you were slaves in Egypt
and the LORD your God redeemed you from there.
That is why I command you to do this.*

DEUTERONOMY 24:18

When Presbyterian clergyman Elijah Lovejoy (1802–1837) left the pulpit, he returned to the printing presses in order to reach more people. After witnessing a lynching, Lovejoy became committed to fighting the injustice of slavery. Threatened by hateful mobs, he did not stop: "If by compromise is meant that I should cease from my duty, I cannot. I fear God more than I fear man. Crush me if you will, but I shall die at my post." Four days later, he was killed at the hands of another angry mob.

Concern about justice for the oppressed is evident throughout Scripture. It was especially clear when God established the rules for His covenant people after they were released from Egyptian bondage (DEUTERONOMY 24:18–22). The Israelites were reminded that they had been slaves in Egypt and should deal justly with the underprivileged in their community (EXODUS 23:9; LEVITICUS 19:34; DEUTERONOMY 10:17–19).

God desires that His people affirm the supreme worth of every individual by fighting against injustice.

❖ *Marvin Williams*

Miracle Material

ISAIAH 46:1–10

"To whom will you compare me?
Or who is my equal?" says the Holy One.

—ISAIAH 40:25

CNN called a derivative of graphite a "miracle material" that could revolutionize our future. Only one atom thick, graphene is being hailed as a truly two-dimensional material in a 3-D world. One hundred times stronger than steel, it is harder than diamond, conducts electricity one thousand times better than copper, and is more flexible than rubber.

In and of themselves, such technological advances are neither moral nor evil. But we are wise to remember the limitations of anything we make for ourselves.

Isaiah spoke to a generation who found themselves carrying into captivity gods they had made with their own hands. The prophet wanted the Israelites to see the irony of needing to care for the silver and gold idols they had crafted to inspire, help, comfort, and protect them.

What was true of Israel holds true for us as well. Nothing we have made or bought for ourselves can meet the needs of our heart. Only God, who has been carrying us "since [we] were born" (ISAIAH 46:3–4), can carry us into the future.

❖ *Mart DeHaan*

Chili Peppers

JAMES 1:22–27

Religion that God our Father accepts as pure and faultless is this:
to look after orphans and widows in their distress
and to keep oneself from being polluted by the world.

JAMES 1:27

"My mother gave us chili peppers before we went to bed," said Samuel, recalling his childhood in sub-Saharan Africa. "We drank water to cool our mouths, and then we would feel full. It did not work well."

Their mother took them to church, but it didn't mean much to Sam, who couldn't see beyond his family's poverty. *How could God allow our family to suffer like this?* he wondered.

One day a man learned about their plight and brought them some medicine to help with a sickness his mother suffered. "On Sunday we will go to this man's church," his mother announced. Right away Sam sensed something different. These people celebrated their relationship with Jesus by loving others.

That was three decades ago. Sam has started more than twenty churches, a large school, and a home for orphans. He's continuing the legacy of true religion taught by James, who urged believers not to "merely listen to the word" but to "do what it says" (JAMES 1:22).

There's no telling what a simple act of kindness done in Jesus's name can do.

❖ *Tim Gustafson*

Porcupine People

1 JOHN 4:16–21

He has given us this command:
Anyone who loves God must also love their brother and sister.

—1 JOHN 4:21

Deep in a Wyoming canyon I came across the biggest porcupine I've ever seen. As he lumbered toward me, I watched him closely and gave him plenty of room. I was not about to get near a guy whose quills looked like missiles. No wonder he was alone!

But he's not alone all the time. Every November and December, porcupines get close enough to produce offspring. During that time they choose to relax their quills, then they return to their prickly selves.

Once in a while, we may encounter a porcupine or two at church—with sharp quills of criticism or sarcasm or arrogance. While we may want to avoid them, God commands us to love one another.

John wrote, "Anyone who loves God must also love their brother and sister" (1 JOHN 4:21). To do this, we need to ask God to help us "relax our quills," even when other people are prickly. The Holy Spirit will help us to love our Christian brothers and sisters. It's the way we show the world that we love God (JOHN 13:35).

❖ *David Egner*

X Prize

For what is our hope, our joy, or the crown in which we will glory in the presence of our Lord Jesus when he comes? Is it not you? Indeed, you are our glory and joy.

—1 THESSALONIANS 2:19–20

The X Prize Foundation attempts to solve the world's problems by offering large cash prizes to whoever can fix them first. Winning teams have built a spacecraft that can fly beyond the earth's atmosphere twice in two weeks and cars that achieve one hundred miles per gallon. People will work hard for $10 million.

The X Prize reminds me that God offers something far greater than money to those who help solve the world's greatest need. God promises us . . .

The joy of leading others to salvation: Paul told the Thessalonians that he gladly endured intense persecution to bring them to Christ—all for the joy of having them stand beside him when the Lord returns (1 THESSALONIANS 2:5–6, 19). What could be more satisfying than bringing someone home to heaven?

The most satisfying words you'll ever hear: If we faithfully use the resources God has given us, we can hear from Him: "Well done, my good and faithful servant. . . . Let's celebrate together!" (MATTHEW 25:21 NLT).

Do you believe these rewards are real? Then run for the prize!

❖ *Mike Wittmer*

On the Wing

MATTHEW 10:27–31

So don't be afraid;
you are worth more than many sparrows.

—MATTHEW 10:31

In his book *On the Wing*, Alan Tennant chronicles his efforts to track the migration of the peregrine falcon. Valued for their beauty, swiftness, and power, these amazing birds of prey were favorite hunting companions of emperors and nobility. Sadly, the effects of the pesticide DDT in the 1950s placed them on the endangered species list.

Interested in the recovery of this species, Tennant attached transmitters to some falcons to track their migration patterns. But when he and his pilot flew their small plane behind the birds, they repeatedly lost the signal and were not always able to track the birds they wanted to help.

It's good to know that God never loses track of us. In fact, Jesus said that not even one sparrow "will fall to the ground outside your Father's care. . . . So don't be afraid; you are worth more than many sparrows" (MATTHEW 10:29–31).

When we face difficulties, we may wonder if God is aware of our situation. Jesus's teaching assures us that God cares deeply and is in control. His tracking of our lives will never fail.

❖ *Dennis Fisher*

Motivated by Love
2 CORINTHIANS 5:11–17

*For Christ's love compels us, because we are convinced
that one died for all, and therefore all died.*

—2 CORINTHIANS 5:14

In the 1920s, Bobby Jones dominated golf, despite being an amateur. In one film about his life, *Bobby Jones: Stroke of Genius*, there is a scene where a pro golfer asks Bobby when he is going to quit being an amateur and grab for the money like everyone else does. Jones answers by explaining that the word *amateur* comes from the Latin *amo*—to love. His answer was clear: He played golf because he loved the game.

Our motives make all the difference—especially as followers of Jesus Christ. In his letter to the Corinthian church, Paul gives us an example of this. Throughout the epistle he defended his conduct, character, and calling as an apostle of Christ. In response to those who questioned his motives, Paul said, "Christ's love compels us, . . . He died for all, that those who live should no longer live for themselves but for him who died for them and was raised again" (2 CORINTHIANS 5:14-15).

Christ's love is the greatest of all motivators. It causes those who follow Him to live for Him, not for themselves.

❖ *Bill Crowder*

Longing for Home

HEBREWS 11:8–16

They were longing for a better country—a heavenly one.
Therefore God is not ashamed to be called their God, for he has prepared a city for them.

—HEBREWS 11:16

When my wife found me poking my head inside the cabinet of our grandfather clock, she wondered, "What are you doing?" Sheepishly I closed the door and replied, "This clock smells just like my parents' house. I guess you could say I was going home for a moment."

We had moved the clock across the country from my parents' house nearly twenty years earlier, but the aroma of the wood inside it still took me back to my childhood.

The writer of Hebrews tells of people who were longing for home in a different way. Instead of looking backward, they were looking ahead to their home in heaven. This seemed a long way off, but they trusted that God was faithful to keep His promise to take them to a place where they would be with Him forever (HEBREWS 11:13–16).

Philippians 3:20 reminds us that "our citizenship is in heaven," and we are to "eagerly await a Savior from there, the Lord Jesus Christ." Looking forward to seeing Jesus helps us keep our focus. The past or the present can never compare with what's ahead!

❖ *James Banks*

Seize the Opportunity

ACTS 8:26–38

Therefore, as we have opportunity, let us do good to all people,
especially to those who belong to the family of believers.

—GALATIANS 6:10

Heavy rain was falling outside as Marcia, the director of the Jamaican Christian School for the Deaf, spoke to our group. Thirty-four teenagers and several adults were visiting the school. But one of our students was not distracted by the rain or the children running around the room.

That teenager heard Marcia say, "My dream for these kids is to have a playground." Lauren took that sentence and through the prompting of the Lord turned it into an idea. Later that day she told me, "We should come back and build them a playground." An opportunity for service was born.

A little over four months later, on another rainy day in Jamaica, we held a celebration in that same room. We had just assembled a wooden playground—complete with slides, a ladder, climbing bars, swings, forts, and a trapeze. One student seized an opportunity, and a dream was fulfilled.

Like Philip in Acts 8 and Lauren in Jamaica, let's honor the Lord by responding with action when God prompts us to serve others. Let's seize the opportunity.

❖ *Dave Branon*

Religious Nuts

MATTHEW 10:16–22

Let your conversation be gracious and attractive
so that you will have the right response for everyone.

—COLOSSIANS 4:6 (NLT)

I have a friend who was invited to a dinner party where he was seated next to a belligerent unbeliever who delighted in taunting Christians.

Throughout the evening, the man baited Matt mercilessly about the evils of Christendom throughout the ages. With each insult, my friend calmly replied, "That's an interesting point of view." And then he deflected the discussion to something else.

At the end of the evening, the man fired a final jab—at which point Matt put his arm around the other man's shoulders and chuckled. "My friend," he said, "all night long you've been trying to talk to me about religion. Are you a religious nut?"

The man's animosity dissolved into laughter. He was indeed a religious nut. We all are. We're insatiably and incurably religious—hounded by the relentless love of God. Matt's kindness and deft humor awakened this man's heart so he could be receptive to the gospel.

Let's be "wise as serpents" (MATTHEW 10:16 NKJV) when dealing with non-Christians, speaking to them with "grace, seasoned with salt" (COLOSSIANS 4:6).

❖ *David Roper*

Fear of the Unknown

HEBREWS 11:8–12

By faith Abraham, when called to go to a place he would later receive as his inheritance, obeyed and went, even though he did not know where he was going.

—HEBREWS 11:8

Has God ever asked you to do something that seemed unreasonable? Something that took you into the territory of the unknown? What if He asked you to refuse a long-awaited promotion or resist a longed-for relationship? What if He called you to a remote part of the world or asked you to release your children to serve Him in a faraway place?

The unknown is full of haunting "what ifs." Yet God often calls us to chart unknown territory as we follow Him. Obeying His commands to forgive, to give away our treasures, or to give up things that provide security and pleasure often leave us in the scary territory of unknown outcomes.

Imagine how Abraham felt when God asked him to move his whole family without telling him where they were going (GENESIS 12:1–3).

Every new day is like entering uncharted territory. The fear of the unknown could cripple our capacity to follow God's leading through the days ahead. Yet, like Abraham, when we cling to the One who knows all things, we're in good hands—regardless of where He leads.

❖ *Joe Stowell*

Choosing the Hard Thing

2 CORINTHIANS 4:5–18

We are hard pressed on every side,
but not crushed; perplexed, but not in despair.

—2 CORINTHIANS 4:8

On September 12, 1962, President John F. Kennedy delivered a speech at Rice University in Houston, Texas, about the difficult challenges facing the nation. He also shared his passion for the United States to place a man on the moon.

Kennedy said, "We choose to go to the moon in this decade. We choose to go to the moon and do the other things, not because they are easy but because they are hard." The nation responded. On July 20, 1969, Neil Armstrong took "one giant leap for mankind" on the surface of the moon.

We need challenges! The apostle Paul found serving Christ hard, but he didn't see it as a cause for discouragement. He continued to focus on Christ, and he wrote, "We are hard pressed on every side, but not crushed; perplexed, but not in despair" (2 CORINTHIANS 4:8). Paul knew that "the one who raised the Lord Jesus from the dead will also raise us with Jesus" (V. 14). The goal was worth the pain.

By the grace of God, may we commit to serving Jesus—not just when it's easy, but also when it's hard.

❖ *Bill Crowder*

Strength in Suffering

*To this you were called, because Christ suffered for you,
leaving you an example, that you should follow in his steps.*

—1 PETER 2:21

When eighteen-year-old Sammy received Jesus as Savior, his family rejected him because their tradition was of a different faith. But the Christian community welcomed him, offering encouragement and finances for his education. Later, when a magazine published his testimony, his persecution intensified.

But Sammy did not stop seeing his family. He visited whenever possible and talked with his father, although his siblings cruelly prevented him from participating in family affairs. When his father fell ill, Sammy attended to him, praying he would get well. When God healed him, the family began to warm up toward Sammy. Over time, his loving witness softened their attitude—and some became willing to hear about Jesus.

When we undergo discomfort or suffering because of our faith, we do so because "Christ suffered for [us], leaving [us] an example, that [we] should follow in his steps" (1 PETER 2:21).

Jesus is our example in suffering. We can turn to Him for strength to continue.

❖ *Lawrence Darmani*

Defending God

LUKE 9:51–56

A gentle answer turns away wrath, but a harsh word stirs up anger.

—PROVERBS 15:1

The anti-God bumper stickers got the attention of a university professor. A former atheist himself, the professor thought the owner wanted to make believers angry. "The anger helps the atheist to justify his atheism," he explained.

In recalling his own journey to faith, this prof noted the concern of a Christian friend who invited him to consider the truth of Christ. His friend's "sense of urgency was conveyed without a trace of anger." He never forgot the genuine respect and grace he received.

Believers in Jesus often take offense when others reject Him. But how does *He* feel about rejection? Jesus constantly faced threats and hatred, yet He never took doubt about His deity personally. Once, when a village refused Him hospitality, James and John wanted instant retaliation. "Lord," they asked, "do you want us to call fire down from heaven to destroy them?" (LUKE 9:54). Jesus "turned and rebuked them" (v. 55). After all, Jesus came not to "condemn the world, but to save" it (JOHN 3:17).

God doesn't need us to defend Him. He wants us to *represent* Him! That takes time, work, restraint, and love.

❖ *Tim Gustafson*

A&M's Twelfth Man

HEBREWS 11:32–12:3

We are surrounded by such a great cloud of witnesses.

—HEBREWS 12:1

A large sign at the Texas A&M University football stadium says, "HOME OF THE 12TH MAN." While each team is allowed eleven players on the field, the "12th Man" is the presence of thousands of A&M students who remain standing the entire game to cheer their team on. The tradition is traced to 1922 when the coach called a student from the stands to suit up and be ready to replace an injured player. Although he never entered the game, his willing presence on the sideline greatly encouraged the team.

Hebrews 11 describes heroes of the faith who faced great trials and remained loyal to God. "We are surrounded by such a great cloud of witnesses" (12:1).

We are not alone on our journey of faith. The people who have been faithful to the Lord encourage us by their example and also by their presence in heaven. They are a spiritual 12th Man standing with us while we are on the field.

As we fix our eyes on Jesus, "the pioneer and perfecter of faith" (12:2), we are spurred on by all those who followed Him

❖ *David McCasland*

The Hand of Comfort

2 CORINTHIANS 1:3–7

Praise be to the God and Father of our Lord Jesus Christ, the Father of compassion and the God of all comfort, who comforts us in all our troubles, so that we can comfort those in any trouble with the comfort we ourselves receive from God.

—2 CORINTHIANS 1:3–4

I was having an allergic reaction as I awakened from a complicated open-heart surgery. I was a mess, with a tube down my throat. My body began shaking violently. At one point, a nurse's assistant to the right side of my bed reached down and simply held my hand. It was an unexpected move, and it struck me as especially gentle. I began to relax, which caused my body to stop shaking.

Having experienced this with other patients, the nurse's assistant knew that a hand of comfort could minister to me as well. It was a vivid example of how God uses comfort when His children suffer.

Comfort is a powerful and memorable tool for any caregiver, and Paul tells us in 2 Corinthians 1:3–4 that it's an important part of God's toolbox. God multiplies the impact of His comfort by telling us to use the memory of the comfort He gives us to comfort others (VV. 4–7). It is another sign of His great love, and it's one we can share with others—sometimes in the simplest of gestures.

❖ *Randy Kilgore*

Twenty-Seven Percent

2 PETER 3:1–13

Since everything will be destroyed in this way, what kind of people ought you to be?
You ought to live holy and godly lives.

—2 PETER 3:11

People's attitudes toward Bible prophecy vary widely. Some believers constantly talk about the latest world events, thinking they are biblical signs that Christ could return at any moment. Others are casual about it—they don't find it relevant to the Christian life.

So is prophecy important? Some facts can put things in perspective: There are 31,124 verses in the Bible. Of these verses, 8,352 have prophetic content of some kind. That's twenty-seven percent of Scripture!

Because prophecy occupies more than a quarter of Scripture, we should value its role in God's revelation. But let's remember why God put it there. After describing how the world will end, Peter concludes, "Since everything will be destroyed in this way, what kind of people ought you to be? You ought to live holy and godly lives" (2 PETER 3:11). We should make choices daily for godly living that conform to our future dwelling place.

God has given us information about the future to glorify himself, to assure us of His sovereign control of history, and to challenge us to godly living.

❖ *Dennis Fisher*

Feeding the Wolf

ROMANS 6:15–23

Clothe yourselves with the Lord Jesus Christ,
and do not think about how to gratify the desires of the flesh.

—ROMANS 13:14

An old Cherokee chief was sitting before a flickering fire with his grandson. The boy had broken a tribal taboo, and his grandpa wanted to help him understand what made him do it. "It's like we have two wolves inside us," said the chief. "One is good, the other is bad. Both demand our obedience."

"Which one wins?" asked the boy.

"The one we feed!" said the chief.

Every follower of Jesus can identify with that struggle. We fight an ongoing battle with selfish and sinful desires. First they are small "harmless" desires, but they grow stronger and can ultimately control us (ROMANS 6:16).

To resist, we must believe what the Bible tells us about temptation's power. We must also believe that the Holy Spirit will help us resist or break free from its power.

Then comes the hard part. When an evil desire demands to be fed, we must say no—perhaps again and again and again. Paul said, "Do not think about how to gratify the desires of the flesh" (13:14).

Remember, what we feed will control us.

❖ *David Egner*

Who Are You?

"Come, follow me," Jesus said, "and I will send you out to fish for people."

—MATTHEW 4:19

If someone were to ask, "Who are you?" my guess is that you would tell what you do—"I'm an electrician" or "I'm a lawyer." But that's not really who you are. Which leads to this question, "If what you do is who you are, who will you be when you stop doing what you're doing?"

Who you are is found in your relationship to Jesus. And this sense of identity will drive your behavior. Take Matthew, for example. As a tax collector during the reign of the Roman Empire, his life was driven by greed. But everything changed the day Jesus showed up and invited Matthew to follow Him (MATTHEW 9:9). Suddenly Matthew had a whole new identity as a follower of Christ!

Jesus is still looking for followers. He wants to make something of your life by giving you the identity of a follower of Jesus. It doesn't mean giving up your career, but it does mean you will do your work—and all of life—according to His will.

So next time someone asks, "Who are you?" I hope you'll answer, "I'm a follower of Jesus!"

❖ *Joe Stowell*

Catch and Release

ROMANS 6:16–23

Jesus replied, "Very truly I tell you, everyone who sins is a slave to sin."

—JOHN 8:34

I'm a "catch and release" fisherman, which means I don't kill the trout I catch. I net them and gently set them free. It's a technique that keeps trout and other target species from disappearing in heavily fished waters.

I rarely release a trout without recalling Paul's words about those who have been "taken captive" by Satan to do his will (2 TIMOTHY 2:26 NKJV). Our adversary the devil does not catch and release but captures to consume and destroy.

We may think we can deliberately sin in a limited way for a short period of time and then get ourselves free. But as Jesus teaches us, "Everyone who sins is a slave to sin" (JOHN 8:34). Even "little" sins lead to greater and greater unrighteousness. We find ourselves entrapped and enslaved.

Sin enslaves us. But when we yield ourselves in obedience to Christ and all upon Him for the strength to do His will, we are "released." The result is increasing righteousness (ROMANS 6:16).

Jesus assures us, "If the Son sets you free, you will be free indeed" (JOHN 8:36).

❖ *David Roper*

The Wonder of Nature

JOB 36:26–33

My ears had heard of you but now my eyes have seen you.

—JOB 42:5

Growing up around the woods and waters of Midwest America, I've been fascinated with the natural wildlife native to our region. But on a trip to the California coast, I found myself staring in breathtaking wonder at snorting elephant seals, barking sea lions, and a forest of silent redwoods. I watched pelicans soar in formation, and I saw migrating whales spouting in the distance. Together they are just a sampling of the millions of species that make up the intricate and delicate balance of nature.

According to the Bible, the variety of the natural world is designed to do far more than inspire childlike wonder. The mysteries of nature can help us come to terms with a God who allows inexpressible, unexplainable pain and suffering.

We see this in the epic story of Job.

What emerges is this eventual, unavoidable conclusion: A Creator who has the wisdom and power to design the wonders of nature is great enough to be trusted with pain and suffering that we can't understand. Job proclaimed, "I know that you can do all things" (42:2). We can trust that kind of God—no matter what.

❖ *Mart DeHaan*

2 CHRONICLES 26:3–19

> *After Uzziah became powerful, his pride led to his downfall.*
> *He was unfaithful to the LORD his God,*
> *and entered the temple of the LORD to burn incense on the altar of incense.*

—2 CHRONICLES 26:16

Dwight L. Moody said, "When a man thinks he has got a good deal of strength and is self-confident, you may look for his downfall. It may be years before it comes to light, but it is already commenced." This was true of King Uzziah. He was obedient, submitted to spiritual mentorship, and sought God's guidance. As long as he asked God for help, God gave him great success—evidenced by his many accomplishments (2 CHRONICLES 26:3–15).

Uzziah's life was one of great power and human success—until he became blinded by it. His pride was evidenced in several ways: he challenged God's holiness by trespassing the temple and presuming upon a position he would never be able to have (V. 16); he viewed God's power as good but not absolutely necessary for his leadership (VV. 5, 16); he refused godly correction and counsel (VV. 18–19); and he bypassed his opportunity to repent (VV. 18–19).

When God gives us success in any area of our lives, let's not forget the Source of our success. May we choose humility, for God gives grace to the humble.

❖ *Marvin Williams*

The Warmth of the Sun

PSALM 6

I am worn out from my groaning.
All night long I flood my bed with weeping and drench my couch with tears.

—PSALM 6:6

In 1963, the Beach Boys' Brian Wilson and Mike Love wrote a song quite unlike the band's typically upbeat tunes. It was a mournful song about love that's been lost. Mike said later, "As hard as that kind of loss is, the one good that comes from it is having had the experience of being in love in the first place." They titled it "The Warmth of the Sun."

Sorrow as a catalyst for songwriting is nothing new. Some of David's most moving psalms were penned in times of deep personal loss, including Psalm 6. Though we aren't told the events that prompted its writing, the lyrics are filled with grief, "I am worn out from my groaning. All night long I flood my bed with weeping" (V. 6).

But that's not where the song ends. David knew pain and loss, but he also knew God's comfort. He wrote, "The LORD has heard my cry for mercy" (V. 9).

Even in grief, there is reason to trust God. In the warmth of His presence, our sorrows gain a hopeful perspective.

❖ *Bill Crowder*

PSALM 139:1–8

You know when I sit and when I rise;
you perceive my thoughts from afar.

—PSALM 139:2

Veteran news reporter Scott Pelley never goes on assignment without his travel essentials—which includes an emergency locator beacon that works anywhere. "You extend the antenna, push two buttons, and it sends a signal to a satellite connected to the National Oceanic and Atmospheric Administration," Pelley says. "It tells them who and where I am. Depending on what country you're in, they'll either send a rescue team—or not." Pelley has never needed to use the beacon, but he never travels without it.

In our relationship with God, we don't need emergency beacons. No matter how precarious our circumstances become, He knows who and where we are. The psalmist wrote, "You have searched me, LORD, and you know me. . . . You are familiar with all my ways" (139:1–3). We are never separated from God's care.

We can say with confidence, "If I rise on the wings of the dawn, if I settle on the far side of the sea, even there your hand will guide me" (VV. 9–10).

The Lord knows all. We are always in His care.

❖ *David McCasland*

Wonders of the Heart

JOB 38:1–11

From birth I have relied on you;
you brought me forth from my mother's womb.
I will ever praise you.

—PSALM 71:6

Our heart beats about 100,000 times every day, pumping blood to every cell in our bodies. This adds up to about 35 million beats a year and 2.5 billion beats in an average lifetime.

Yet as amazing as our heart is, it is only one example of a natural world that is designed to tell us something about our Creator. This is the idea behind the story of a man named Job.

Broken by a series of mounting troubles, Job felt abandoned. When God finally spoke, He didn't tell Job why he was suffering. Nor did the Creator tell him that someday He would suffer for Job. Instead, He drew Job's attention to a series of natural wonders that are always whispering to us—and sometimes shouting—about a wisdom and power far greater than our own (JOB 38:1–11).

So what can we learn from the complexity of this hardworking muscle, the heart? The message may be similar to the sound of waves coming to shore and stars quietly shining in the night sky. The power and wisdom of our Creator give us reason to trust Him.

❖ *Mart DeHaan*

Beyond Amazing!

PSALM 19:1–6

In the beginning you laid the foundations of the earth,
and the heavens are the work of your hands.

—PSALM 102:25

In 1977, the US launched a small spacecraft called *Voyager I* to explore the planets. After *Voyager* was done sending back photos and data from Jupiter and its neighbors, it just kept going.

Today, more than *forty years* after launch, that tiny vehicle is still going—traveling at over 38,000 miles per hour. It is more than 13 billion miles from the earth. Brilliant scientists sent a spaceship into interstellar space! It's amazing.

But it's absolutely puny when compared with what God has done. It would be like hearing someone brag to the architect of the Empire State Building that he had traveled to the second floor.

We have barely begun to explore the vastness of God's creation. But every small step by mankind should put us in absolute awe of God's power and creativity. Think of this: While we have left the realm of one star with a spaceship, the Creator of the stars "calls forth each of them by name" (ISAIAH 40:26). After all, He made them.

Exploring the universe is amazing. But exploring the God who made it all: That's beyond amazing!

❖ *Dave Branon*

A Putt, a Pad . . . but No Peace

JOHN 14:25–31

Peace I leave with you; my peace I give you.
I do not give to you as the world gives.
Do not let your hearts be troubled and do not be afraid.

—JOHN 14:27

I've helped at many funeral services, but the one I did for a member of a motorcycle gang was by far the most memorable. It was held in a park where there's a natural grassy bowl surrounding a small lake. The man's friends parked their bikes in a circle and sat on the grass while a friend and I conducted the service. We spoke simply about the inner peace that Jesus's love can bring.

Afterward, a motorcycle gang member thanked us, started to walk away, but then turned back. He said that he had "a putt, a pad, and an old lady" (a bike, apartment, and girlfriend), and then added, "But I ain't got no peace." So we talked about Jesus who is our peace.

Whether we've got a chopper or a Lexus, a mansion or a tiny apartment, a loved one or no one—it makes no difference. Without Jesus, there is no peace. He said, "Peace I leave with you, my peace I give you" (JOHN 14:27). This gift is for all who trust in Him. Have you asked for His peace?

❖ *David Roper*

Lifting a Burden

GENESIS 45:1–5

And now, do not be distressed and do not be angry with yourselves for selling me here,
because it was to save lives that God sent me ahead of you.

—GENESIS 45:5

It was the last weekend of the 1964 baseball season. Bill Valentine was umpiring a game between the Detroit Tigers and the New York Yankees.

Dave Wickersham was pitching for Detroit, and he had nineteen victories for the season. One more would be a sign of stardom.

After a close play, Wickersham tapped the umpire on the shoulder to ask for a time-out. Touching an umpire is against the rules, so Valentine tossed Wickersham from the game—depriving him of his chance for a twenty-win season.

For thirty-nine years, Valentine lived with a gnawing regret for booting the pitcher in that split-second decision. Finally, Wickersham wrote the umpire a note, telling him he was right and that he held no hard feelings. That note lifted a weight from Valentine's shoulders.

In Genesis 45, Joseph lifted a burden of guilt from his brothers, who had sold him into slavery. He was willing to forgive them.

Does someone need to hear a forgiving word from you that would lift a burden of regret?

❖ *Dave Branon*

The Mess
2 SAMUEL 22:26–37

*You, LORD, are my lamp;
the LORD turns my darkness into light.*

—2 SAMUEL 22:29

A major theme of the book of 2 Samuel could easily be "Life is a mess!" It has all the elements of a blockbuster TV miniseries. As David sought to establish his rule as king of Israel, he faced military challenges, political intrigue, and betrayal by friends and family members. And he was certainly not without guilt as his relationship with Bathsheba clearly showed (CHAPTERS 11–12).

Yet near the end of 2 Samuel we find David's song of praise to God for His mercy, love, and deliverance. "You, LORD, are my lamp; the LORD turns my darkness into light" (22:29).

We identify with David's struggles because he, like us, was far from perfect. Yet he knew that God was greater than the most chaotic parts of his life.

With David we can say, "As for God, his way is perfect: . . . he shields all who take refuge in him" (V. 31). Life is messy, but God is greater than the mess.

❖ *David McCasland*

Ernie's Farewell

2 CORINTHIANS 5:6–8; PHILIPPIANS 1:22–23

For he says, "In the time of my favor I heard you,
and in the day of salvation I helped you." I tell you,
now is the time of God's favor, now is the day of salvation.

—2 CORINTHIANS 6:2

On September 30, 2009, columnist Mitch Albom sat on stage at the Fox Theater in Detroit, Michigan, to interview Ernie Harwell, who had spent more than fifty years as a radio play-by-play announcer, mostly for the Detroit Tigers. His kindness, humility, and warmth as a broadcaster left an indelible impression on all who knew him or listened to him on the radio.

Ernie was 91 years old and had just announced he had incurable cancer. As Ernie talked, he wasn't about to let people feel sorry for him. Instead, he talked about the day he trusted Jesus Christ as Savior. Then he concluded, "I don't know how many days I've got left . . . but I know . . . whose arms I'm going to end up in, and what a great, great thing heaven is going to be."

Ernie knew that God had a glorious eternal home prepared for him (JOHN 14:2–3; PHILIPPIANS 1:21–23), so he could look death in the face and praise God. Is that your confidence? Do you know that His arms are waiting to welcome you home? At the end, that's what matters.

❖ *Dave Branon*

Broken Bones

Let me hear joy and gladness;
let the bones you have crushed rejoice.

—PSALM 51:8

I played goalkeeper for my college soccer team. It was more fun than I can describe here, but that fun came at a hefty price—one I continue to pay today. Being a goalie meant I threw my body into harm's way to prevent the other team from scoring, often resulting in injuries. During one season, I suffered a broken leg, several cracked ribs, a separated shoulder, and a concussion! Today, especially on cold days, I am visited by painful reminders of those broken bones.

David also had reminders of broken bones, but his injuries were spiritual. After David's moral collapse: an affair with Bathsheba and the murder of her husband, God firmly disciplined him. But David repented, praying, "Let me hear joy and gladness; let the bones you have crushed rejoice" (PSALM 51:8).

God's chastening was so crushing that David felt as if his bones were broken. Yet he trusted God to both repair his brokenness and rekindle his joy. In our own failure, it's a comfort to know that God loves us enough to pursue and restore us with His loving discipline.

❖ *Bill Crowder*

Cricket and Christianity

ROMANS 3:21–28

*But now apart from the law the righteousness of God has been made known,
to which the Law and the Prophets testify. This righteousness is given through faith
in Jesus Christ to all who believe. There is no difference between Jew and Gentile.*

—ROMANS 3:21–22

While visiting Jamaica on a mission trip, I noticed how much the people love cricket. So I asked a Jamaican teenager to explain the game to me. We sat on the ground, and he used rocks and sand drawings to help me understand it. Later, I watched a televised match while a coach pointed out what was happening. Yet I still didn't understand the game.

I'm sure some Jamaicans feel that way about American football. And millions of people worldwide consider baseball a mystery. One reason we may not like one another's sports is that we don't understand them.

Could that be true of the way some view Christianity—that it seems too complicated to enjoy? Maybe it seems to be about rules and a big thick book with words people don't understand.

Actually, Christianity is simple: We can be made right with a holy God through faith in Jesus's death and resurrection. Our sins can be forgiven (SEE ROMANS 3:24, 28; 10:9–10). Check it out. Discover why believers love Jesus, and you can learn to love Him too.

❖ *Dave Branon*

Fleeing to Strength

1 CORINTHIANS 6:12–20

You were bought at a price. Therefore honor God with your bodies.

—1 CORINTHIANS 6:20

"Parry four!"

When I began fencing in high school, my coach would shout the correct defensive position ("parry") against the move he was making. When he extended his weapon and lunged, to repel the attack I had to listen and respond immediately.

That active listening brings to mind the prompt obedience Scripture calls for in the area of sexual temptation. Paul writes to believers tempted to solicit pagan temple prostitutes, telling them to "flee from sexual immorality" (1 CORINTHIANS 6:18). The Bible practically shouts our best defense: *"Run away!"*

Immediate action guards against compromise. Small compromises can lead to devastating defeats. An unrestrained thought, a glance in the wrong place on the internet, a flirting friendship when you're married—each are steps that take us where we shouldn't go and put distance between us and God.

When we flee temptation, God provides a place to run. Jesus offers us hope, forgiveness, and a new beginning—no matter where we've been or what we've done. When we run to Jesus in our weakness, He sets us free to live in His strength.

❖ *James Banks*

Crashing Down

OBADIAH 1–14

"Though you soar like the eagle and make your nest among the stars,
from there I will bring you down," declares the LORD.

—OBADIAH 4

"We got really good," Raleigh Becket bragged. He and his brother Yancy piloted a Jaeger, a huge robot that fought massive, dinosaur-like creatures named Kaiju in the movie *Pacific Rim.* The brothers defied orders and went on a reckless mission to battle a Kaiju alone. The beast destroyed their Jaeger. Yancy was killed while Raleigh could only watch in horror.

Obadiah knew all about arrogance. Called by God to deliver words of condemnation to the nation of Edom, he proclaimed, "You have been deceived by your own pride" (V. 3 NLT). The people of Edom lived "in a rock fortress . . . high in the mountains" (V. 3 NLT). But God said the perceived security of their lofty lair couldn't save them. "I will bring you crashing down," He told the Edomites (V. 4 NLT).

God's prophetic words came true. Just thirty-three years after Jerusalem fell to Babylon (aided by Edom), the Babylonians burned the Edomite cities to the ground. The not-so-mighty had fallen.

Pride will ultimately destroy you even if you think you're "really good." Humble yourself under His "mighty hand" today (1 PETER 5:6).

❖ *Tom Felten*

A Happy Ending
EPHESIANS 4:20–32

Be kind and compassionate to one another,
forgiving each other, just as in Christ God forgave you.

—EPHESIANS 4:32

A friend told me he was watching football on TV as his young daughter played nearby. Angered by his team's poor play, he grabbed the closest thing and threw it down. His little girl's favorite toy was shattered, along with her heart. My friend immediately embraced her and apologized. He replaced the toy and thought all was well. But he had frightened his four-year-old, and the pain lingered. In time, however, forgiveness came.

Years later he sent an identical toy to his daughter when she was expecting a baby. She posted a photo of the toy on Facebook, saying, "This gift has a long story going back to my childhood. It wasn't a happy story then, but it has a happy ending now! Redemption is a beautiful thing. Thanks, Grandpa!"

The Bible urges us to avoid angry outbursts, for we are "created to be like God in true righteousness and holiness" (EPHESIANS 4:24). And if we are the victim of anger, God asks us to forgive each other (SEE V. 32).

Restored relationships aren't easy, but they're possible by the grace of God.

❖ *David McCasland*

Peacocks and their Kin

2 CORINTHIANS 12:7–10

But he said to me, "My grace is sufficient for you,
for my power is made perfect in weakness." Therefore I will boast
all the more gladly about my weaknesses, so that Christ's power may rest on me.

—2 CORINTHIANS 12:9

Male peacocks are resplendent creatures with iridescent blue-green plumage and elongated trains tipped with "eyes" colored in hues of gold, red, and blue. They are strikingly beautiful birds! But they have ugly feet.

To be honest, most of us have some type of physical limitation. It may be something we've borne all our lives or one we've recently acquired.

Paul described his deficiency as a "thorn in my flesh" that kept him humble (2 CORINTHIANS 12:7–9). Three times he asked the Lord to remove it, but the Lord assured him, "My grace is sufficient for you, for my power is made perfect in weakness." Paul replied, "Therefore I will boast all the more gladly in my weaknesses, so that Christ's power may rest on me."

One of the ironies of faith is that God often chooses us to accomplish His most important tasks despite our imperfections. Hudson Taylor said, "God was looking for someone weak enough to use, and he found [you and me]!" When we find our strength in Him, He can use us in ways we could never imagine (V. 9).

❖ *David Roper*

The Worst Defeat

2 KINGS 25:1–21

*It was because of the LORD's anger that all this happened to Jerusalem and Judah,
and in the end he thrust them from his presence.*

—2 KINGS 24:20

There have been some horrendous defeats in sports history, but none more devastating than Cumberland's 222-0 loss to Georgia Tech in 1916. It was the worst college football defeat ever.

Another kind of loss happened to the people of Jerusalem in 586 BC—much worse than any sports defeat. Because of their disobedience, God allowed them to be defeated by the Babylonian army (2 KINGS 24:20).

Led by Nebuchadnezzar, the Babylonians left the Holy City in ruins. They burned the majestic temple, the palace of the king, and the people's homes. And the people were led into exile.

It was one of the worst defeats in the tragic history of God's people. Their continued disobedience had devastating consequences. Through it all, God urged them to repent and turn back to Him.

It's sobering to see how much the Lord longs for His people to live in a way that glorifies Him. We need to remind ourselves of our duty to live as God wants us to live because of how much it means to Him.

Judah's terrible loss can challenge us to live in obedience to God.

❖ *Dave Branon*

Standing in the Fire

DANIEL 3:10–25

If we are thrown into the blazing furnace,
the God we serve is able to deliver us from it,
and he will deliver us from Your Majesty's hand.

—DANIEL 3:17

Wrapped in blankets in my grandparents' pickup, I watched as fire consumed our home. My father says I had slept soundly as he carried my brother and me and our puppies out to safety. When I woke up and saw the huge blaze, I was already safe. I was too curious and too young to be scared.

Later, I learned that in the chaos my father raced into the fire to look for my grandfather, which prompted my grandfather (who was not inside the house) to race in to get my father. Their courage affected all who saw it that night.

I'm reminded of that fire every time I read the story of Shadrach, Meshach, and Abed-Nego. When challenged with the decree to bow to the king or face execution (DANIEL 3:10–12), these three bravely faced the fire for the One they loved (VV. 16–18). And the Lord stood with them in the flames (V. 25).

When life's "flames" test us, may those who observe our choices recognize our love for each other and for our God.

❖ *Randy Kilgore*

Worth It All

How foolish!
What you sow does not come to life unless it dies.

—1 CORINTHIANS 15:36

By the end of the fourth century in Rome, games of death in the arena were still taking place—until the day Telemachus showed up.

Telemachus, a desert monk, had come to Rome for the holidays—only to find himself unable to tolerate the bloodlust of this popular pastime. According to fifth-century church historian Theodoret, Telemachus cried out for the violence to stop but was stoned to death by the crowd. Emperor Honorius heard about his courageous act and ordered an end to the games.

Was Telemachus's action the only way to protest a tragic blood sport? Similarly, the apostle Paul asked, "Why do we stand in jeopardy every hour?" (1 CORINTHIANS 15:30 NKJV). In 2 Corinthians 11:22–33, he chronicled some of his travails for the love of Christ, many of which could have killed him. Had it all been worth it?

In Paul's mind the matter was settled. Trading temporary things for eternal honor is a great investment. In the resurrection, a life lived in behalf of Christ and others is seed for an eternity we will never regret.

❖ *Mart DeHaan*

Losing Our Way

1 TIMOTHY 6:6–10

The love of money is a root of all kinds of evil. Some people, eager for money, have wandered from the faith and pierced themselves with many griefs.

—1 TIMOTHY 6:10

An online survey conducted by a New York law firm revealed that fifty-two percent of Wall Street financial service professionals have either engaged in illegal activity or believe they may need to do so in order to be successful. The survey concludes that these financial leaders "accept corporate wrongdoing as a necessary evil."

In mentoring young Timothy, Paul warned that the love of money and the desire to get rich had caused some to lose their way. They had yielded to temptations and embraced many "foolish and harmful" desires (1 TIMOTHY 6:9). Paul saw "the love of money" (not money itself) as a source of "all kinds of evil" (V. 10), especially the evil of trusting in money rather than depending on Christ.

As we recognize that Christ is the source of all we have, we will find contentment in Him rather than in material possessions. When we seek godliness rather than riches, we gain a desire to be faithful with what we have been given.

Let's cultivate an attitude of contentment in God and faithfully submit to Him. Our Provider will care for us.

❖ *Marvin Williams*

Always on the Bridge
JOSHUA 1:1–9

No one will be able to stand against you all the days of your life.
As I was with Moses, so I will be with you;
I will never leave you nor forsake you.

—JOSHUA 1:5

My friend had the thrilling experience of taking a short cruise on the aircraft carrier USS *John F. Kennedy*. He saw jet fighters take off, land, and demonstrate maneuvers. He was told that whenever the planes are taking off or landing—dangerous operations—the captain watches. Even if the planes are flying continually, he stays on the bridge, cat-napping between runs if necessary. The pilots know that the captain is always on duty.

When it was time for Joshua to take over as leader of Israel, he needed reassurance that God would be with him as He had been with Moses. The Israelites knew that Moses had divine direction during their wilderness journey because God led them by a pillar of fire and a cloud.

But what about Joshua? God promised him, "As I was with Moses, so I will be with you; I will never leave you nor forsake you" (JOSHUA 1:5). Joshua could lead Israel with absolute confidence that God was watching over him.

We can have that same confidence. God is watching—guiding, protecting, and leading. He's always on the bridge!

❖ *David Egner*

The Money

MATTHEW 6:24–34

"No one can serve two masters. Either you will hate the one and love the other, or you will be devoted to the one and despise the other. You cannot serve both God and money."

—MATTHEW 6:24

Early in my career while doing work that I saw as more of a mission than a job, another company offered me a more lucrative position. Our family could surely have used the money. There was one problem. I hadn't been looking for another job, because I loved my current role, which was growing into a calling.

But the money . . .

I called my father, then in his seventies, and explained the situation. His answer was crisp and clear: "Don't even think about the money. What would you do?" In an instant, my mind was made up. The money would have been my only reason for leaving the job I loved! Thanks, Dad.

Jesus devoted a substantial section of His Sermon on the Mount to money. He taught us to pray not for an accumulation of riches but for "our daily bread" (MATTHEW 6:11). He warned against storing up treasures on earth (V. 19). "Seek first his kingdom and his righteousness," Jesus said (V. 33).

Money matters. But money shouldn't rule our decision-making process.

❖ *Tim Gustafson*

The Great Creator-Healer

PSALM 139

I praise you because I am fearfully and wonderfully made;
your works are wonderful, I know that full well.

—PSALM 139:14

A few years ago, I had a rather serious skiing accident and severely tore the muscles in one of my legs. In fact, my doctor told me that the tear caused excessive bleeding. The healing process was slow, but during that time of waiting I found myself in awe of our great Creator (SEE COLOSSIANS 1:16).

I've wrinkled a few car fenders in my lifetime and dropped more than my allotment of dishes. They've always stayed broken. Not so with my leg. As soon as the tearing of my muscles occurred, the internal healing mechanisms that Christ created in my body went to work. Invisibly, down deep in my throbbing leg, the medics of His marvelous design were mending the tear. Before long, I was up and running again with a whole new sense of what the psalmist meant when he said that we are "fearfully and wonderfully made" (PSALM 139:14).

The next time you face an unwanted interruption—no matter its cause—focus your attention on Jesus's wonderful love, and let Him lift your heart to grateful worship in the midst of the pain!

❖ *Joe Stowell*

Follow the Instructions

MATTHEW 7:24–29

*Therefore everyone who hears these words of mine and puts them into practice
is like a wise man who built his house on the rock.*

—MATTHEW 7:24

One of my boyhood hobbies was building model planes. At first I didn't think I needed the instructions; I knew exactly how to put the model together. Not until I had glued a few pieces together did I realize I had skipped an important step, like putting the pilot in the cockpit.

It's easy to think we have no need for instructions in life, only to later realize we've messed things up.

Jesus advised that following His instructions is the way for wise people to build a safe, solid, and significant life (MATTHEW 7:24–29). But just getting the instructions isn't enough. The key is to follow them. "Whoever hears these sayings of mine and puts them into practice is like a wise man who built his house on the rock" (7:24).

Those who don't follow the instructions are, as Jesus put it, "foolish" (V. 26). To the world, forgiving your enemies and giving to the poor may seem like a silly way to build a life, but, take it from Jesus, it's the wise way.

❖ *Joe Stowell*

Already Settled

I write these things to you who believe in the name of the Son of God
so that you may know that you have eternal life.

—1 JOHN 5:13

I love watching soccer, and I'm a fan of Liverpool in England's Premier League. When the Reds are playing, I'm filled with anxiety. Because one play can change the game's outcome, I feel constant tension. Recently, though, I saw a tape-delayed replay of one of Liverpool's games. I was surprised how much calmer I felt seeing the replay. Why? I already knew the outcome!

Life is often like observing live sporting events. There are shocks and surprises, frustrations and fears, because we are unsure of the outcome. Followers of Christ can draw comfort, however, from the fact that though many of life's situations are uncertain, our eternal outcome is settled by the work of Jesus Christ on the cross.

The apostle John wrote, "I write these things to you who believe in the name of the Son of God so that you may know that you have eternal life" (1 JOHN 5:13). Life may present us with surprises along the way, but because of Christ's work we can have peace. He has already settled our eternal outcome.

❖ *Bill Crowder*

It's Good to Be Home

PSALM 73:21–28

You guide me with your counsel,
and afterward you will take me into glory.

—PSALM 73:24

One of my favorite pastimes as a boy was walking the creek behind our home. Those walks were high adventure for me: rocks to skip, birds to watch, dams to build. And if I made it to the mouth of the creek, my dog and I would sit and share lunch. We'd linger as long as we could, but my father wanted me home before sunset. The shadows grew long and the hollows got dark fast in the woods. I'd soon be wishing I was already home.

Often my father would be sitting on the back porch, reading the paper and waiting for me. "How did it go?" he would ask. "Pretty good," I'd say. "But it sure is good to be home."

Those memories make me think of another journey—the one I'm making now. It isn't always easy, but I know at the end there's a caring Father and my eternal home. I can hardly wait.

I'm expected there. And my heavenly Father is waiting for me. I suppose He'll ask, just like my father used to, "How did it go?" "Pretty good," I'll say. "But it sure is good to be Home."

❖ *David Roper*

Must-See Destinations

ROMANS 8:19–25

*The creation itself will be liberated from its bondage to decay
and brought into the freedom and glory of the children of God.*

—ROMANS 8:21

A special edition of *LIFE* magazine: *"Heaven on Earth: The World's Must-See Destinations"* contains stunning photography of places such as the Grand Canyon, Alaska's Denali, Petra in Jordan, and Rio de Janeiro.

This magazine caught my attention shortly after the death of my parents. I found myself grieving over all the "must-see destinations" my folks were never able to visit. The hope, however, of a renewed earth brought me great comfort.

Jesus died on the cross to save us from our sins (1 PETER 3:18). One day we will join Him in His mission to reclaim, liberate, and restore this physical world, which currently groans under the crushing weight of sin and decay (ROMANS 8:21–22).

When the Lord comes back to dwell with us forever, He'll bring heaven to earth. The broken effects of sin will be gone forever and Jesus will renew all things (REVELATION 21:1–5), including the physical earth—reclaiming its original goodness (GENESIS 1:31).

My parents (and all of God's forgiven children) will have eternity to enjoy all of the "must-see destinations" the new heaven and earth will offer.

❖ *Jeff Olson*

Job Envy

NUMBERS 4:17–32

So that they may live and not die when they come near the most holy things,
do this for them: Aaron and his sons are to go into the sanctuary
and assign to each man his work and what he is to carry.

—NUMBERS 4:19

While in college, my friend Charlie and I worked for a furniture store. We often made deliveries accompanied by an interior decorator who talked with the people who had purchased the furniture while we carried it in from the truck. Charlie and I often wished we had the decorator's job instead of ours!

During Israel's forty years of wandering in the wilderness, three clans from the priestly tribe of Levi—the Kohathites, Gershonites, and Merarites—were assigned the job of transporting the Tent of Meeting (tabernacle). They put it up, took it down, and carried it to the next place—over and over. Their job description was simple: Carry the things assigned to you (SEE NUMBERS 4:32).

I wonder if these "custodians" ever envied the "clergymen" who offered sacrifices and incense in the sanctuary (VV. 4–5, 15). But both assignments were important and came from the Lord.

We don't always get to select the work we do. But we *can* choose our attitude. How we do the job God gives us reveals our service to Him.

❖ *David McCasland*

Why Cause Grief?

Have confidence in your leaders and submit to their authority,
because they keep watch over you as those who must give an account.
Do this so that their work will be a joy, not a burden, for that would be of no benefit to you.

—HEBREWS 13:17

Pastors make an easy target for criticism. Every week they are on display, carefully explaining God's Word, challenging us toward Christlike living. But sometimes we look to find things to criticize. It's easy to overlook all the good things a pastor does and focus on our personal opinions.

Like all of us, our pastors are not perfect. So I'm not saying that we should follow them blindly and never confront error through the proper channels. But the writer of Hebrews may help us find the right way of thinking about our leaders who are presenting God's truth and modeling servant leadership: "Have confidence in your leaders and submit to their authority, because they keep watch over you as those who must give an account" (13:17).

Before God, our pastor is responsible for guiding us spiritually. We should want that burden to be joyous, not grievous. Causing grief for the pastor "would be of no benefit" (v. 17).

We make things better for our church when we respect those He has called to lead.

❖ *Dave Branon*

True Prosperity

MARK 10:17–23

Jesus looked around and said to his disciples,
"How hard it is for the rich to enter the kingdom of God!"

—MARK 10:23

A few years ago, the banking empire Citicorp ran a series of billboards about money. One said, "Money changes hands—just be sure it doesn't change the rest of you!" This ad gave a refreshingly new perspective on riches.

God also has a surprising spin on wealth. From His perspective, you can be "well off" in worldly treasures yet be in dire poverty in your soul. Or you can be poor in earthside stuff yet be lavishly rich by God's standards.

This reminds me of the rich young ruler. After a discussion about eternal life, Jesus asked him to sell his possessions, give to the poor, and follow Him. Unfortunately, the man "went away sad, because he had great wealth" (MARK 10:22). This prompted Jesus's comment: "How hard it is for the rich to enter the kingdom of God!" (V. 23).

Jesus is not against wealth, but He is grieved by anything we value more than Him. If working hard and making money are the main pursuits of life, Jesus isn't. Placing Him first and foremost in our lives is the key to true prosperity.

❖ *Joe Stowell*

Foolish Baggage

*Therefore, since we are surrounded by such a great cloud of witnesses,
let us throw off everything that hinders and the sin that so easily entangles.
And let us run with perseverance the race marked out for us.*

—HEBREWS 12:1

In 1845, the ill-fated Franklin Expedition sailed from England, searching for the Northwest Passage.

The crew loaded their two sailing ships with things they didn't need: a 1,200-volume library, fine china, crystal goblets, and engraved sterling silverware for each officer. Amazingly, each ship took only a twelve-day supply of coal for their auxiliary steam engines.

When the ships became trapped in vast frozen plains of ice, the men decided to trek to safety in small groups, but none of them survived.

One story is especially heartbreaking. Two officers pulled a large sled more than sixty-five miles across the treacherous ice. When rescuers found their bodies, they discovered that the sled was filled with table silver.

Those men were carrying what they didn't need. Don't we sometimes do the same? Don't we drag baggage we don't need? Evil thoughts that hinder us. Bad habits that drag us down. Grudges that we won't let go.

Let's "throw off everything that hinders and the sin that so easily entangles" (HEBREWS 12:1).

❖ *David Egner*

The Trail of Tears

REVELATION 21:1–7

He will wipe every tear from their eyes.
There will be no more death or mourning or crying or pain,
for the old order of things has passed away.

—REVELATION 21:4

A tragic event in US history was the forced relocation of thousands of Native Americans in the early nineteenth century. Native American tribes, who had struck treaties with and fought alongside the burgeoning white population, were driven out of their ancestral lands. In the winter of 1838, thousands of Cherokee were forced to embark on a brutal 1,000-mile march known as The Trail of Tears. This injustice resulted in the deaths of thousands of people.

The world continues to be filled with injustice, pain, and heartache. And many today may feel as if they are leaving a trail of tears—unnoticed tears and unassisted grief. But our Lord sees our tears and comforts our weary hearts (2 CORINTHIANS 1:3–5). He also declares the hope of a future time not marked by the stains of sin or injustice. In that day and in that place, "God will wipe away every tear from their eyes; there shall be no more death" (REVELATION 21:4 NKJV).

The God who offers freedom from tears in the future is the only One who can fully comfort our tears now.

❖ *Bill Crowder*

Benefits of Friendship

ECCLESIASTES 4:9–12

Two are better than one,
because they have a good return for their labor.

—ECCLESIASTES 4:9

Cicero was one of the greatest thinkers of the Roman Empire. He was a skilled orator, lawyer, politician, linguist, and writer. Still today he is quoted for his clear prose and practical wisdom.

For instance, regarding friends he wrote: "Friendship improves happiness and abates misery, by the doubling of our joy and the dividing of our grief." He understood the double benefits of friendship along life's journey.

Nearly a millennium earlier, King Solomon had also written about the value of friends: "Two are better than one, because they have a good return for their labor: If either of them falls down, one can help the other up. But pity anyone who falls and has no one to help them up" (ECCLESIASTES 4:9–10). Certainly a life without friends makes our sojourn lonely and more difficult.

Cicero and Solomon were right: Friends are important. Friends serve as confidants, counselors, and burden-sharers.

Why not seek out one of your friends for fellowship this week. Remember, "two are better than one," because a friend can double our joy and divide our grief.

❖ *Dennis Fisher*

NUMBERS 5:5–8

*"Say to the Israelites: 'Any man or woman who wrongs another in any way
and so is unfaithful to the LORD is guilty and must confess the sin they have committed.
They must make full restitution for the wrong they have done,
add a fifth of the value to it and give it all to the person they have wronged'"*

—NUMBERS 5:6–7

Researchers at the University of Toronto reported that people who suffer from a guilty conscience experience "a powerful urge to wash themselves." To study this effect, the researchers asked volunteers to recall past sins. They were then given an opportunity to wash their hands as a symbol of cleansing their conscience. Those who had recalled their sins washed their hands at "twice the rate of study subjects who had not imagined past transgressions."

The Bible proposes the only effective way of dealing with sin—confession. In the Old Testament, one of the ways the Israelites were supposed to cleanse themselves and maintain purity before God and in their community was by confessing their sins (NUMBERS 5:5–8). Their confession was a demonstration of a change of heart. Refusing to confess their sins allowed sin to take deeper root within their lives and community.

Admitting our sin unlocks the gate to forgiveness, joy, and peace. If we confess our sins, God is faithful to forgive (1 JOHN 1:9).

❖ *Marvin Williams*

The Circle of the Wise

1 JOHN 2:12–17

I am writing to you, fathers,
because you know him who is from the beginning.
I am writing to you, young men, because you have overcome the evil one.

—1 JOHN 2:13

I used to serve on the elder board of a church in California. One elder, Bob Smith, who was older than most of us, frequently called us back to the Word of God for guidance.

On one occasion we were discussing a leadership shortage in the church and had spent an hour or more working through various solutions. Bob was silent throughout the discussion. Finally, he said quietly, "Gentlemen, we've forgotten Jesus's solution to our leadership issue. Before we do anything, we must first 'ask the Lord of the harvest . . . to send out workers'" (LUKE 10:2). We were humbled, and we spent the rest of our time praying that God would raise up workers.

Proverbs 1:5 says, "Let the wise listen and add to their learning." Bob's comment exemplifies the value of wise men and women who "have known who is from the beginning" (1 JOHN 2:13–14) and whose minds are saturated with the Word of God.

Let's take to heart the counsel of those who have lived in the Lord's presence and are mature in His wisdom.

❖ *David Roper*

The Challenge of Transition OCTOBER 26

JOSHUA 1:6–11

"Be strong and very courageous. Be careful to obey all the law
my servant Moses gave you; do not turn from it to the right or to the left,
that you may be successful wherever you go."

—JOSHUA 1:7

After NFL wide receiver Chris Sanders suffered a career-ending injury, he told a group of military veterans that although he had never experienced combat, "I understand the pressures of transitions."

Whether it's the loss of a job, the loss of a marriage, or a financial setback, every major change brings challenges. Sanders said the key to success when transitioning into a new way of living is to seek help.

The book of Joshua is recommended reading for all in transition. After forty years, God's people were poised to enter the Promised Land. Moses, their great leader, had died, and Joshua, his assistant, was in charge.

God told Joshua to "be strong and very courageous . . . do not turn from it to the right or to the left" (JOSHUA 1:7). God's words of direction were to be the bedrock of Joshua's leadership.

The Lord's charge and promise to Joshua apply to us as well: "Be strong and courageous. . . . for the LORD your God will be with you wherever you go" (V. 9).

He's with us in every transition.

❖ *David McCasland*

Is Ambition Wrong?

Whatever you do, work at it with all your heart,
as working for the Lord, not for human masters.

—COLOSSIANS 3:23

Is ambition wrong? Is it wrong to be driven, to push to be the best? It can be. The difference between right and wrong ambition is in our goal and motivation—whether it's for God's glory or our own.

In 1 Thessalonians 4:1, Paul tells us that Christians are to live "to please God."

So, in the workplace we ask: "How will that job change help me serve others and glorify God?" Ambition oriented toward God is focused outward on Him and others, always asking how He has gifted us and wants to use us.

Paul suggests we work with "sincerity of heart and reverence for the Lord" (COLOSSIANS 3:22). Whatever we're doing—in the boardroom, on the docks, wherever we're working—we're to serve as if doing it for God (VV. 23–24).

We glorify Him most and enjoy Him most when we work with fervor and excellence for His pleasure, not ours. For His service and the service of others, not self-service and personal gain—because He deserves our all.

❖ *Randy Kilgore*

Belonging

JOHN 14:1–11

My Father's house has many rooms; if that were not so,
would I have told you that I am going there to prepare a place for you?

—JOHN 14:2

My dad was full of stories about his hometown. So you can imagine how excited I was as a child when he took our family there every summer. We fished the St. Joseph River together and visited his boyhood farm where his stories came to life. Although that place was never really my home, whenever I visit that town—it fills me with a nostalgic sense of belonging.

Jesus talked with His disciples about His home in heaven, which He left to come and live among us. What a joy it must have been for Him to tell His disciples, "I go to prepare a place for you, . . . that where I am, there you may be also" (JOHN 14:2–3 NKJV). No doubt Jesus was looking forward to returning to His heavenly home and taking His Father's sons and daughters there to be with Him.

The thought of Jesus taking us to His Father's home fills us with great anticipation and compels us to tell others the good news about the Son who came to rescue us from this fallen place.

❖ *Joe Stowell*

For Example

Be shepherds of God's flock that is under your care, watching over them—not because you must, but because you are willing, as God wants you to be; not pursuing dishonest gain, but eager to serve; not lording it over those entrusted to you, but being examples to the flock.

—1 PETER 5:2–3

A mother cheetah brought a live gazelle fawn to her five-month-old cubs and released it. After the cubs made several unsuccessful attacks, the mama cheetah intervened and showed them how to "catch dinner."

I observed a similar technique used by a life insurance salesman. After he told me about the benefits of a particular policy, he shared how much coverage he had for his own family. His words took on new meaning because he demonstrated by his own example how to insure a family adequately.

If we want to teach others the art of knowing God and serving Him, we can't overemphasize the power of example. That's how Christ and His apostles communicated. Their obedience to God was seen in flesh-and-blood terms that were easily understood.

Paul said the Thessalonians, who had become "imitators of us and of the Lord," were "a model to all the believers in Macedonia" (1 THESSALONIANS 1:6–7).

Leadership doesn't come automatically. To lead, we must first be good examples.

❖ *Mart DeHaan*

Tackling Taunting

NEHEMIAH 4:1–10

Those who hope in the LORD will renew their strength.
They will soar on wings like eagles; they will run and not grow weary,
they will walk and not be faint.

—ISAIAH 40:31

Boxing legend Muhammad Ali used several ring tactics to defeat his opponents; one tactic was taunting. In his fight with George Foreman in 1974, Ali taunted Foreman, "Hit harder! Show me something, George. That don't hurt. I thought you were supposed to be bad." Fuming, Foreman punched away furiously, wasting his energy and weakening his confidence.

It's an old tactic. By referring to Nehemiah's efforts at rebuilding the broken wall of Jerusalem as nothing more than a fox's playground (NEHEMIAH 4:3), Tobiah intended to weaken the workers with words of discouragement. Goliath tried it on David by despising the boy's simple weapons of a sling and stones (1 SAMUEL 17:41–44).

Nehemiah refused to surrender to Tobiah's discouragements, and David rejected Goliath's diabolical teasing. By focusing on God and His help, David and Nehemiah both achieved victory.

Responding to taunts only saps our energy. God encourages us through His promises: He will never forsake us (PSALM 9:10; HEBREWS 13:5), and He invites us to rely on His help (HEBREWS 4:16).

❖ *Lawrence Darmani*

Suit Up

EPHESIANS 6:13–21

Put on the full armor of God, so that when the day of evil comes,
you may be able to stand your ground, and after you have done everything, to stand.

—EPHESIANS 6:13

When I played American football as a kid, one thing that took some getting used to was all the equipment we had to wear. Running effectively in a helmet, shoulder pads, and other protective items can feel awkward and clumsy at first. But soon the protective gear becomes like a familiar friend providing welcome protection. When a football player suits up, he knows that his equipment is designed to protect him in battle against a dangerous opponent.

As followers of Christ, we also face a dangerous foe—a spiritual enemy who seeks our downfall and destruction. Fortunately, our Lord has provided us with protection, and He challenges us to suit up.

In Ephesians 6:13, we read, "Put on the full armor of God, so that when the day of evil comes, you may be able to stand your ground." Paul then describes our armor—helmet, breastplate, shield, sword, belt, and shoes, which we must put on and use. Faithfulness in the Word (V. 17), in prayer (V. 18), and in witness (VV. 19–20) are critical to making our armor feel like a part of us. So suit up! The battle is on!

❖ *Bill Crowder*

Rising Above

1 TIMOTHY 6:11–16

*Fight the good fight of the faith. Take hold of the eternal life
to which you were called when you made your good confession
in the presence of many witnesses.*

—1 TIMOTHY 6:12

Kris Silbaugh played football with just one hand. What's more, he played *receiver*—a position that's all about using two hands. In 2015, the young man set the all-time receiving yards record at his high school. Born without a left hand due to a birth defect, Silbaugh says, "It has never stopped me. I just don't let it—never have."

New Testament character Timothy didn't let challenges stop him either. He faithfully served God and the church at Ephesus. Paul identified two difficulties for Timothy—youthfulness and the fact that he was "sick so often" (SEE 1 TIMOTHY 4:12, 5:23). Timothy was probably about thirty—quite young to be leading a dynamic and immature church. Facing a chronic illness certainly didn't help.

You and I also face challenges. May we, as Timothy did, "Fight the good fight of the faith" (1 TIMOTHY 6:12). In our Lord we find the strength to rise above the challenges of today.

❖ *Tom Felten*

Pursuing Unity

COLOSSIANS 3:9–17

Here there is no Gentile or Jew, circumcised or uncircumcised,
barbarian, Scythian, slave or free, but Christ is all, and is in all.

—COLOSSIANS 3:11

Growing up during the 1950s, I never questioned racism and the segregation practices that permeated daily life in the city where we lived.

My attitude changed in 1968 when I entered the US Army. Our company included young men from different cultural groups, and we learned that we needed to understand and accept each other and work together to accomplish our mission.

When Paul wrote to the first-century church at Colossae, he was aware of the diversity of its members. He reminded them, "Here there is no Gentile or Jew, circumcised or uncircumcised, barbarian, Scythian, slave or free, but Christ is all, and is in all" (COLOSSIANS 3:11). Paul urged them to "clothe [themselves] with compassion, kindness, humility, gentleness and patience" (V. 12). And over these virtues, he told them to put on love "which binds them all together in perfect unity" (V. 14).

This is what Jesus calls us to: Pursue understanding, peace, and unity. Amid all our wonderful diversity, we pursue an even greater unity in Christ.

❖ *David McCasland*

Jesus: Unique in all the World

PHILIPPIANS 2:5–11

For in Christ all the fullness of the Deity lives in bodily form.

—COLOSSIANS 2:9

Someone commented: "I struggle with the claim of other Christians that Jesus Christ is the only way to heaven and to God. What will happen to those who believe otherwise?"

A scriptural review of Jesus and His uniqueness can help us stand strong in our belief that He is the only way.

Jesus is unmatched in history—His very being cries out for us to entrust our lives to Him. Jesus Christ is:

Unique in substance: He alone is both God and man (JOHN 10:30). *Unique in prophecy*: No other leader's life was foretold so clearly and accurately (MICAH 5:2). *Unique in mission*: Jesus alone came to save us from our sins (MATTHEW 1:21). *Unique in birth*: Only Jesus was born of a virgin (MATTHEW 1:23). *Unique in ability*: No one but Jesus has the power to forgive sins (MARK 2:10). *Unique in position*: No one else is equal with God (PHILIPPIANS 2:5–6). *Unique in reign*: Only Jesus reigns forever (HEBREWS 1:8).

No one in history is like Jesus. He alone deserves our trust, and He alone is the path to God.

❖ *Dave Branon*

A Matter of Perspective
REVELATION 3:14–22

"You say, 'I am rich; I have acquired wealth and do not need a thing.'
But you do not realize that you are wretched, pitiful, poor, blind and naked."

—REVELATION 3:17

One of my favorite stories is about the Texas rancher who was doing agricultural consulting for a farmer in Germany. He asked the German farmer about the size of his property, to which he replied, "About a mile square." When the German asked the Texan about the size of his ranch, the rancher explained that if he got in his pick-up truck at dawn and drove until sunset he would still be on his ranch. Not to be outdone, the farmer replied, "I used to have an old truck like that!"

All joking aside, it's important to have the right perspective. Unfortunately, the Christians in Laodicea had the wrong perspective about wealth (REVELATION 3:14–22). By all appearances, they were rich. So they thought they needed nothing—not even Jesus. But Jesus saw their flaws (V. 17). So He invited them to become truly rich by seeking what only He could provide: purity, character, righteousness, and wisdom.

True wealth is not measured by what you have but by who you are in Christ.

❖ *Joe Stowell*

Home

EPHESIANS 2:11–22

You are no longer foreigners and strangers, but fellow citizens with God's people and also members of his household.

—EPHESIANS 2:19

Steven, a young African refugee, was a man without a country. He thought he may have been born in Mozambique or Zimbabwe. But he was separated from his parents in his country's civil war. So Steven walked into a British police station and asked to be arrested. Jail seemed better to Steven than trying to exist on the streets without any identification or without the rights and benefits of citizenship.

The plight of living without a country was on Paul's mind as he wrote his letter to the Ephesians. His non-Jewish readers knew what it was like to live as aliens and outsiders (2:12). Only since finding life and hope in Christ (1:13) had they discovered what it meant to belong to the kingdom of heaven (MATTHEW 5:3). In Jesus, they experienced being known and cared for by the Father Jesus revealed (MATTHEW 6:31–33).

May our God help us to live in security—to experience the belonging we have as members of His family—by faith in Jesus Christ. We have the rights and benefits of having our home in Him.

❖ *Mart DeHaan*

Reach Out to the Little Guy

God does not show favoritism.

—ROMANS 2:11

A Michigan high school basketball coach had won the state championship with his team, and he was on top of the world. Named coach of the year, he felt like a hero. But then one day his study hall students were filling out a form when a shy girl who sat in the back row all year timidly raised her hand. "Excuse me, sir," she began. "There's one thing I don't know on this form. What's your name?"

The coach realized that despite his success he had failed to reach that girl. In eight months he had never taken the time to even talk to her.

Jesus was followed by the masses and His name was known far and wide. But He was never too busy to care for individuals. How surprised Zacchaeus, an unpopular little tax collector, must have been when Jesus called out his name!

Our Savior was concerned about all people—both great and small. Is there someone we've neglected because he is in the wrong group or lives in the wrong place? Let's be more like Jesus and reach out to the little guy.

❖ *Dave Branon*

Make a Joyful Shout

PSALM 100

Shout for joy to the LORD, all the earth.

—PSALM 100:1

Duke University's basketball fans are known as "Cameron Crazies." When Duke plays archrival North Carolina at the Cameron Indoor Arena, the Crazies are given these instructions: "This is the game you've been waiting for. No excuses. Give everything you've got." Clearly, Duke fans take allegiance seriously.

The songwriter of Psalm 100 took his allegiance to the Lord seriously and wanted others to do the same. "Shout for joy to the LORD!" he exclaimed (V. 1). His people were to freely express their praise to Him because He was the covenant God of Israel. They were called to focus all their energies on Him and His goodness.

God's goodness should motivate us to freely express our love and allegiance to Him. This may mean that those who are more reserved must push back the boundaries of restraint and learn what it means to be expressive in their praise. Those who are so expressive that they miss the beauty of silence may need to learn from those whose style is more reflective.

Worship is a time to focus on our Creator, Redeemer, and Shepherd, and to celebrate what He has done.

❖ *Marvin Williams*

Decisive

I, even I, am he who blots out your transgressions,
for my own sake, and remembers your sins no more.

—ISAIAH 43:25

The line between victory and defeat can be quite slim. Did the winning shot leave his hands before the buzzer sounded? Sure, "a win is a win," but many contests could have gone either way.

Aren't you glad God always wins decisively? He doesn't squeak by His opponents—He obliterates them. Look at His resumé:

Egypt. God didn't sneak Israel out in the middle of the night. He delivered His children in broad daylight, enticed the Egyptian army to follow, then drowned them "beneath the waves" (ISAIAH 43:17 NLT).

Baal. God won this one big-time! He allowed the false prophets to embarrass themselves, and then He sent down fire from heaven to consume Elijah's water-soaked sacrifice (1 KINGS 18:1–40).

Sin, Death, and Satan. God sent Jesus to decisively defeat His strongest opponents: sin, death, and Satan. Jesus didn't merely slip past the devil. "He shamed [the spiritual rulers and authorities] publicly by his victory over them on the cross" (COLOSSIANS 2:15 NLT). When He arose, He left Satan in the dust.

If you have trusted Jesus, you're totally and decisively forgiven.

❖ *Mike Wittmer*

Solving the Mystery

ROMANS 5:1–11

But God demonstrates his own love for us in this:
While we were still sinners, Christ died for us.

—ROMANS 5:8

One of the most popular tourist attractions in England is Stonehenge. Its massive pieces of granite are a great source of mystery. Every year, people travel to Stonehenge with questions such as: Why were they erected? Who built this? How did they do it? But visitors leave having received no answers from the silent stones. The mystery remains.

The Scriptures speak of a greater mystery—the fact that God came to live among us as a man: "Great is the mystery of godliness: God was manifested in the flesh, justified in the Spirit, seen by angels, preached among the Gentiles, believed on in the world, received up in glory" (1 TIMOTHY 3:16 NKJV).

This brief overview of the life of Christ—the mystery of godliness—is remarkable. What prompted the Savior's great sacrifice, however, is not a mystery. "But God demonstrates His own love toward us, in that while we were still sinners, Christ died for us" (ROMANS 5:8 NKJV). God's great love is at the root of the mystery of godliness. The cross has made it plain for all to see.

❖ *Bill Crowder*

The Last Call

2 SAMUEL 1:17–27

"How the mighty have fallen! The weapons of war have perished!"

—2 SAMUEL 1:27

After serving his country for two decades as a helicopter pilot, James took a job flying medical evacuations for a local hospital. He flew until late in his life.

Now it was time to say a final goodbye to him. As friends and family stood vigil at the cemetery, a colleague called in one last mission over the radio. Soon the distinctive sound of rotors beating the air could be heard. A helicopter circled over the memorial garden, hovered briefly to pay its respects, then headed back to the hospital. Not even the military personnel who were present could hold back the tears.

When Jonathan was killed in battle, David honored him with an elegy for the ages called "the lament of the bow" (2 SAMUEL 1:17). "A gazelle lies slain on your heights," he sang. "How the mighty have fallen!" (V. 19). Jonathan was David's closest friend and brother-in-arms. "I grieve for you, Jonathan my brother," David wrote (V. 26).

Even the best goodbyes are oh-so-difficult. How good it is when we can honor those who have served others!

❖ *Tim Gustafson*

The Eleventh Hour

MATTHEW 24:3–14

He will judge between the nations and will settle disputes for many peoples.
They will beat their swords into plowshares and their spears into pruning hooks.
Nation will not take up sword against nation, nor will they train for war anymore.

—ISAIAH 2:4

World War I has been ranked by many as one of the deadliest conflicts in human history. Millions lost their lives in the first global modern war. On November 11, 1918, a ceasefire was observed on the eleventh hour of the eleventh day of the eleventh month. During that historic moment, millions around the world observed moments of silence while they reflected on the war's terrible cost. It was hoped that "the Great War," as it was called, would truly be "the war that would end all wars."

The Bible offers a hopeful and realistic promise that someday wars will finally end. At Jesus's second coming, Isaiah's prophecy will come true: "Nation will not take up sword against nation, nor will they train for war anymore" (ISAIAH 2:4). The first hour of lasting peace in a new heaven and new earth will begin.

Until that day, those who follow Christ are to be people who represent the Prince of Peace in the way we conduct our lives.

❖ *Dennis Fisher*

A Serving Leader
1 KINGS 12:1–15

Not so with you.
Instead, whoever wants to become great among you must be your servant.

—MATTHEW 20:26

In traditional African societies, leadership succession is a serious decision. Besides being from a royal family, the successor must be strong, fearless, and sensible. Candidates are questioned to determine if they will serve the people or rule with a heavy hand. The king's successor needs to both lead and serve.

Even though Solomon made his own bad choices, he worried over his successor. "Who knows whether that person will be wise or foolish?" (ECCLESIASTES 2:19). His son Rehoboam was that successor, and he demonstrated a lack of sound judgment and ended up fulfilling his father's worst fear.

When the people requested more humane working conditions, it was an opportunity for Rehoboam to show servant leadership. "If today you will be a servant to these people and serve them . . . ," the elders advised, "they will always be your servants" (1 KINGS 12:7). But he rejected their counsel. His harsh response to the people divided the kingdom (12:14–19).

In the family, the workplace, at church, or in our neighborhood—we need His wisdom for the humility to serve rather than be served.

❖ *Lawrence Darmani*

All Safe! All Well!

HEBREWS 11:8–16

Now faith is confidence in what we hope for
and assurance about what we do not see.

—HEBREWS 11:1

On April 24, 1916, twenty-two men watched as Ernest Shackleton and five comrades set out in a tiny lifeboat for South Georgia, an island 800 miles away. These twenty-eight men had reached nearly uninhabitable Elephant Island after their ship *Endurance* was destroyed near Antarctica. The odds of this new mission succeeding seemed impossible. If the men failed to find South Georgia—their only hope—they would all certainly die. What joy, then, when more than *four months* later a boat appeared on the horizon with Shackleton on its bow shouting, "Are you all well?" And the call came back, "All safe! All well!"

What kept those men alive? Faith and hope placed in one man. They believed Shackleton would find a way to save them.

This human example of hope echoes the faith of the heroes listed in Hebrews 11. Their faith in the "substance of things hoped for, the evidence of things not seen" kept them going through great difficulties (HEBREWS 11:1 NKJV).

As we look out upon the horizon of our own problems, may we have hope through the certainty of our faith in One Man: Jesus.

❖ *Randy Kilgore*

A Walk with Whitaker

He makes me lie down in green pastures,
he leads me beside quiet waters.

—PSALM 23:2

When my dog Whitaker and I take early morning walks through the woods, he runs ahead while I amble along, meditating or praying. I know where we're going; he's not sure. I stay on the trail and he trots ahead—sniffing, investigating, and taking occasional forays into the forest to chase real or imagined chipmunks.

Although Whit is ahead, I'm leading. Every so often he checks to see where I am. If I've turned toward home or gone on to another trail, I hear his pounding feet as he races to catch up with me. If I hide behind some brush, he runs to the last place he saw me and tracks me down. Then we walk the trail together again.

It's like that with God's leading. He knows the way. But sometimes we may not see Him—so we do our best to go where He wants by following the guidance of His Word.

Just as Whitaker keeps looking back at me, we need to look to God and His Word at every important juncture. We must rely on the direction of His Spirit.

❖ *David Egner*

Another Walk with Whitaker

GENESIS 1:20–25

And God said, "Let the water teem with living creatures, and let birds fly above the earth across the vault of the sky."

—GENESIS 1:20

As Whitaker and I take another walk through the deep woods of Michigan's Upper Peninsula, the air is filled with sound. Birds of many species break the early morning silence.

Sometimes it's a steady chirp-chirp-chirp—probably a sparrow. It could be the lilting melody of a robin or the happy trill of a cardinal. At times it's a sustained, single-note call from some unfamiliar bird. Then a little group of chickadees will flit their way through the trees, repeating their "chick-a-dee-dee-dee" sounds.

"Isn't God great!" I say to Whit, who seems to have chipmunks on his mind. I thank God for the great gift of hearing and the wonderful variety of sounds with which He fills His woods. He created hundreds of varieties of birds, each with its own color and habits and call (GENESIS 1:20–21).

As I continue my walk with Whitaker, my heart is filled with thankfulness for the sights and sounds and colors and species that enrich our world. I praise Him for His creativity in not only forming our world but in also making it so beautiful.

❖ *David Egner*

The Power of a Promise

GENESIS 2:18–25

For this reason a man will leave his father and mother and be united to his wife, and the two will become one flesh.

—MATTHEW 19:5

I wear only two pieces of jewelry: a wedding band on my finger and a small Celtic cross on a chain around my neck. The ring represents my vow to be faithful to Carolyn, my wife. The cross reminds me that it is not for her sake alone, but for Jesus's sake that I do so. He has asked me to be faithful to her until death shall separate us.

A marriage vow is more than a contract. It's a unique vow that's explicitly intended to be binding until death separates us (MATTHEW 19:6). The words "for better, for worse; for richer, for poorer; in sickness and in health" take into consideration the probability that marriage won't be easy. Circumstances may change and so may our spouses.

Marriage is hard at best; disagreements and difficult adjustments abound. While no one must live in an abusive and dangerous relationship, accepting the difficulties of poverty, hardship, and disappointment can lead to happiness. As a friend of mine once put it, "This is the vow that keeps us faithful even when we don't feel like keeping our vows."

❖ *David Roper*

Comfort Shared

2 CORINTHIANS 1:1–10

Jesus said, "Peace be with you!
As the Father has sent me, I am sending you."

—JOHN 20:21

"God sent you to me tonight!"

Those were the parting words from a woman who sat across the aisle from me on our flight to Chicago. I learned that she was headed home after several flights in a one-day round-trip. When I inquired about the quick turn-around, she glanced downward: "I just put my daughter in rehab for drug abuse today."

I gently shared the story of my son's struggle with heroin addiction and how Jesus had set him free. As she listened, a smile broke through her tears. After the plane landed we prayed together before parting, asking God to break her daughter's chains.

Later that evening I thought of Paul's reminder that "the Father of compassion and the God of all comfort, . . . comforts us in all our troubles, so that we can comfort those in any trouble with the comfort we ourselves receive from God" (2 CORINTHIANS 1:3–4).

All around us are people who need to be encouraged with the comfort only God can give. May God send us to those who need His comfort today!

❖ *James Banks*

Bring It On!
2 CORINTHIANS 11:22–12:10

*Three times I was beaten with rods, once I was pelted with stones,
three times I was shipwrecked, I spent a night and a day in the open sea,
I have been constantly on the move. I have been in danger from rivers, in danger from bandits,
in danger from my fellow Jews, in danger from Gentiles; in danger in the city,
in danger in the country, in danger at sea; and in danger from false believers.*

— 2 CORINTHIANS 11:25–26

A TV program on the History Channel featured the world's most extreme airports. One that caught my attention was Kai Tak Airport, an East Asian facility that closed in 1998. That was definitely a thrill ride for passengers and surely a challenge for pilots. If you came in from one direction, you had to fly over skyscrapers and then hope the plane stopped before it plunged into the sea. If you came in the other way, it seemed as if you were going to smack into a mountain.

One pilot who flew planeloads of people into Kai Tak said, "I miss flying into that airport." As a pilot, he relished the challenge.

The apostle Paul courageously faced many challenges (2 CORINTHIANS 11:25–26). Christ's promise to Paul and to us is this: "My grace is sufficient for you, for my power is made perfect in weakness" (2 CORINTHIANS 12:9). Like Paul, in the confidence of God's care we can say to the next challenge: Bring it on!

❖ *Dave Branon*

Longing for Rescue

MATTHEW 1:18–25

"She will give birth to a son, and you are to give him the name Jesus,
because he will save his people from their sins."

—MATTHEW 1:21

When the movie *Man of Steel* was released, it was a fresh imagining of the Superman story. Filled with breathtaking special effects and nonstop action, it drew crowds to movie theaters around the world. Some said the film's appeal was rooted in its amazing technology. Others pointed to the enduring appeal of the "Superman mythology."

Amy Adams, the actress who plays Lois Lane, says it is about a basic human longing: "Who doesn't want to believe that there's one person who could come and save us from ourselves?"

That's a great question. And the answer is that someone has: Jesus. Several announcements were made regarding the birth of Jesus. One was from the angel Gabriel to Joseph: "She [Mary] will give birth to a son, and you are to give him the name Jesus, because he will save his people from their sins" (MATTHEW 1:21).

Jesus came—He did so to save us from our sin and from ourselves. His name means "the Lord saves"—and our salvation was His mission. The longing for rescue that fills the human heart ultimately is met by Jesus.

❖ *Bill Crowder*

The Power of Love

*This is love: not that we loved God, but that he loved us
and sent his Son as an atoning sacrifice for our sins.*

—1 JOHN 4:10

In Henri Nouwen's book *In the Name of Jesus: Reflections on Christian Leadership*, the former university professor, who spent many years serving developmentally disabled adults, says: "The question is not: How many people take you seriously? How much are you going to accomplish? Can you show some results? But: Are you in love with Jesus? . . . In our world of loneliness and despair, there is an enormous need for men and women who know the heart of God, a heart that forgives, that cares, that reaches out and wants to heal."

John wrote, "This is how God showed his love among us: He sent his one and only Son into the world that we might live through him. This is love: not that we loved God, but that he loved us and sent his Son as an atoning sacrifice" (1 JOHN 4:9-10).

"The Christian leader of the future," writes Nouwen, "is the one who truly knows the heart of God . . . in Jesus." In Him, we discover and experience God's unconditional, unlimited love.

❖ *David McCasland*

All the Comforts of Home

NOVEMBER 21

JOHN 14:1–6

There is more than enough room in my Father's home.

—JOHN 14:2 (NLT)

Once, during my time as a human resource officer for a construction company, we took some jobs in a neighboring state. This meant our workers would face a two-hour commute each way. To ease the burden, we booked motel rooms but also offered vans for those who decided to commute. Almost every worker took the vans!

One of our grumpiest workers described the thrill and surprise of his wife and four boys on the first night. He hadn't told them he had an option to come home, so he showed up unexpectedly to surprise them. Later his wife called to thank the company owner for understanding how important home was to workers.

Anyone who has been deprived of home, even for a short time, will understand the comfort Jesus's disciples drew from His words when He promised that an eternal home awaited them (JOHN 14:2). Then Jesus told them He would prepare that home and guide them to it. And, joy of joys, He would be there too (V. 3).

Remember the greatest comfort of this life: Jesus promised that one day we will go home to be with Him.

❖ *Randy Kilgore*

Recalculating Relationships

GALATIANS 5:13–15

You, my brothers and sisters, were called to be free.
But do not use your freedom to indulge the flesh; rather, serve one another humbly in love.

—GALATIANS 5:13

A comedian once mused that he wished someone would make a Global Positioning System (GPS) for husbands. *GPS:* "Compliment your wife's appearance." *Comedian:* "Hey, honey, you look really good." *GPS:* "Ask her about her day." *Comedian:* "How was your day, sweetheart?" *GPS:* "Pretend to be listening." *Comedian:* "Oh . . . Really." *GPS:* "Flatter your wife." *Comedian:* "Um . . . Hey, you're gonna look really good once you put all your make-up on." *GPS:* "Recalculating!"

The Bible is much more than a GPS. But it does record that Jesus dropped many GPS-like directives—instructions that help us recalculate how relationships should work. Here are a couple: "Love your enemies and pray for those who persecute you!" (MATTHEW 5:44); "Do to others as you would have them do to you" (LUKE 6:31).

The life, death, and resurrection of Jesus opened a new way of relating to others and to God. Selfishness, revenge, and pride were replaced with love, grace, and humility.

Of Jesus's way, theologian N. T. Wright said, "It's a way nobody's ever tried before. . . . Precisely. Welcome to Jesus's new world!"

❖ *Jeff Olson*

Getting Beyond Ourselves

2 CORINTHIANS 3:7–18

We all, who with unveiled faces contemplate the Lord's glory,
are being transformed into his image with ever-increasing glory,
which comes from the Lord, who is the Spirit.

—2 CORINTHIANS 3:18

I have one of those friends who seems to be better than I am at just about everything. He is smarter; he thinks more deeply; and he knows where to find better books to read. He is even a better golfer. Spending time with him challenges me to become a better, more thoughtful person. His standard of excellence spurs me on to greater things.

That highlights a spiritual principle: It's crucial for us to spend time in God's Word so we can connect with the person of Christ. Reading about the impact of Jesus's unconditional love for us compels me to love without demand. His mercy and His free distribution of grace to the most undeserving make me ashamed of my tendency to withhold forgiveness and seek revenge.

The apostle Paul calls us to the joy of beholding Christ. As we do so, we are "being transformed into his image with ever-increasing glory" (2 CORINTHIANS 3:18).

❖ *Joe Stowell*

The Advocate

1 JOHN 1:8–2:2

My dear children, I write this to you so that you will not sin.
But if anybody does sin, we have an advocate with the Father—
Jesus Christ, the Righteous One.

—1 JOHN 2:1

From a Florida prison cell in June 1962, Clarence Earl Gideon wrote a note asking the US Supreme Court to review his conviction for a crime he said he didn't commit. He added that couldn't afford a lawyer.

One year later, in the historic case of *Gideon v. Wainright*, the Supreme Court ruled that people who can't pay for their own defense must be given a public defender—an advocate—provided by the state. With this decision, and with the help of a court-appointed lawyer, Clarence Gideon was retried and acquitted.

But what if we are not innocent? According to the apostle Paul, we are all guilty. But the court of heaven provides an Advocate who, at God's expense, offers to defend and care for our soul (1 JOHN 2:2). On behalf of His Father, Jesus comes to us offering a freedom that even prison inmates have described as better than anything they've experienced on the outside. It is a freedom of heart and mind.

Jesus, our Advocate, can turn a prison of lost hope, fear, or regret into the place of His presence.

❖ *Mart DeHaan*

Star Shepherd

ISAIAH 40:25–27

Lift up your eyes and look to the heavens: Who created all these?
He who brings out the starry host one by one and calls forth each of them by name.
Because of his great power and mighty strength, not one of them is missing.

—ISAIAH 40:26

Some night when you're away from city lights, "lift up your eyes and look to the heavens" (ISAIAH 40:26).

If you have good eyes, you can see about 5,000 stars, according to astronomer Simon Driver. There are, however, far more that you cannot see. The Hubble Deep Field Study space probe concluded that there are billions of galaxies, each containing billions of stars. By one estimate, there are more than ten stars in the universe for every grain of sand on the earth.

Yet each night, without fail, God "brings out the starry host one by one. . . . Because of his great power and mighty strength, not one is missing" (V. 26).

Why then do people say, "My way is hidden from the LORD"? (V. 27). No one has been forgotten by God. He knows "those who are his" (2 TIMOTHY 2:19). If He can bring out the incalculable hosts of heaven each night one by one, He can bring you into His light.

Are the stars out tonight? Rejoice! God cares for you.

❖ *David Roper*

The Variety of Creation

JOB 12:7–13

In his hand is the life of every creature and the breath of all mankind.

—JOB 12:10

Think about the amazing features God placed in the animals He created. Job wrote about several of them, including the ostrich. Despite its apparent lack of good sense and its eccentric parenting skills, its offspring survive (39:13–16). And despite its membership in the bird family, it can't fly—but it can outrun a horse (V. 18).

Another remarkable creature is the bombardier beetle. This African insect shoots two common materials, hydrogen peroxide and hydroquinone, from twin storage tanks in its back, blinding the beetle's predators. A special nozzle inside the beetle mixes the chemicals, enabling it to bombard its foe at amazing speeds! The little guy can rotate his "cannon" to fire in any direction.

How can this be? How is it that a rather dull-witted ostrich survives despite a seeming inability to care for its young while the bombardier beetle needs a sophisticated chemical reaction to ensure its continued presence on earth? It's because God's creative abilities know no boundaries. "At his command they were created," the psalmist tells us (148:5). God's creative work is clear for all to see.

❖ *David Egner*

Big Spring

JOHN 4:7–14

"Whoever drinks the water I give them will never thirst. Indeed, the water I give them will become in them a spring of water welling up to eternal life."

—JOHN 4:14

In Michigan's Upper Peninsula is a remarkable natural wonder—a pool about forty feet deep and three hundred feet across, which Native Americans called "Kitch-iti-kipi," or "big cold water." Today it's known as Big Spring. Underground springs push more than 10,000 gallons of water a minute through the rocks below and up to the surface. The water maintains a temperature of forty-five degrees Fahrenheit. Even in the brutally cold winters of the Upper Peninsula the pool never freezes. Tourists can enjoy viewing the waters of Big Spring during any season of the year.

When Jesus encountered a woman at Jacob's well, He talked to her about another source of water that would always satisfy. He said, "Whoever drinks the water I give them will never thirst. Indeed, the water I give them will become in them a spring of water welling up to eternal life" (JOHN 4:14).

Far greater than any natural spring is the refreshment we have been offered in Christ himself. Jesus alone, the Water of Life, can quench our thirst. Praise God, for Jesus is the source that never runs dry.

❖ *Bill Crowder*

The Debt of Leadership

Guard my life, for I am faithful to you;
save your servant who trusts in you. You are my God.

—PSALM 86:2

Examine Psalm 86, and you might forget that you're reading the musings of a good leader. David prayed, "Hear me, LORD, and answer me, for I am poor and needy" (V. 1). Then the king of Israel refers to himself as a "servant" and pleads for mercy. Think of it! The man God had chosen to lead His people identified as a servant and pled for God's help. Wow!

Let's review what leadership means. According to businessman Max De Pree, whose leadership moved his company near the top of the Fortune 500: "The first responsibility of a leader is to define reality. The last is to say thank you. In between the two, the leader must become a servant and a debtor." Those two words, *servant* and *debtor*, describe David's view of himself as he asked God for help.

All of us who lead—whether a family, a church, a classroom, or a business—need Psalm 86 as our guide. The "poor and needy" (V. 1) servant-leader who trusts God is the one who, in the end, can say as David did, "You, LORD, have helped me and comforted me" (V. 17).

❖ *Dave Branon*

Legacy

PSALM 127

Children are a heritage from the LORD,
offspring a reward from him.

—PSALM 127:3

A friend of mine wrote recently, "If we died tomorrow, the company that we are working for could easily replace us in a matter of days. But the family left behind would feel the loss for the rest of their lives. Why then do we invest so much in our work and so little in our children's lives?"

Why do we sometimes exhaust ourselves rising up early and going late to rest, "eating the bread of anxious toil" (PSALM 127:1–2 ESV), busying ourselves to make our mark on this world, and overlooking the one investment that matters beyond everything else—our children?

Solomon declared, "Children are a heritage from the Lord"—an invaluable legacy He has bequeathed us. "Like arrows in the hand of a warrior are children born in one's youth" (V. 4) is his striking simile. Nothing is more worthy of our energy and time.

We need to make time for our children and trust that the Lord will provide for all of our physical needs. Children, whether our own or those we disciple, are our lasting legacy—an investment we'll never regret.

❖ *David Roper*

NOVEMBER 30

Time to Flourish

*Since you are precious and honored in my sight, and because I love you,
I will give people in exchange for you, nations in exchange for your life.*

—ISAIAH 43:4

To celebrate Winston Churchill's eightieth birthday on November 30, 1954, the British parliament commissioned artist Graham Sutherland to paint a portrait of the celebrated statesman.

Churchill was not happy with the results. Sutherland's portrait had Churchill slumped in a chair wearing his trademark scowl—true to reality, but hardly flattering. After its official unveiling, Churchill hid the painting in his cellar. It was later secretly destroyed.

Like Churchill, most of us have an image of ourselves we want others to have of us. Perhaps deep down we fear we won't be loved if the real us is known.

When the Israelites were taken captive by Babylon, they were seen at their worst. Because of their sins, God allowed their enemies to conquer them. But He told them not to fear; He was with them in every trial (ISAIAH 43:1–2). They were secure in His hands (V. 13) and "precious" to Him (V. 4). Despite their ugliness, God loved them.

Remember this: God knows the real us and still loves us immeasurably (EPHESIANS 3:18).

❖ *Sheridan Voysey*

The Path of Wisdom

PSALM 38:1–15

LORD, I wait for you; you will answer, Lord my God.

—PSALM 38:15

Albert Einstein was heard to say, "Only two things are infinite, the universe and human stupidity, and I'm not sure about the former." Sadly, it does seem that far too often there's no limit to the damage we create by our foolishness.

It was in such a season of regret that David poured out his struggle to God in Psalm 38. As he recounted his failings, as well as the painful consequences of those failings, the shepherd-king made an insightful comment: "My wounds fester and are loathsome because of my sinful folly" (V. 5). Although the psalmist does not give us the details of his worsening wounds, one thing is clear—David recognized his own foolishness as their root cause.

The answer for such foolishness is to embrace God's wisdom. Proverbs 9:10 reminds us, "The fear of the LORD is the beginning of wisdom, and knowledge of the Holy One is understanding." Only by allowing God to transform us can we overcome the foolish decisions that cause so much trouble. With His loving guidance, we can follow the pathway of godly wisdom.

❖ *Bill Crowder*

True Sacrifice

PHILIPPIANS 2:17–30

He almost died for the work of Christ.
He risked his life to make up for the help you yourselves could not give me.

—PHILIPPIANS 2:30

Teenagers amaze me. Many of them love life with grand passion and face it with unrelenting optimism. Sometimes they demonstrate the Christian life in ways adults can only hope to emulate.

Such is the case with Carissa, a teen who loved soccer, basketball, friends, family, and Jesus. When she was just twelve, her mother was diagnosed with cancer. Carissa began immediately to help care for her mom.

During the next few years, Carissa often fed her mom, dressed her, and helped her do anything she couldn't do for herself. "It was so hard to learn," she said. "Can you imagine, a mother and daughter literally changing roles? I learned to be a humble servant."

Sometimes, while her friends were out having fun, Carissa was helping her dad care for her mom, which she did until the family said goodbye for the last time. As Carissa puts it, "God took her home and made her perfect."

Carissa reminds me of Epaphroditus, who sacrificially cared for Paul's needs (PHILIPPIANS 2:25–30). Their examples of caring, love, and compassion can teach us all about the value of servanthood.

❖ *Dave Branon*

Acts of Kindness

ACTS 4:1–13

Then know this, you and all the people of Israel:
It is by the name of Jesus Christ of Nazareth, whom you crucified
but whom God raised from the dead, that this man stands before you healed.

—ACTS 4:10

I was traveling with some men when we spotted a family stranded alongside the road. My friends immediately pulled over to help. They got the car running and gave the people some money for gasoline. When the people thanked them over and over, they replied, "We're glad to help out, and we do it in Jesus's name." I was impressed with how natural it was for these friends to help people in need and acknowledge the Lord as the source of their generosity.

Peter and John exhibited that same joyful generosity when they healed a lame man in Jerusalem (ACTS 3:1–10). This led to their arrest and appearance before the authorities who asked, "By what power or what name did you do this?" Peter replied, "Know this, you and all the people of Israel: It is by name of Jesus Christ of Nazareth, . . . that this man stands here before you healed" (ACTS 4:7–10).

Kindness is a powerful context in which to genuinely speak to others about the Lord.

❖ *David McCasland*

What Money Can't Buy

EPHESIANS 1:3–14

In him we have redemption through his blood, the forgiveness of sins,
in accordance with the riches of God's grace.

—EPHESIANS 1:7

"There are some things money can't buy—but these days, not many" accoring to Michael Sandel, author of *What Money Can't Buy*. A person can buy a prison-cell upgrade for $90 a night and your doctor's cell phone number for $1,500. It seems that "almost everything is up for sale."

But one thing money can't buy is *redemption*—freedom from the stranglehold of sin. When Paul began writing about the rich nature of God's plan of salvation through Jesus, his heart erupted in praise: "In him we have redemption through his blood, the forgiveness of sins, in accordance with the riches of God's grace that He lavished on us" (EPHESIANS 1:7–8).

Jesus's death on the cross was the high cost of delivering us from sin. And only He could pay that price because He was the perfect Son of God. The natural response to such free but costly grace is spontaneous praise from our hearts and commitment to God (VV. 13–14).

Praise to our loving God—He has come to set us free!

❖ *Marvin Williams*

Growing in the Wind

MARK 4:36-41

They were terrified and asked each other,
"Who is this? Even the wind and the waves obey him!"

—MARK 4:41

Who would expect trees to suddenly fall over in a windless environment? That's what happened in a three-acre glass dome in the Arizona desert. Trees growing inside Biosphere 2 grew faster than normal, but they collapsed under their own weight. Researchers discovered that these trees needed wind stress to grow strong.

Jesus let His disciples experience gale-force winds to strengthen their faith (MARK 4:36–41). During a night crossing of familiar waters, wind and waves swamped their boat while Jesus slept in the stern. In a panic they woke Him. *Didn't it bother Him that they were about to die? What was He thinking?* Then they began to find out. Jesus told the wind and waves to be quiet—and asked His friends why they still had no faith in Him.

If the wind had not blown, these disciples would never have asked, "Who is this? Even the winds and the waves obey him!" (MARK 4:41).

Life in a protective bubble might sound good. But how strong would our faith be if we couldn't discover for ourselves His reassuring "be still" when the winds of circumstance howl?

❖ *Mart DeHaan*

Built to Last
EPHESIANS 4:7–16

*In him you too are being built together
to become a dwelling in which God lives by his Spirit.*

—EPHESIANS 2:22

When explorers entered Peru, they found huge, impressive buildings that may have been standing for 2,000 years. These ancient Inca structures were built of hand-hewn rocks of varied sizes and shapes. Without the use of mortar, they were fitted together so perfectly that they stood for many centuries.

God builds His church in much the same way. The Bible pictures the church of Jesus Christ as a building, and each believer is a block in that building. Peter said that we, "like living stones, are being built up into a spiritual house" (1 PETER 2:5). And Paul said we are "joined together" (EPHESIANS 2:21) and "are being built together to become a dwelling in which God lives by his Spirit" (V. 22).

People with a variety of backgrounds, abilities, interests, and needs make up Christ's church, so uniting in a common purpose is not an easy process. Yet when we let the Lord shape us and assign our place in the structure, we become part of a strong, solid edifice.

God is building an enduring church—a church that is built to last.

❖ *David Egner*

This Do in Remembrance

1 CORINTHIANS 11:23–24

When he had given thanks, he broke it and said,
"This is my body, which is for you; do this in remembrance of me."

—1 CORINTHIANS 11:24

When a US Navy vessel arrives or departs from military bases in Pearl Harbor, the crew of that ship lines up in dress uniform. They stand at attention at arm's length on the outer edges of the deck, in salute to the soldiers, sailors, and civilians who died on December 7, 1941. It is a stirring sight.

Even for spectators on shore, the salute triggers an incredible emotional connection, but especially between the service personnel of today and those of yesterday. It grants nobility to the work of today's sailor, while giving dignity to the sacrifice of those from the past.

When Jesus instituted the Lord's Supper (MATTHEW 26:26–29), it was surely with an eye toward creating this same kind of emotional bond. Our participation in communion honors His sacrifice while also granting us a connection to Him unlike any other act of remembrance.

Just as the Navy carefully prescribes the way it salutes the fallen, so too Scripture teaches us how to remember Jesus's sacrifice (1 CORINTHIANS 11:26–28). These acts of reverence honor past action while giving purpose to present service.

❖ *Randy Kilgore*

Like Sheep
ISAIAH 53:1–6

We all, like sheep, have gone astray, each of us has turned to our own way;
and the LORD has laid on him the iniquity of us all.

—ISAIAH 53:6

One of my daily chores when I lived in northern Ghana was taking care of sheep. Each morning I took them out to pasture and returned by evening. That was when I noticed how stubborn sheep can be. Whenever they saw a farm, for instance, their instinct drove them right into it, getting me in trouble with the farmer.

Sometimes when I was tired from the heat and resting under a tree, sheep slipped off into the bushes and headed for the hills. I had to chase them—scratching my skinny legs in the shrubs. I had a hard time directing the animals away from danger and trouble.

So I quite understand when Isaiah says, "We all, like sheep, have gone astray, each of us has turned to our own way" (53:6). We stray. We behave like sheep in the field.

Fortunately, we have the Good Shepherd who laid down His life for us (JOHN 10:11) and who carries our sorrows and our sins (ISAIAH 53:4–6). And as our shepherd, He calls us back to safe pasture that we might follow Him more closely.

❖ *Lawrence Darmani*

"Go Fever"

NUMBERS 14:39–45

Be still before the LORD and wait patiently for him;
do not fret when people succeed in their ways, when they carry out their wicked schemes.

—PSALM 37:7

In early 1986, after five weather-related delays, the space shuttle *Challenger* lumbered heavenward amid a thunderous overture of flame. A mere seventy-three seconds later, a systems failure tore the shuttle apart, and all seven crew-members perished. Insiders referred to the fatal decision to launch as "go fever"— the tendency to ignore vital precautions in the rush to a grand goal.

Our ambition can tempt us to make ill-advised choices, yet we are also prone to a fear that can make us overly cautious. The Israelites demonstrated both traits. When the twelve scouts returned from spying out the Promised Land, ten of them saw only obstacles (NUMBERS 13:26–33). After a rebellion against the Lord that led to the death of the ten spies, the people suddenly developed "go fever." They said, "Now we are ready to go up to the land the LORD promised" (14:40). Without God, the ill-timed invasion failed (VV. 41–45).

When we take our eyes off the Lord, we'll either impatiently rush ahead without Him, or we'll cower and complain in fear. Focusing on Him brings courage tempered with His wisdom.

❖ *Tim Gustafson*

Power That Disrupts

MATTHEW 20:20–28

"The Son of Man did not come to be served,
but to serve, and to give his life as a ransom for many."

—MATTHEW 20:28

What does it take to disrupt the good work of a church? Just one power-hungry person.

One of my college friends, a pastor, wrote to me about a disruption in his church. People had come to faith in Christ, and membership had quadrupled. The members were active in serving the church and community.

But then one man in a leadership position began to envy the pastor's influence. He felt he deserved more power, so he began to tear down the pastor. He wanted power and recognition. He caused such an uproar that my friend finally had to resign.

When it comes to serving Christ, we have no right to seek power. We have no calling for prestige. We have no reason to look for self-aggrandizement and recognition. Our task is to serve quietly in the background, keeping in mind that Jesus, our example, "did not come to be served, but to serve" (MATTHEW 20:28).

Are you a pastor? A teacher? A deacon? A missionary? A church member? If you look for power, you may get it, but it will become power that disrupts the good work of God's people.

❖ *Dave Branon*

Our Best Friend

HEBREWS 10:9–13

Yet to all who did receive him, to those who believed in his name,
he gave the right to become children of God.

—JOHN 1:12

When I was twelve, our family moved to a town in the desert. After gym classes in the hot air at my new school, we rushed for the drinking fountain. Being skinny and young for my grade, I sometimes got pushed out of the way. One day my big, strong friend Jose saw this happening. He stuck out his arm to clear my way. "Hey!" he exclaimed. "Let Banks get a drink first!" I never had trouble at the drinking fountain again.

Jesus understood what it was like to face the ultimate unkindness of others: "He was despised and rejected by mankind" (ISAIAH 53:3). But He was also our advocate. By giving His life, Jesus opened a "new and living way" for us to enter into a relationship with God (HEBREWS 10:20). He did for us what we could never do for ourselves, offering us the gift of salvation when we repent and trust in Him.

Others may hold us at arm's length or even push us away, but God has opened His arms to us through the cross. How is that for a best friend!

❖ *James Banks*

Living Life to the Max

JOHN 10:7–11

The thief comes only to steal and kill and destroy;
I have come that they may have life, and have it to the full.

—JOHN 10:10

A veteran mountain climber was sharing his experiences with a group of novices preparing for their first major climb. "Remember this," he said, "your goal is to experience the exhilaration of the climb and the joy of reaching . . . the peak. Each step draws you closer to the top. If your purpose for climbing is just to avoid death, your experience will be minimal."

I see an application to the Christian's experience. Jesus did not call us to live the Christian life just to escape hell. It's not to be a life of minimum joy and fulfillment, but a life that is full and overflowing.

The Lord promised us "life . . . to the full" (JOHN 10:10). We cannot experience a full and abundant life if we are living in fear. When we walk by faith, we will see each day of the Christian life as a challenge to be met and as one more upward step to glory!

Do not live minimally. Live life to the max! Climb that mountain with confidence!

❖ *David Egner*

Pain's Purpose

HEBREWS 12:7–11

No discipline seems pleasant at the time, but painful. Later on, however,
it produces a harvest of righteousness and peace for those who have been trained by it.

—HEBREWS 12:11

Affliction, when we accept it with patience and humility, can lead us to a deeper, fuller life. "Before I was afflicted I went astray," David wrote, "but now I obey your word" (PSALM 119:67).

Pain can be a pathway to our growth instead of an obstacle to it. If we allow pain to train us, it can lead us closer to God and into His Word. It is often the means by which our Father graciously shapes us to be like His Son, gradually giving us the courage, compassion, contentment, and tranquility we long and pray for. Without pain, God would not accomplish all He desires to do in and through us.

Is God instructing you through suffering and pain? By His grace, you can endure His instruction patiently (2 CORINTHIANS 12:9). He can teach you the lessons He intends for you to learn and give you His peace in the midst of your difficulties.

The Bible says, "Consider it pure joy . . . whenever you face trials of many kinds" (JAMES 1:2). God is making more out of you than you ever thought possible.

❖ *David Roper*

Out of the Ruins

LAMENTATIONS 5:8–22

Though we are slaves, our God has not forsaken us in our bondage.
He has shown us kindness in the sight of the kings of Persia:
He has granted us new life to rebuild the house of our God and repair its ruins,
and he has given us a wall of protection in Judah and Jerusalem.

—EZRA 9:9

In the Jewish Quarter of Jerusalem is Tiferet Yisrael Synagogue. This nineteenth-century synagogue was dynamited by commandos during the 1948 Arab-Israeli War.

It lay in ruins until 2014, when rebuilding began. As city officials set a piece of rubble as the cornerstone, one quoted from Lamentations: "Restore us to yourself, Lord, that we may return; renew our days as of old" (5:21).

Lamentations is Jeremiah's funeral song for Jerusalem. The prophet graphically describes the impact of war on his city. Verse 21 is his heartfelt prayer for God to intervene. Decades later, God did answer that prayer as the exiles returned to Jerusalem.

Our lives too may seem to be in ruins. Difficulties may leave us devastated. But we have a Father who understands. Gently, patiently, He clears away the rubble, repurposes it, and builds something better. It takes time, but we can always trust Him. He specializes in rebuilding projects.

❖ *Tim Gustafson*

Winning the Big One

PHILIPPIANS 3:7–14

I press on toward the goal to win the prize
for which God has called me heavenward in Christ Jesus.

—PHILIPPIANS 3:14

In every field of endeavor, one award is considered the epitome of recognition and success. An Olympic gold medal, a Grammy, an Academy Award, or a Nobel Prize are among "the big ones." But there is a greater prize anyone can obtain.

Paul was familiar with first-century athletic games in which competitors gave their full effort to win the prize. With that in mind, he wrote to a group of followers of Christ in Philippi: "Whatever were gains to me I now consider loss for the sake of Christ" (PHILIPPIANS 3:7). Why? Because his heart had embraced a new goal: "I want to know Christ—yes, to know the power of his resurrection and participation in his sufferings" (V. 10). His trophy for completing the race would be the "crown of righteousness" (2 TIMOTHY 4:8).

Each of us can aim for that prize, knowing that we honor the Lord in pursuing it. Every day, in our ordinary duties, we are moving toward "the big one"—"the heavenly prize for which God, through Christ Jesus, is calling us" (PHILIPPIANS 3:14 NLT).

❖ *David McCasland*

Kingdom Living
COLOSSIANS 1:3–14

For he has rescued us from the dominion of darkness
and brought us into the kingdom of the Son he loves.

—COLOSSIANS 1:13

A man I know transplanted his family to the inner city. One day as he was walking down the hallway in his apartment building, he noticed two guys smoking crack cocaine. Not wanting his kids to see this, he asked them to stop. The next thing he knew, one of their fists had found its way to his jaw. Through the blood, he responded, "If Jesus shed His blood for me, I can shed my blood for you."

The two men fled. Later, one of them returned, knocked on my friend's door, and said, "I have not forgotten your words. If your God is that real to you, then I want to know Him." That day, he was "rescued . . . from the dominion of darkness," and brought into "the kingdom of the Son he loves" (COLOSSIANS 1:13).

Those of us who have been rescued from the darkness can bring a bit of heaven to earth when we're willing to demonstrate the power of God's unique approach to life. We prove the power and strength of God's forgiveness by showing His love for our enemies.

❖ *Joe Stowell*

Brotherhood of the Sea

EPHESIANS 2:14–22

*Consequently, you are no longer foreigners and strangers,
but fellow citizens with God's people and also members of his household.*

—EPHESIANS 2:19

On August 8, 2005, the world learned of the dramatic rescue of seven Russian sailors trapped in a small sub entangled in a fishing net. The men had survived three cold, dark days on the bottom of the ocean and had less than six hours of oxygen left. Meanwhile, a frantic, unified rescue effort by Russian, Japanese, British, and American personnel was underway. Finally, the sub was freed. The Russian defense minister proclaimed, "We have seen in deeds, not in words, what the brotherhood of the sea means."

Ephesians talks about the unity of believers in Jesus by referring to the oneness of "his household" (2:19). The Gentiles—once "foreigners" (V. 12)—were now "brought near by the blood of Christ" (V. 13), uniting them with their Jewish brothers and sisters. This unity should mark the Christian community today.

Believers are called to undertake a most important rescue effort: rescuing people who are dying without Christ. Those united mission efforts are bringing hope, salvation, and relief to desperate people everywhere. That's the brotherhood of Christ!

❖ *David Egner*

Mom's Finish Line

I have fought the good fight,
I have finished the race, I have kept the faith.

—2 TIMOTHY 4:7

When Jeff learned that his mother's health was rapidly declining, he caught a plane to be with her. He sat at her bedside comforting her and expressing his love for her. She passed away, and at her funeral many people told Jeff what a blessing his mother had been. She was gifted in Bible teaching, counseling others, and leading prayer groups until near the end of her life. She finished strong for Christ.

To honor his mother's life, Jeff ran in a marathon. During the race he thanked God for her life and grieved her loss. When he crossed the finish line, Jeff pointed his index finger toward heaven—"Where Mom is," he said. She had honored Christ to the end, which reminded him of Paul's words: "I have fought the good fight, I have finished the race, I have kept the faith. " (2 TIMOTHY 4:7).

We are involved in a "long-distance race." Let's run in a way that we may obtain the prize of "a crown that will last forever" (1 CORINTHIANS 9:25). What could be more desirable than to finish strong for Christ!

❖ *Dennis Fisher*

The Great Comeback

ACTS 2:14–21, 37–41

Then Peter stood up with the Eleven, raised his voice and addressed the crowd:
"Fellow Jews and all of you who live in Jerusalem,
let me explain this to you; listen carefully to what I say."

—ACTS 2:14

In the 1940s, a reluctance by leadership to modernize nearly destroyed the Ford Motor Company. In fact, the government almost took over the company lest its demise threaten the US war effort. But when Henry Ford II was released from his military duties to run the company, things turned around. Ford became one of the biggest corporations in the world.

Occasionally, we need a comeback in life. We have an example in Peter, who had failure written all over him. First, he nearly drowned when his faith faltered (MATTHEW 14:30). Then he said things that were so wrong Jesus called him "Satan" (16:22–23). And when Jesus needed Peter the most: three denials (26:74).

But that's not the end of the story. In the power of the Spirit, Peter made a comeback. On the Day of Pentecost, he preached and 3,000 people came to faith in Christ (ACTS 2:14, 41). Peter returned to effectiveness because his faith was renewed, he guarded what he said, and he stood up for Jesus.

Struggling? If Peter can come back, so can you.

❖ *Dave Branon*

Probing Questions

*In your hearts revere Christ as Lord. Always be prepared to give an answer
to everyone who asks you to give the reason for the hope that you have.
But do this with gentleness and respect.*

—1 PETER 3:15

While riding on a train a few years after the Civil War, General Lew Wallace of the Union Army encountered a fellow officer, Colonel Robert Ingersoll. Ingersoll was a leading agnostic, and Wallace was a man of faith. As they talked, Wallace realized he wasn't able to answer the questions and doubts raised by Ingersoll. Wallace began searching the Scriptures for answers. The result was his confident declaration of the person of the Savior in his classic historical novel *Ben-Hur: A Tale of the Christ*.

Probing questions from skeptics don't have to be a threat to our faith. Instead, they can motivate us to seek a deeper understanding of our faith. The apostle Peter encouraged us to pursue the wisdom of God in the Scriptures when he wrote, "Always be prepared to give an answer to everyone who asks you to give a reason for the hope that you have" (1 PETER 3:15).

We don't have to have an answer for every question, but we need the courage, confidence, and conviction to share our love for Christ and the hope that is in us.

❖ *Bill Crowder*

The Mark of Leadership

MARK 10:35–45

Whoever wants to be first must be slave of all.

—MARK 10:44

While visiting Purdue University on a frigid winter day, I came upon two young men chipping ice from the sidewalk next to a fraternity house. Thinking they must be underclassmen assigned the tough job by older fraternity brothers, I said, "They didn't tell you about this when you joined, did they?" One looked up with a smile and said, "Well, we're upperclassmen. I'm the fraternity vice-president and my friend here is the president." I thanked them for their hard work and went on my way having been reminded that serving others is the mark of a true leader.

When two of Jesus's disciples asked Him for positions of honor in His coming kingdom, He told His twelve closest followers, "Whoever wants to become great among you must be your servant, and whoever desires to be first must be slave of all" (MARK 10:43–44). Then He reminded them He had not come to be served but to serve others (V. 45).

The mark of godly leadership is not power and privilege, but humble service. God gives us strength to follow Jesus's example and to lead His way.

❖ *David McCasland*

Not Much in Between

EPHESIANS 3:14–21

To know this love that surpasses knowledge—
that you may be filled to the measure of all the fullness of God.

—EPHESIANS 3:19

In the western panhandle of Texas is a small town named Texline. It had an ostentatious beginning in the late 1800s as a thriving center along a new railroad line. Within a few years, though, most of the shops had closed and the town's population shriveled. Recently, the population was just over 500.

One online description of Texline says that it has "a city limits sign at one end, another at the other end, and not much in between."

What a shame if that description could be given of our spiritual journey! Our earthly Christian life journey begins at the moment of faith in Jesus and ends when we go to be with the Lord. But what happens in between?

A rich and full life is available to all who believe in and serve Jesus. Paul prayed that believers would "be filled to the measure of the fullness of God" (EPHESIANS 3:19). He wanted them to know life "to the full" (JOHN 10:10).

God desires to give us a marvelous beginning with salvation and a great ending in Glory—with much in between.

❖ *David Egner*

GENESIS 3:1–10

This is how God showed his love among us:
He sent his one and only Son into the world that we might live through him.

—1 JOHN 4:9

One morning my phone rang, and as I answered it I heard my eleven-month-old grandson's voice. He had his mom's cellphone, and he somehow hit my number. What followed was a "conversation" I will long remember. He could only say a few words, but he knew my voice and responded to it. So I talked to him and told him how much I love him.

The joy I felt at hearing my grandson's voice was a reminder of God's deep desire for a relationship with us. From the beginning, God actively pursued us. Even after Adam and Eve sinned and hid from God, "the LORD God called" to Adam (GENESIS 3:9).

God continued to pursue humanity through Jesus. He sent Jesus to earth to pay the penalty for our sin by His death on the cross. He made that sacrifice "to clear away our sins and the damage they've done to our relationship with God" (1 JOHN 4:9–10 MSG).

God wants us to respond to His love through Jesus. Even when we don't quite know what to say, our Father longs to hear from us!

❖ *James Banks*

Just a Bunch of Shepherds

LUKE 2:8–20

This will be a sign to you: You will find a baby
wrapped in cloths and lying in a manger.

—LUKE 2:12

The angel announcing Jesus's birth bypassed Jerusalem, the religious center of Israel. He didn't go to Herodium, Herod's villa near Bethlehem. He appeared instead to a bunch of shepherds tending their flocks (LUKE 2:8–9).

Back then no one thought God would be interested in shepherds, or that shepherds would be interested in God. Shepherds were notoriously irreligious, ranked by the rabbis with prostitutes and other "habitual sinners."

They were outcasts, barred from the synagogue and polite society. They assumed that God would never accept them, and they feared Him.

But God spoke to them. All of us—shepherds included—have a longing for something more in life. No matter how hard we try to appear self-sufficient, sooner or later we run out of something essential—love, money, time, or life. Isolation, loneliness, and fear of death lead us to acknowledge our need for a Savior.

The angel's words to the shepherds were simple and direct: "Today in the town of David a Savior has been born to you; he is the Messiah, the Lord" (LUKE 2:11). That's what we all need!

❖ *David Roper*

The Heavens Declare

PSALM 19:1–6

The heavens declare the glory of God;
the skies proclaim the work of his hands.

—PSALM 19:1

You don't have to gaze long at the night sky to marvel at the wonder of God's awe-inspiring handiwork. The massive stretch of galaxies and the cloudy mass of our own Milky Way remind us of the spectacular creation and the sustaining work of Jesus by whom it is all held together (COLOSSIANS 1:16–17).

But the nightly show we experience is nothing compared with the glory that God displayed when He sent His Son to Earth. While shepherds were watching their flocks, the sky was suddenly ablaze with angelic messengers praising God and saying, "Glory to God in the highest!" (LUKE 2:14). Even Magi from a foreign land came and worshiped the King when God planted the brightest of stars in the east, leading them to Bethlehem.

While "the heavens declare the glory of God" nightly (PSALM 19:1), never before or since has the theater of the universe been more alive with His glory than when the Creator loved us enough to come to our planet to save us from our sin. Keep that in mind the next time you marvel at the stars!

❖ *Joe Stowell*

The Gift of Time

A generous person will prosper;
whoever refreshes others will be refreshed.

—PROVERBS 11:25

I headed into the post office in a big hurry. I had a number of things on my to-do list, but as I entered I was frustrated to find a long line backing up all the way to the door.

My hand was still on the door when an elderly stranger approached me. "I can't get this copier to work," he said, pointing to the machine behind us. "It took my money and I don't know what to do." Immediately I knew what God wanted me to do. I stepped out of line and was able to fix the problem in ten minutes.

The man thanked me and then left. As I turned to get back in line, it was gone. I walked straight to the service counter.

My experience that day reminds me of Jesus's words: "Give, and it will be given to you. A good measure, pressed down, shaken together and running over, will be poured into your lap. For with the measure you use, it will be measured to you" (LUKE 6:38).

My wait seemed shorter because God interrupted my hurry. By turning my eyes to others' needs and helping me give of my time, He gave me a gift. It's a lesson I hope to remember next time I look at my watch.

❖ *James Banks*

Eric's Hymn

PSALM 46

He says, "Be still, and know that I am God;
I will be exalted among the nations, I will be exalted in the earth."

—PSALM 46:10

Eric Liddell, memorialized in *Chariots of Fire*, won a gold medal in the 1924 Paris Olympics before going to China as a missionary. Years later, with the outbreak of World War II, Liddell sent his family to safety in Canada, but he remained in China. Soon Liddell and other missionaries were interned in a Japanese detainment camp, where he developed a brain tumor.

Every Sunday afternoon a band would play near his hospital. One day Liddell requested "Be Still, My Soul." As he listened, I wonder if Eric pondered these words: "Be still, my soul: the hour is hastening on / When we shall be forever with the Lord. / Be still, my soul: when change and tears are past / All safe and blessed we shall meet at last."

That beautiful hymn, so comforting to Eric as he would face death just three days later, expresses a great reality of Scripture. In Psalm 46:10, David wrote, "Be still, and know that I am God." In our darkest moments, we can be still and allow Him to calm our greatest fears.

❖ *Bill Crowder*

Everything We Need

2 PETER 1:1–11

*His divine power has given us everything we need for a godly life
through our knowledge of him who called us by his own glory and goodness.*

—2 PETER 1:3

D o you ever feel inadequate for the things life is throwing your way? I often do. Like Peter, I have a lot to learn.

The New Testament reveals Peter's shortcomings. While walking on water to Jesus, Peter began to sink (MATTHEW 14:25–31). When Jesus was arrested, Peter swore he didn't know Him (MARK 14:66–72). But Peter's encounter with the risen Christ and the power in the Holy Spirit changed his life.

Peter came to understand that God's "divine power has given us everything we need for a godly life" (2 PETER 1:3). An amazing statement from a man who had many flaws!

"[God] has given us his very great and precious promises, so that through them you may participate in the divine nature" (V. 4).

Our relationship with the Lord Jesus Christ is our source for meeting the challenges of today. Through Him, we can overcome our hesitations and feelings of inadequacy.

He has given us everything we need to serve and honor Him.

❖ *David McCasland*

Load Line

1 PETER 5:5–9

Humble yourselves, therefore, under God's mighty hand,
that he may lift you up in due time.
Cast all your anxiety on him because he cares for you.

—1 PETER 5:6–7

In the nineteenth century, ships were often overloaded, resulting in sinkings and loss of life. In 1875, to remedy this negligent practice, British politician Samuel Plimsoll led the charge for legislation to create a line on the side of a ship to indicate if the ship was overloaded. That "load line" continues to mark the hulls of ships today.

Sometimes, like those ships, our lives can seem overloaded—perhaps with fears, struggles, and heartaches. We can even fear "going under." In those times, it's reassuring to remember our remarkable resource: a heavenly Father who stands ready to help us carry that load. The apostle Peter said, "Humble yourselves, therefore, under God's mighty hand, that he may lift you up in due time. Cast all your anxiety on him because he cares for you" (1 PETER 5:6–7).

Though the testings of life may feel like a burden too heavy to bear, we can have full assurance that our heavenly Father loves us deeply and knows our load limits. Whatever we face, He will help us stay above the load line.

❖ *Bill Crowder*

More

Yet when I surveyed all that my hands had done
and what I had toiled to achieve, everything was meaningless,
a chasing after the wind; nothing was gained under the sun.

—ECCLESIASTES 2:11

Tom Brady has model-like good looks, is married to supermodel Gisele Bundchen, and has led his football team to several Super Bowl wins. But it's still not enough. Brady confessed during an interview, "Why do I have [these] Super Bowl rings and still think there's something greater out there for me? I think, 'It's got to be more than this.' I mean this isn't—this can't be what it's all cracked up to be." The interviewer asked, "What's the answer?" Brady responded, "I wish I knew. I wish I knew."

Brady's befuddlement sounds similar to the complaint found in Ecclesiastes. Solomon sought fulfillment in pleasure, wine, women, projects, gardens, music, and excessive wealth. He wrote, "Anything I wanted, I would take. I denied myself no pleasure" (ECCLESIASTES 2:9–10 NLT). Yet he discovered that nothing in this life ultimately satisfies. It's not supposed to.

Isn't it comforting to know the true meaning of success: The only thing that was ever meant to satisfy the human heart is God.

❖ *Mike Wittmer*

"The Guy Who Ran the Wrong Way"

COLOSSIANS 1:9–14

In [Jesus] we have redemption, the forgiveness of sins.

—COLOSSIANS 1:14

It was New Year's Day 1929. The University of California at Berkeley was playing Georgia Tech in college football's Rose Bowl. Roy Riegels, a California defender, recovered a Georgia Tech fumble, turned, and scampered sixty-five yards in the wrong direction! One of Riegels' teammates tackled him just before he reached the wrong goal line. On the next play, Georgia Tech scored and went on to win.

From that day on, Riegels was saddled with the nickname "Wrong-way Riegels." For years, whenever he was introduced, people would exclaim, "I know who you are! You're the guy who ran the wrong way in the Rose Bowl!"

We've all gone the wrong way, and the memories haunt us. Recollections of sin and failure rise up to taunt us. If only we could begin again!

We can. When we confess our sins and repent before God, He forgives our past. In Christ, "we have redemption, the forgiveness of sins"—*all* our sins (COLOSSIANS 1:14; 2:13).

A new year lies ahead. It's a good time to remember that it's never too late to begin again.

❖ *David Roper*

THE WRITERS

James Banks, who is pastor of Peace Church in Durham, North Carolina, has a favorite exercise workout he does with his dog, Max. Along a river near their home, James and his 90-pound Labrador retriever do a three-mile "fetch run." James throws a stick into the woods, which Max fetches and then drops on the trail. Then James throws a second stick, and off goes Max after that one—and on it goes. Back at the house, James enjoys tinkering with old diesel engines with the goal of keeping them running for hundreds of thousands of miles. James is the author of several books, including *Praying Together*, *Praying the Prayers of the Bible*, and *Prayers for Prodigals*. He and his wife, Cari, have two adult children. And one stick-fetching dog.

Dave Branon spent countless hours as a kid trying to emulate his basketball hero Pete Maravich, but when it became clear that his small-college basketball experience at Cedarville University would never lead to the NBA, he had to choose a different career path. For several years, he was a high school English teacher and basketball coach (he was Tom Felten's varsity hoops coach) before entering the publishing world at Our Daily Bread Ministries as an assistant editor for *Our Daily Bread*. Later, Dave spent eighteen years as managing editor of *Sports Spectrum* magazine, which features top Christian athletes and their testimony of faith. Dave has written seventeen books, including Zondervan's Sports Devotional Bible, *Stand Firm*, *Heads Up!*, and *Beyond the Valley*. Dave and his wife, Sue, have four children and eight grandchildren and live in Grand Rapids, Michigan.

Bill Crowder is a Bible teacher and writer with a deep love of sports. He played intercollegiate soccer (goalkeeper) followed by decades of slow-pitch softball, and now he plays golf whenever possible (though never often enough due to Michigan winters, he says). He also follows college and professional sports—especially Liverpool Football Club of the English Premier League, West Virginia University (his home state), and the Los Angeles Angels (among others!). For more than forty years, his wife, Marlene, has endured his passion for sports with a smile, and his five kids have (mostly) willingly accepted his coaching in soccer, track, and baseball. Now he is working to build a love for sports in the grandkids. Bill has written several books, including *Let's Talk*, *For This He Came*, and *Windows on Christmas*.

Lawrence Darmani has enjoyed bird-watching since he was a kid growing up in Ghana. He has since added another item he loves to observe: good architecture—which will cause him to pause and enjoy a building's composition. Lawrence also loves to drop a line in the water and see what is biting. Over the years, Lawrence has established himself as an award-winning author. His first novel, *Grief Child*, won a British Commonwealth Writers Prize. Some of his books include *One for the Road*, *Strength for the Journey*, and *Palm-Tree Parables*. Lawrence and his wife, Comfort, have two daughters. The family lives in Accra, Ghana, where Lawrence is editor of *Step* magazine and CEO of Step Publishers.

Mart DeHaan has followed in the footsteps of his grandfather, Dr. M. R. DeHaan, by being an avid fisherman and an active observer of the natural world. Mart says some of his warmest memories over the years have been the hours spent with his son or his daughter fly-fishing the lily pads of a quiet lake, stalking white tail deer, and kayaking local rivers. Now that his kids are grown, his pursuits include trying to catch wildlife with a camera, survive ping-pong marathons with his son, or chase pars and birdies on a golf course with friends. Mart was the president of Our Daily Bread Ministries for many years, and he has written dozens of the ministry's Discovery Series booklets. Currently, he teams up with Elisa Morgan, Bill Crowder, and Daniel Ryan Day on the ODB Ministries weekday radio program *Discover the Word*, hosted by Brian Hettinga. Mart and his wife, Diane, live in Grand Rapids and have two grown children.

Prior to retirement, **David Egner** enjoyed nothing better than taking a break from his work schedule to spend time at his rustic cabin on Piatt Lake in Michigan's Upper Peninsula. There he could wander the woods with his dog, put a line in the water to catch some Piatt Lake largemouth bass, or just sit and share a cup of coffee with his wife, Shirley. For many years, David was an editor with Our Daily Bread Ministries. He also wrote many Discovery Series booklets for the ministry, and he began writing for *Our Daily Bread* in the 1980s. Dave and Shirley have been married for more than sixty-six years. They have three children, ten grandchildren, and three great-grandchildren. Dave volunteers at the Michigan Blood Center and teaches Bible classes at his church in Grand Rapids.

Tom Felten is one of those diehard lifetime Detroit Lions fans who still clings to hopes of a Super Bowl appearance. Tom, who is the executive editor of *Our Daily Bread*, was a talented high school basketball player—and he still enjoys playing lunchtime pickup ball three times a week. A five-time cancer survivor, Tom is extremely active in his local congregation—leading music and sometimes teaching the Word. He and his wife, Lynn, who have three adult sons, enjoy leadership roles at Michigan's Upper Peninsula Bible Camp. Recently, Tom hiked to the summit of the massive Haleakala Volcano on Maui. Tom and Lynn live in Grand Rapids.

Dennis Fisher and his dad bonded, as many sons and dads do, as they hunted the fields and fished the rivers of his boyhood. Whether they were taking salmon from the Sacramento River or downing pheasant from nearby fields, Dennis and his dad found both enjoyment of each other's company and thankfulness to God in their adventures. These days, Dennis plays a mean banjo—an instrument he once got to use to help entertain for an event attended by Ronald Reagan. Today, many of the songs Dennis composes relate to C. S. Lewis, about whom Fisher has become an expert. Dennis used his expertise as a former college professor and his doctorate in ministry during his years at Our Daily Bread Ministries as a research editor and writer. Dennis and his wife, Janet, a former college professor, live in California, and they enjoy using music in a variety of fun settings.

Tim Gustafson had the special privilege of growing up as a missionary kid in Ghana (which explains why he was bummed that neither the US nor Ghana qualified for soccer's 2018 World Cup). Tim would accompany his dad on hunts in Ghana, where Pop would carry a .308 and an eight-gauge shotgun. ("Hey, the critters could be large," Tim says.) Back stateside, Tim graduated from Michigan State University before serving in the US military—Active Army plus Army and Navy Reserves for many years. He served in places such as the Philippines, Turkey, Singapore, and the Caribbean. Tim is currently a senior content editor and writer for Our Daily Bread Ministries. He and his wife, Leisa, have eight children—all of whom are girls except for the last seven.

Randy Kilgore is the son, nephew, and grandson of truck drivers and coal miners, and he loves the rich heritage of those two professions. In fact, he often lists "truck driver" as the favorite job he's ever had. An avid baseball fan of the Kansas City Royals, Randy coached Little League baseball for six years as well as softball for two years. He worked as a senior human resource manager for many years before earning a seminary master's degree. From his experience in HR and as a workplace chaplain, Randy wrote *Made to Matter: Devotions for Working Christians*. He, his wife, Cheryl, and their two children live in Massachusetts.

Albert Lee served admirably in the Singapore Armed Forces, earning the Best Recruit and Best Non-Commissioned Officer awards while completing his national service. In his youth, he was also a rugby player, and he still enjoys watching Rugby Sevens, which is a variant of the fifteen-man game. It is played by seven rugby players in two seven-minute halves. Another of Albert's interests is swimming—but he has cut down from his hundred-laps-a-day pace to swimming once a week with a friend. He also enjoys art and photography. Albert has been the national director of Singapore Youth for Christ and the director of international ministries for Our Daily Bread Ministries. He and his wife, Catherine, have two children.

David McCasland grew up in Oklahoma City, graduated from Oklahoma State University, and earned his master's degree in communications from Wheaton College. David taught in public schools in Colorado Springs, at Daystar University in Nairobi, Kenya, and at the US Air Force Academy Preparatory School. He also served in the US Army and is a Vietnam veteran. Among the books David has written are *Blind Courage*, which told the story of Bill Irwin, the first blind person to hike the Appalachian Trail; *Oswald Chambers: Abandoned to God*, the life story of the writer of *My Utmost for His Highest*; and *Eric Liddell: Pure Gold*, the story of the Olympic gold medalist about whom the movie *Chariots of Fire* was written. He and his wife, Luann, live in Colorado Springs, Colorado, and have four grown children and six grandchildren.

Jeff Olson's fishing boat gets a workout during Michigan's mild-weather seasons—many times out on Lake Michigan angling for salmon and trout. When he's not fishing, Jeff is a licensed counselor who maintains a private practice. He was an editor and writer for Our Daily Bread Ministries, and he has written several Discovery Series booklets. Although his playing days are over, Jeff remains an avid baseball, basketball, and football fan (he and his good friend Tom Felten live and die by the Detroit Lions together). When Jeff gets outdoors, besides boating, he enjoys bow hunting for whitetail deer and walking the woods with Chester, his English Labrador retriever. Jeff and his wife, Diane, have been married for over thirty years and are the parents of two adult daughters.

David Roper has spent a lifetime as an avid outdoorsman. One of his great joys was being an expert fly fisherman, fly tier, and fly rod builder. His friends designated one stretch of his favorite trout stream "Roper's Hole" because he fished it almost every Thursday for nearly twenty years. He also enjoyed hiking and biking. David refers to himself a "less than successful athlete in high school and college." He was planning to become a coach before he got drafted into the US Army, which changed his direction. For thirty years, David was a pastor. He and his wife, Carolyn, opened a mountain lodge called Shepherd's Rest as a place for pastors to go for rest, recreation, and counsel. Of course, David made sure they found out about activities such as fly-fishing, hiking, and cross-country skiing. David has written several books, including *The Strength of a Man*, *Teach Us to Number Our Days*, and *A Burden Shared*. He and Carolyn live in Boise, Idaho.

Joe Stowell has served as president of two Midwestern Christian institutions of higher learning: Moody Bible Institute and Cornerstone University. Before that, he pastored churches in Ohio, Michigan, and Indiana. Joe played soccer in both high school and in college at Cedarville University. He enjoys cross-country skiing, mountain and coastal path trekking, gardening, and following Big Ten basketball and football. He has also been able to cheer on Cornerstone University's national championship men's basketball teams (NAIA) in 2011 and 2015. Among Joe's many published books are *Strength for the Journey*, *The Upside of Down*, and *Jesus Nation*. He and his wife, Martie, have three children and ten grandchildren and live in Grand Rapids, Michigan.

———————————

Herb Vander Lugt remained a vital contributor to *Our Daily Bread* up to the time he went to be with his Lord and Savior on December 2, 2006. He served as senior research editor for Our Daily Bread Ministries and had been with the ministry since 1966, when he became the third author to contribute to *Our Daily Bread* (after editor Henry Bosch and ministry founder Dr. M. R. DeHaan). In addition to his devotional articles, he wrote numerous Discovery Series booklets and reviewed all study and devotional materials for theological accuracy. Herb pastored six churches and held three interim ministerial positions after retiring from the pastorate in 1989. An avid baseball fan and former catcher, Herb regaled his co-workers with stories of attending Detroit Tigers games when his favorite player, Hall of Fame first baseman Hank Greenberg played. Herb and his wife, Virginia, had two children.

Sheridan Voysey is an author and broadcaster on the subjects of faith and spirituality. His books include *Resilient: Your Invitation to a Jesus-Shaped Life*; *Resurrection Year: Turning Broken Dreams into New Beginnings*; and the award-winning *Unseen Footprints: Encountering the Divine Along the Journey of Life*. He is a regular contributor to Britain's largest national network, *BBC Radio 2*. He also speaks at conferences and events around the world. Among Sheridan's interests are photography, Thai food, dark chocolate, funk and soul, and long hikes in England's rugged north. He has renovated two homes (and quite nicely too, if he does say so himself). Although born in Australia and living in England, he never did get the cricket bug. But he keeps that a secret from the neighbors. Sheridan is married to Merryn, a medical researcher, and they reside in Oxford, United Kingdom.

Marvin Williams should write an autobiography called *My Life at 11,000 Feet*. That number seems rather significant, since he has jumped out of an airplane at that height (and survived), and he has climbed to the height of 11,000 feet on Mt. Kenya, the highest mountain in Kenya. When Marvin is closer to sea level, his other pursuits include running a 25k race and being, in his own words, "a grill master." Earlier in his life, he was a martial arts champion. He also claims to have conquered another manly feat: changing his kids' dirty diapers "without covering my nose or holding my breath." That is something any dad can relate to and be proud of! Marvin is senior teaching pastor of Trinity Church in Lansing, Michigan. He and his wife, Tonia, have three children.

Mike Wittmer's down-to-earth writing style and his sense of humor as a speaker belie his position has a noted Bible scholar. Mike did his undergraduate work at Cedarville University, and he received his doctorate at Calvin College. He is a longtime professor at Grand Rapids Theological Seminary and is in demand as an expositor of the Bible and as someone who can address key issues in the church. On the downside, he calls himself a "miserable Cleveland sports fan whose high point is always next year's NFL draft." When he is not grading papers or writing books, he likes to cross-country ski, ride his mountain bike, kayak, and play backyard whiffle ball. His high school sport was basketball, and his position on the church softball team is second base. Mike loves to build things, but he admits that when he made an ottoman for his wife, Julie, she insisted it was merely an "ottoboy." Mike has written several books, including *The Last Enemy*, *Despite Doubt*, *Becoming Worldly Saints*, and *Heaven Is a Place on Earth*. Mike and Julie have three children.

Help us get the word out!

Our Daily Bread Publishing exists to feed the soul with the Word of God.

If you appreciated this book, please let others know.

- Pick up another copy to give as a gift.
- Share a link to the book or mention it on social media.
- Write a review on your blog, on a bookseller's website, or at our own site (ourdailybreadpublishing.org).
- Recommend this book for your church, book club, or small group.

Connect with us:

 @ourdailybread

 @ourdailybread

 @ourdailybread

Our Daily Bread Publishing
PO Box 3566
Grand Rapids, Michigan 49501 USA

 books@odb.org